Conrad's *Heart of Darkness* and Contemporary Thought

RELATED TITLES

Conrad's Heart of Darkness, Allan Simmons

Heart of Darkness, Ashley Chantler

Reading Derrida's Of Grammatology, Ian Maclachlan
and Sean Gaston

Conrad's *Heart of Darkness* and Contemporary Thought

Revisiting the Horror with Lacoue-Labarthe

Edited by

Nidesh Lawtoo

B L O O M S B U R Y

LONDON • NEW DELHI • NEW YORK • SYDNEY

Bloomsbury Academic

An imprint of Bloomsbury Publishing Plc

50 Bedford Square   175 Fifth Avenue

London   New York

WC1B 3DP   NY 10010

UK   USA

www.bloomsbury.com

First published 2012

British Library Cataloguing-in-Publication Data

A catalogue record for this book is available from the British Library.

ISBN: HB: 978-1-4411-2461-6

PB: 978-1-4411-0100-6

Library of Congress Cataloging-in-Publication Data

Conrad's 'Heart of darkness' and contemporary thought : revisiting the horror with Lacoue-Labarthe / edited by Nidesh Lawtoo.

p. cm.

Includes bibliographical references and index.

ISBN 978-1-4411-2461-6 (hardcover: alk. paper) –

ISBN 978-1-4411-0100-6 (pbk.: alk. paper) –

ISBN 978-1-4411-0376-5 (ebook pdf: alk. paper) –

ISBN 978-1-4411-2377-0 (ebook epub: alk. paper)

1. Conrad, Joseph, 1857-1924. Heart of darkness. 2. Psychological fiction, English–History and criticism. 3. Lacoue-Labarthe, Philippe. 4. Africa–In literature. I. Lawtoo, Nidesh.

PR6005.O4H4755 2012

823'.912–dc23

2012005162

Typeset by Deanta Global Publishing Services, Chennai, India

Printed and bound in India

CONTENTS

ACKNOWLEDGEMENTS

This book is the product of a communal spirit I believe to be in line with both Conrad's and Lacoue-Labarthe's *ethos*. In addition to all the authors who gave voice to this book, I wish to thank Arnaud Dubois, Mikkel Borch-Jacobsen and Gary Handwerk for encouraging this project at a time it was still untimely; Brian Richardson, Allan Simmons, Wieslaw Krajka and Andrea White for their timely support. Many thanks to Camille Marshall, Philip Lindholm and Marie-Emile Walz for helping with formatting and bibliography and to Martine Hennard Dutheil de la Rochère for suggesting the image that 'envelops' the book. I wish to say *merci à* Claire Nancy, Leonid Kharlamov and Michel Surya for granting permission to translate 'L'horreur occidentale'; David Avital, at Bloomsbury, for his flexibility and precious editorial suggestions. Special thanks go to Hannes Opelz for first calling my attention to 'L'horreur occidentale' and for his friendly collaboration in translating it *à quatre mains*; to Anne Luyat, for suggesting this project in the first place, and for her enthusiastic support all along; to J. Hillis Miller for the gift of an ideal *ouverture* to read Conrad with Lacoue-Labarthe. Heart felt thanks go to Michaela Lawtoo, for the company that nourishes my emotion of thought.

PREFACE

ANNE LUYAT

It is the task of the translator to release in his own language
that pure language which is under the spell of another.
WALTER BENJAMIN, *'The Task of the Translator'*

Walter Benjamin, whose counsel on translation the French
philosopher Philippe Lacoue-Labarthe adopted as his own in
order to translate Hölderin as well as Nietzsche, believed that 'it
is the task of the translator to release in his own language that
pure language which is under the spell of another'.[1] The linguistic
mantle of concision, precision and incisiveness which characterizes
'L'horreur occidentale', the French philosopher's explication of
Joseph Conrad's novella, *Heart of Darkness*, now enters the English
language for the first time with the essence of its thought and the
spell of its language respected in their vivid integrity.

It was the actor David Warrilow's reading of Conrad's text
in French at a Paris theatre in 1992 which led Philippe Lacoue-
Labarthe to comment on the metaphysical nature of *Heart of
Darkness*. As a direct consequence of the reading, Professor Lacoue-
Labarthe announced in the context of a seminar on *Psychiatry,
Psycho-Therapy and Culture(s)* a few years later his firmly held
belief that *Heart of Darkness* was 'one of the greatest texts of
Western literature' (112) and a great 'event of thought' because of
its '*mythical* power' (112). In the published version of his address,
he was careful to preserve the spontaneous nature of his remarks, a
choice which Nidesh Lawtoo and Hannes Opelz faithfully respected
in establishing the English version. Inscribed from its inception in an
oral tradition, 'The Horror of the West' is a scholarly performance
of unusual force and persuasion which brings to the fore the oral
qualities Joseph Conrad utilized in writing *Heart of Darkness*.

Philippe Lacoue-Labarthe worked within a modern philosophical and literary tradition which he cites as one which puts European culture in perspective with the African one. The period begins in France with Michel de Montaigne's *Essais* in the sixteenth century, extends to the publication of Claude Lévi-Strauss's *Tristes Tropiques* in 1955, and stretches to the opening of the Museum of Primitive Arts in Paris in 2006. Because of his direct influence on Claude Lévi-Strauss, Joseph Conrad is also considered to be part of a current of French and European thought which seeks out what Lévi-Strauss called the 'world of the other'. In explicit homage to Joseph Conrad when he wrote the first three chapters of *Tristes Tropiques*, Lévi-Strauss recognized the oral wisdom of the unlettered Nambikwara of Brazil.[2] The Prix Goncourt Jury regretted in 1955, when the French *ethnologue* published *Tristes Tropiques,* that it was not a novel, for if it had been a work of fiction, it would have been awarded the prize for literature. The world of the other that was so extensively investigated in the human sciences looks directly to Joseph Conrad's *Heart of Darkness* for the source of its inspiration.

Recognizing from the outset the essential role played by voice in *Heart of Darkness*, Philippe Lacoue-Labarthe in his discussion of the complex narrative structure of the tale – whose mimetic passages alternate with Marlow's diegetic narrative – suggests that the 'oratorio' is 'perhaps the true form of th[is] work' (114). As Lacoue-Labarthe points out, an oratorio, which functions with minor characters in choric roles, also offers the possibility of composing major pieces – Lacoue-Labarthe uses the word 'arias' – for major characters in extended moments of dramatic eloquence. The musical structure creates a memorable unity of tone in which the dissonant voices of Europe and Africa present in the narrative can be heard. This volume respects this musical frame: the heterogeneous voices that compose it create an echo that resonates, sometimes in unison, sometimes contrapuntally, with Lacoue-Labarthe's voice, structuring the different parts (or 'arias') of this book.

Lacoue-Labarthe's appreciation of Conrad's sense of narrative form and the multiple responses he generated, transform what has long been a familiar story for English readers into one which becomes strange and unfamiliar. As the voyage of initiation progresses towards its tragic end, the voices clash, become more intense, more desperate and more violent until the moment when Kurtz sees and voices 'the horror'. If this experience is a deeply singular and interior one in Conrad's tale, it becomes a plural, shared experience [*expérience partagée*] in what is aptly titled, 'Conrad's *Heart of Darkness* and Contemporary Thought'.

Philippe Lacoue-Labarthe's explication of *Heart of Darkness* has become a controversial one, for he employs the personal pronoun 'us' to explain the source of the horror which Kurtz perceives in the story: '[W]hat is at stake in the horror', the French philosopher writes, 'is the savagery in us' (120). The tragedy in *Heart of Darkness* springs from the aspiration of Kurtz to become an artist, 'the *figure* par excellence of the West', the guardian of 'the gift of gifts: language' (115). The Western culture that Kurtz represents possesses the advantage of a written language, but as its representative, he respects the truth of neither the written nor the spoken word. As Lacoue-Labarthe admirably shows, the Greek gift of *techne* becomes a two-edged sword capable of savagery if it is ill-used.

Conrad's rendering of late nineteenth-century voices meeting in Africa becomes palpable when Philippe Lacoue-Labarthe explores the multiple facets of its metaphysical dimension and undeniable historic complexity. He also insists that tragedy, whether it springs from a written plot or an oral fable, is essentially political. Its source is the horror which we recognize both within and without, the horror to which this volume faithfully bears witness.

Notes

1   Walter Benjamin, 'The Task of the Translator,' in *Illuminations*, ed. Hannah Arendt, trans. Harry Zohn (New York: Schocken Books, 2007), 80.

2   Claude Lévi-Strauss, *Tristes Tropiques*, (Paris: Terre Humaine, 1955), 349–50.

Introduction: 'An emotion of thought'

NIDESH LAWTOO

Encounters

The origin of this volume lies in what could be called 'a lucky encounter', the encounter with what is, in all probability, the first reading of Joseph Conrad offered by a professional philosopher. 'Philosophical' is, indeed, a term that has often been used to account for Conrad's *Heart of Darkness*. Soon after its initial appearance in *Blackwood's Magazine* in 1899, reviewers commented on 'Mr. Conrad's philosophy' and the 'metaphysics' it entails. And subsequent critics were quick to align Conrad's insights behind the veil of darkness with continental philosophers such as Arthur Schopenhauer and Friedrich Nietzsche. More recently, influential theorists such as Frederick Jameson, Edward Said and J. Hillis Miller among others, have done much to provide a solid conceptual frame to open up a number of theoretical questions that are far from being disconnected from what goes under the rubric of 'continental philosophy': from the subject to the other, language to power, sameness to difference. So, philosophy is not new to Conrad studies, just as Conrad critics are not new to readings of Conrad with philosophical underpinnings. And yet, until now, philosophers by training and profession have themselves remained silent on the theoretical implications of Conrad's most influential tale. One of the goals of this book is to break this silence and inaugurate a new literary-philosophical line of inquiry that revisits *Heart of Darkness* in light of contemporary thought.

The author who provides this volume with a springboard to read Conrad philosophically is the increasingly influential French thinker Philippe Lacoue-Labarthe (1940–2007). Late professor of Aesthetics at the Université Marc Bloch (Strasburg) and former president of the *Collège International de Philosophie* (Paris), Lacoue-Labarthe has been an important figure on the philosophical scene over the past three decades. With Jean-Luc Nancy, he was among the very first to promote the work of Jacques Derrida, and with René Girard he is currently considered one of the founding figures of the emerging field of 'mimetic theory'. One of the first critical readers of Jacques Lacan, personal friend of Jacques Derrida, Sarah Kofman and Jean-Luc Nancy (with whom he co-edited the Collection *La philosophie en effet*), privileged interlocutor of Jean-François Lyotard, Luce Irigaray and Alain Badiou, mentor and colleague of Mikkel Borch-Jacobsen, Christopher Fynsk, Avital Ronell and many others, it is not surprising that Lacoue-Labarthe's name is often associated with what currently goes under the general rubric of 'French Theory'.

And yet, like so many of his generation, Lacoue-Labarthe did not identify within the confines of a given school or movement but preferred to align himself with the tradition of Western thought itself. An acute commentator of the origins of literary theory in Greek philosophy (Plato and Aristotle), Lacoue-Labarthe is one of the leading authorities on what he calls 'the metaphysics of the moderns', a metaphysics that includes key figures in the Western philosophical tradition (from Nietzsche to Heidegger, Benjamin to Derrida) and stretches to include their literary counterparts or doubles (from Bataille to Hölderlin, Baudelaire to Blanchot). Conrad also now belongs to this tradition. In fact, in the last decade of his career, the French philosopher turned to *Heart of Darkness* in order to align Joseph Conrad with these influential figures in Western thought.

Lacoue-Labarthe's reading of *Heart of Darkness* is one of those precious pearls whose discovery comes as a surprise and, what is more, at a moment one expects it less. A few months after his disappearance, in January 2007, the Journal *Lignes* published a special volume devoted to his memory titled, *Philippe Lacoue-Labarthe.*[1] In addition to numerous moving homages, the concluding section of the volume (titled, 'Textes de Philippe Lacoue-Labarthe') included unpublished or hard to find essays by the French philosopher. Among them was a piece with an open yet intriguing title, especially for Conradian ears: 'L'horreur occidentale'. The content of the essay revealed what one could only have hoped for: a sustained, impressively dense and truly thought-provoking reading of *Heart of Darkness*. After rereading it with increasing enthusiasm, I sent the article to Hillis Miller. We exchanged a few e-mails and he confirmed my sense that something important was at stake as he remarked: 'so far as I know, it is not quite like anything anyone else has said on Conrad before'. This book introduces Lacoue-Labarthe's philosophical reading of *Heart of Darkness* for the first time to the English speaking world and provides a critical and theoretical context for the initial reception of what is now called 'The Horror of the West' (translated by Hannes Opelz and Nidesh Lawtoo).

The translation of a piece on Conrad's most celebrated and controversial text from an internationally renowned philosophical figure such as Lacoue-Labarthe could not fail to generate a chorus of theoretical responses across both sides of the Atlantic, voices eager to engage with what has already been called an 'event' for literary studies (Hillis Miller). Following Miller's *ouverture*, the volume includes 11 essays that pick up, from different angles, Lacoue-Labarthe's invitation to consider Conrad's tale not only as a literary event but – as he puts it in one of his memorable phrases – also as 'an event of thought' [*événement de pensée*] (112). Critics and theorists who have written influentially on Conrad's *Heart of Darkness* before and are well-read in the tradition of thought Lacoue-Labarthe convokes, join arms in order to respond, further and, at times, challenge Lacoue-Labarthe's insights into what he calls, echoing Conrad, 'the horror of the West'. The main aim of this book is to revisit Conrad's untimely account of 'the horror' in the illuminating presence of Philippe Lacoue-Labarthe in order to open up *Heart of Darkness* to current theoretical tendencies in contemporary thought.

The moon and the halo

The intellectual unity of this book is guaranteed by the centralizing force of its 'centrepiece', as well as by the single, yet protean problematic that informs all the essays that surround it. As Lacoue-Labarthe puts it at the beginning of 'The Horror of the West', his fundamental concern is to explore what he calls the 'emotion of thought' [*émotion de la pensée*] (111) *Heart of Darkness* has the power to generate. This characteristic oxymoronic phrase joins two registers of experience that, from the beginning of Western thought, have tended to be considered in opposition, due to an 'ancient quarrel' between philosophy and literature. Lacoue-Labarthe's phrase, thus, makes clear that his reading of *Heart of Darkness* is part of his career-long effort to overturn this ancient antagonism in order to establish a critical dialogue between these exemplary traditions. As he puts it in *L'imitation des modernes*, his fundamental concern is to address 'the question of the relation [*rapport*] between literature and philosophy'.[2] Thus, throughout his career, Lacoue-Labarthe consistently argued that emotion and thought, specialists of affect (or *pathos*) and specialist of concepts (or *logos*) are far from being mutually exclusive but gain from being considered in relation to each other. This structural polarity is at the heart of 'The Horror of the West' and provides this volume with a specific conceptual/affective line of inquiry.

This book's single concern with the relation between emotion and thought and, more generally, literature and philosophy, functions as a centripetal, unifying force that connects all the essays that follow. But it is important to stress that this force opens up a panoply of decentralizing, centrifugal questions located at the uneasy juncture where different disciplines, perspectives and areas of thought meet, interpenetrate and fertilize each other. Aesthetic and politics, ethics and psychology, theology and economics and mythology and ontology are but some of the areas of knowledge that Lacoue-Labarthe and his commentators rely on in order to revisit *Heart of Darkness* in light of contemporary horrors.

Conrad's tale addresses problems that continue to make the headlines of our contemporary world, such as racial and gendered oppression, colonial and imperial power, material exploitations and genocidal horrors. This volume not only addresses these problems but also questions the underlying emotional and conceptual logic that informs the horrors that ensue from them. Contributors are thus particularly attentive to the complex relation that ties myth to violence, desire to ideology, contagion to (will to) power, colonial ideas to fascist practices and the death drive to collective traumas. If *Heart of Darkness* constitutes an 'event of thought', then, it is also because it is a text that strives to make us see that 'the West is the *horror*' or, as Lacoue-Labarthe also says, that the horror is what the West 'must necessarily think of itself'(112).

In a way, the questions that guide the different sections of this book all aim to reveal the theoretical implications of such a striking affirmation. They include the following: What does *Heart of Darkness* teach us about the relation between the psychic and the social? What is the link between aesthetics and politics? What is the role of *techne* in the exploitation of nature and people? Why does ideology need the *pathos* of voice and the *logos* of myth in order to gain power over the modern masses? What does the horror of colonial practice tell us about the horrors of the twentieth century and the traumas that ensue? And what is the ethical responsibility of the West for more contemporary genocidal terrors? These and other characteristically Lacoue-Labarthian questions open up Conrad's celebrated novella to a multiplicity of innovative perspectives which all eventually lead us back to the singular–plural problematic that runs through the entire volume, namely, how to respond, engage with and address the 'emotion of thought' (111) that, according to the French philosopher, renders *Heart of Darkness* both a literary event and 'an event of thought' (112)?

Taking their clues from 'The Horror of the West', contributors to the volume address problems in Conrad's tale that are often treated in isolation but that, after Lacoue-Labarthe, must be reconsidered in relational, interdisciplinary terms. This involves exploring the uneasy cross-road where affect and thought, literature and philosophy, politics and ethics meet, confront and address each other. Some of the articles do so by aligning themselves with Lacoue-Labarthe, others are ambivalent in their evaluation and still others position themselves contra Lacoue-Labarthe. And yet, all the essays fundamentally engage with the line of inquiry the French philosopher opens up in order to further his insights into 'the horror of the West'. For instance, Stephen Ross argues *with* Lacoue-Labarthe that affect and ideology as they operate in *Heart of Darkness* need to be understood in relation to each other and suggests that Kurtz's insatiable desire for ivory reveals a wider, catastrophic desire that drives capitalist ideology *tout court*. Along similar lines, but in a different context, Beth Ash articulates her *différend* from Lacoue-Labarthe by considering the traumatic, melancholic affects that emerge from Western horrors, while at the same time furthering the psychoanalytical line of inquiry that informs 'The Horror of the West'. On the philosophical front, Henry Staten argues, this time *contra* Lacoue-Labarthe, that Conrad's artistic craft (*techne*) is not so much concerned with the metaphysical voice of nature (*physis*) but, rather, with phallocentric phantasies about what nature is, or should be. These are but some of the specific articulations of the 'emotion of thought' that suddenly become visible if we revisit Conrad's tale 'in the company of Lacoue-Labarthe' (Miller's phrase). Since all the essays draw their source of inspiration from the conceptual landscape mapped by the French philosopher, a continuous, organic argument that connects the different sections of the book naturally ensues as we move from the mythic to the ideological, ethical, political and metaphysical implications of the horror.

At the level of method, contributors adopt different perspectives, from deconstruction to psychoanalysis, feminism to cultural materialism, Marxism to narratology and postcolonial studies to trauma studies. This heterogeneity is, once again, in line with Lacoue-Labarthe's philosophical approach in general and with his effort to reveal the multilayered implications of Conrad's elusive insights into the 'the horror' in particular, implications that cannot easily be contained within a single, totalizing, homogeneous perspective.

Readers of this volume might worry that, in what follows, theoretical approaches will simply be mapped onto literature, thought onto emotion. But it is important to stress that Lacoue-Labarthe's investigation of the relation between emotion and thought in *Heart of Darkness* is in line with aesthetic principles that are already *intrinsic* to Conrad's poetic thought itself. In *A Personal Record*, for instance, Conrad makes clear that one of his major preoccupations concerns precisely that 'interior world where *his* [the artist's] *thought and his emotions* go seeking for imagined adventures' (my emphasis).[3] For Conrad then, as for Lacoue-Labarthe after him, there is no thought without emotion, no literary adventure without conceptual explorations. This dual emphasis on both feeling and thought is central to Conrad's literary project, so central that he does not hesitate to reiterate it in what is probably the most-often quoted passage of his poetics. As he famously writes in the 'Preface' of *The Nigger of the 'Narcissus'*: 'My task which I am trying to achieve is, by the power of the written word, to make you hear, to make you feel – it is, before all, to make you *see*'.[4] As Marlow's voice also makes clear in *Heart of Darkness*, feeling is far from being antithetical to seeing; the darkness of bodily senses are far from being opposed to the more rational or luminous senses.[5] Rather, it is the conjunction between 'feeling' and 'seeing', 'emotion' and 'thought', 'moon-like' senses and 'sun-like' senses that, in Conrad's view, gives readers the possibility to catch 'that glimpse of truth for which [we] have forgotten to ask'.[6] Or, to put it in the language of *Heart of Darkness*, this literary-philosophical conjunction allows us to approach 'the appalling face of a glimpsed truth' that is at the heart of Kurtz's confrontation with the horror.[7] Lacoue-Labarthe's account of what he calls, in a phrase that will require further explication, the 'truth of the West', is there to make sure we do not forget to ask this essentially Conradian question and that we do so in light of our contemporary preoccupations.

In the spirit of Lacoue-Labarthe's conviction that literature does not need philosophy to think, let alone make readers think,[8] the essays in this book refrain from applying a theoretical perspective to a literary text, mapping concepts from the outside in order to solve problems inside. Instead, contributors cast light on the thoughts which, in their views, are already internal to Conrad's tale itself. This also means that the so-called *conceptual* meaning of the text cannot easily be detached from the linguistic *form* that would supposedly contain it. Hence this meaning cannot be summed up in neat philosophical 'theses' that would nicely stand apart, once the 'literary shell' has been cracked open. This point is, once again, in line with the poetics that informs *Heart of Darkness*. In order to account for the distinctive characteristic of Marlow's yarns, the frame narrator famously says:

> to him the meaning of an episode was not inside like a kernel but outside, enveloping the tale that brought it out only as a glow brings out a haze, in the likeness of one of these misty halos that, sometimes, are made visible by the spectral illumination of moonshine. (48)

This striking Conradian image illustrates, perhaps better than any other, the spirit, inspiration (both affective and conceptual) and the implicit methodological assumptions of this book. In fact, the task critics and theorists set themselves is not so much to crack philosophical riddles hidden inside the tale but, rather, to provide the proper background, one might even say, the right atmosphere, for these riddles to appear and be made visible first, and subsequently be revisited in a new literary/philosophical light.

Given the pervasive use of this analogy in the essays that follow, it is perhaps not surprising that Conrad's impressionistic metaphor eventually came to give form to the general outline of this book, delineating its figure (or *Gestalt*) from the inside-out. Thus, if the volume situates Philippe Lacoue-Labarthe's essay at its *centre*, it is surely not to signify that the philosophical 'meaning' or 'truth' of *Heart of Darkness* is neatly contained within it – no matter how penetrating Lacoue-Labarthe's reading of Conrad is. Rather, this is to suggest that 'The Horror of the West' provides a powerful, stimulating and, above all, illuminating philosophical reflection *on* – as well as *of* – Conrad's tale. Furthermore, if all the other essays are positioned *around* 'The Horror of the West', this is surely not to suggest that they simply serve as an external frame for Lacoue-Labarthe's central piece – no matter how effective such a framing is. Rather, their position at the 'margins' is to better 'centre', 're-centre' and, at time, 'decentre' specific claims made in the centrepiece. Above all, this positioning is instrumental in bringing out the meaning of the horror that informs Conrad's tale itself – the real throbbing heart of the book and direct source of light around which everything else turns.

The chorus

This book, then, turns around two main voices: the voice of the French philosopher situated at the centre of the volume and the chorus of theoretical voices situated all around it. Together they resonate in a multiplicity of ways in order to make us both feel and see the 'emotion of thought' that a mythic text like *Heart of Darkness* continues to generate in the twenty-first century.[9] In order to frame this chorus of singular–plural voices, the volume is book-ended by two influential theoretical figures who are ideally positioned to comment on the importance of Lacoue-Labarthe's reading of *Heart of Darkness*: the literary critic and theorist J. Hillis Miller and the philosopher Avital Ronell. These figures are intimately familiar with Lacoue-Labarthe's work. They are not only among the most respected and influential theoretical voices in contemporary thought but, like Lacoue-Labarthe himself, they also belong to the same generation of thinkers who contributed to opening up literary analysis to its philosophical 'outside'. It is thus an honour to have their voices open and conclude the book.

Miller's 'Prologue' starts by emphasizing his sense of admiration for Lacoue-Labarthe's essay as well as its critical and philosophical importance for contemporary thought. Thus, he does not hesitate to call 'The Horror of the West' 'one of the best [essays] ever written' on Conrad's novel (18). This is not a minor compliment, especially given the impressive amount of criticism *Heart of Darkness* has generated over more than a century. And yet, Miller's reading of Lacoue-Labarthe is not only laudatory but also critical. This is certainly a type of engagement Lacoue-Labarthe would have welcomed – if only because for the French philosopher, as for Nietzsche before him, thinking was also thinking *against* himself. In a second moment, thus, Miller tactfully but incisively engages with the political, aesthetic and metaphysical implications of 'The Horror of the West', delineating major conceptual and methodological differences between his own (Biblical) approach to *Heart of Darkness* and Lacoue-Labarthe's (Hellenic) approach. Miller's response to the emotion of *thought Heart of Darkness* ('revisited in the company of Lacoue-Labarthe') generates, opens up fundamental questions concerning the relation between truth and revelation, affect and the rhetorical power of language. Above all, Miller paves the way for future engagements with 'The Horror of the West', sets the theoretical tone of the volume and inaugurates a philosophical dialogue with Lacoue-Labarthe for contemporary thought to continue exploring. In the 'Postface', Avital Ronell, a privileged interlocutor of Lacoue-Labarthe, both echoes and balances Miller's opening piece by accounting for the *emotion* of thought that ties her to the French philosopher, while, at the same time, articulating the theoretical urgency for us today to engage with this untimely thinker whose 'worthy *oeuvre*' is barely beginning to be discovered.

Part 1, 'Mythic Darkness', includes contributions by three influential Anglo-American theorists and critics who join their philosophical and literary sensibility in order to engage with the religious or, as Lacoue-Labarthe would prefer to say, 'mythic' implications of *Heart of Darkness*. Hillis Miller's now canonical essay '*Heart of Darkness* Revisited' has been reprinted in other collections before, but it gains a second life from being positioned right after his new 'Prologue' (aptly titled 'Revisiting "*Heart of Darkness* Revisited"') in a contrapuntal relation to 'The Horror of the West.' According to Miller, both his and Lacoue-Labarthe's essays illustrate two different, yet related, hermeneutical principles that run deep in Western philosophical thought: Lacoue-Labarthe belongs to the Hellenic/Heideggerian tradition, whereas Miller belongs to the Biblical/Derridean one. The difference that underscores their reading of 'the horror' rests on two distinct, yet related ontologies, ontologies that question the possibility or impossibility to reveal the 'essence' of the West. The two authors, however, ultimately agree in taking seriously the metaphysical implications of *Heart of Darkness* and in revealing the ethical and political horrors this apocalyptic/mythic text gives us to think. Michael Bell pursues this mythological line of inquiry by situating Conrad's tale (as well as Lacoue-Labarthe's discussion of 'myth') in a wider modernist context that includes European literary figures such as Thomas Mann, W. B. Yeats and D. H. Lawrence but also theoretical figures such as Nietzsche and Freud. Bell argues that the category of 'the myth of the West' Lacoue-Labarthe invokes to account for *Heart of Darkness*'s 'mythic power' needs to be qualified by considering what he calls the 'struggle of rival myths' that informs the modernist *Weltanschauung*. Finally, cultural critic Jonathan Dollimore furthers this Freudian/Nietzschean line of inquiry by diagnosing the degenerative forces that infect Western civilization and generate perverse figures *à la Kurtz*. Giving cultural 'density' to Lacoue-Labarthe's claim that the horror emerges from a psychic 'void', Dollimore pushes psychic categories beyond the pleasure principle and reveals the metaphysics of oblivion that haunts both *Heart of Darkness* and Western civilization as a whole. Dollimore provocatively combines psychology with sociology and theology with ontology in order to unmask the contradictory push-pulls towards/away from the threatening forces of 'self-dissolution' that, in his view, are constitutive of the metaphysics of darkness we repress yet secretly and perversely desire. These essays are not uncritical of specific aspects of 'The Horror of the West'; yet, they all share the Lacoue-Labarthian concern to read literature philosophically and philosophy poetically in order to reveal the mythic forces that continue to affect and infect the West.

   These initial contributions articulate the implicit philosophical assumptions of 'The Horror of the West' and prepare the ground to approach the second and central section of the book, where the encounter of 'Conrad *avec* Lacoue-Labarthe' takes place. Since Lacoue-Labarthe's reading of *Heart of Darkness* is extremely dense, theoretically multi-layered and relies on a conceptual apparatus the philosopher assumes his audience to be already familiar with, I open this section with a preface to 'The Horror of the West'. The aim of this piece is not so much to offer an original interpretation of Lacoue-Labarthe's account of Conrad's tale but to offer what Jacques Derrida would call a 'doubling commentary' [*commentaire redoublant*].[10] This frame situates some of the main concepts Lacoue-Labarthe mobilizes in his reading of *Heart of Darkness* in the context of the general economy of his thought.

Then follows the centrepiece around which all the essays revolve. 'The Horror of the West' is unique in both style and approach and escapes easy summaries. It offers no neat, pre-packaged theses for me to sum up here, except the one stated in the title: Lacoue-Labarthe argues that the horror is 'of the West' because the West – from the Roman conquest to the Holocaust – continues to generate horrors, for others. In order to support this claim, he aligns Conrad with an impressive number of figures in the Western philosophical tradition (from Plato to Augustine, Diderot to Nietzsche, Benjamin to Lévi-Strauss and Heidegger to Lacan) and argues that 'the horror of the West' cannot be dissociated from an essential 'void' at the heart of Western subjectivity, an 'absence of any proper being [*être-propre*]' (116). This lack of being, in his view, renders the modern subject radically vulnerable to all kinds of psychic infiltrations, incantations and mimetic manipulations by charismatic leader figures like Kurtz endowed with the (will to) power to subjugate the modern masses.

For the French philosopher, then, 'the horror' Conrad makes us see is both interior and exterior, subjective and objective, psychic and social and political and ontological. It is a horror that is located not only at the heart of subjectivity but also at the heart of empires and continues to be responsible for Western atrocities. Above all, Lacoue-Labarthe strives to make us see that *Heart of Darkness* is a (mythic) tale that reveals the devastating (philosophical) 'truth' about the West, namely that the 'West is the *horror*' (112). Lacoue-Labarthe finds evidence to support this point in the 'technique of death' [*technique de la mort*] (119) massively used in the twentieth century. This is not the first time that Lacoue-Labarthe addresses these problems. They constitute a *Leitmotif* in his thought and are at the heart of his confrontation with Heidegger's take on *techne*, the latter's complicity with Nazism and his refusal to address the horrors of mass-extermination in the aftermath of Auschwitz. Lacoue-Labarthe's reading of *Heart of Darkness*, as so many of his late texts, is haunted by the most harrowing horrors the West ever managed to produce: the horror of the Holocaust.

Philippe Lacoue-Labarthe is an ideal candidate to open up Conrad studies to this heavy dossier, whereby aesthetic, psychic, ethical, political and metaphysical principles come together in order to re-evaluate the origins of Western techniques of will to power. As Jacques Derrida reminds us in 'Desistance': 'on these grave and formidable problems, I know no judgment more sure than Lacoue-Labarthe's, none more rigorous and prudent.'[11] That Conrad was among the first to foresee and denounce the implications of this apocalyptic event testifies to what Lacoue-Labarthe calls 'an event of thought' (112). This is by no means the only contribution of Lacoue-Labarthe's reading of *Heart of Darkness*. 'The Horror of the West' offers radically new insights on philosophical/literary concepts as diverse as 'myth', 'affect', 'ideology', 'mimesis', 'art', 'genius' and 'techne', to name a few—insights that open up an entirely new conceptual register to continue to talk critically about Conrad in the twenty-first century.

As a coda to this central section, the French philosopher, specialist of African thought and intimate friend of Lacoue-Labarthe, François Warin, offers a deeply felt homage to the dead friend. He does so by revisiting their 'African adventures', whereby the two philosophers were confronted to a Dagara funeral ceremony, in the company of Conrad's novella. The first part of the essay bears witness to the sacred horror of sacrificial death; in the second part, Warin extends Lacoue-Labarthe's considerations on Western 'techniques of death' by offering a philosophical/postcolonial reading of how the West continues to be implicated with, and partly responsible for, recent genocidal horrors perpetuated on African soil. As he provocatively asks: 'what closer reenactment of Kurtz's atrocities than the Rwandan genocide?' The horror, Warin argues, has not stopped to plague Africa and is still, in many ways, the horror *of* the West.

Part 3, 'The Affect of Ideology', concentrates on the affective dimension of Lacoue-Labarthe's reading of the horror and argues that the psychic dimension of *Heart of Darkness* needs to be reconsidered in the context of larger social forces that affect the entire body politic. Jacques Lacan is a key reference in 'The Horror of the West', and the contributors in this section do much to account for catastrophic forms of desires that haunt Western culture as a whole. Thus, Stephen Ross builds on Lacoue-Labarthe's reference to the Lacanian *la Chose* and argues – via Derrida, Levinas and

Marx – that the logic of desire in *Heart of Darkness* and in the West needs to be reframed within a larger lack of an 'ethics of alterity' that should denounce the horrors of 'global capitalism' and the fetishism for capital it continues to generate. Along similar psychoanalytical lines, but writing from a perspective informed by narratology, Claude Maisonnat zeroes in on Lacoue-Labarthe's take on 'voice' and argues that a polyphony of different voices, including French ones, operate in *Heart of Darkness* and must be taken into consideration in order to fully hear the haunting power of 'the horror'. Beth Sharon Ash concludes this psychoanalytical section from the perspective of the emerging field of trauma studies. While agreeing with Lacoue-Labarthe's reading of Kurtz as a 'tragic hero' confronted with the horror of death, her psychoanalytical *différend* leads Ash to focus on Marlow as traumatized subject and to argue that the horror of trauma and the melancholy it generates requires communal working-through first, in order to subsequently face 'the horror of the West'. These essays all acknowledge their debts to Lacoue-Labarthe's *psychic* insights into the horror and do much to articulate the complex logic that ties ideology to affect, the social to the psychic and the political to the personal.

Part 4, 'The Echo of the Horror', includes three essays concerned with an intrinsic (formal) perspective on *Heart of Darkness* that is equally attentive to the extrinsic (gendered, ethico-political and metaphysical) implications of the tale. Henry Staten opens this part by acknowledging the importance of Lacoue-Labarthe's attempt to articulate 'the very essence' of Conrad's text but then continues in a more critical vein. Articulating his resistance to Lacoue-Labarthe's (Heideggerian) reading of the horror allows Staten to propose a (Nietzschean) reading of the human, all too human phantasies that resonate in Marlow's phallocentric view of nature, revealing what he calls 'the most mystified level' of Marlow's experience, a Dionysian experience with the horror of death that structures the tale as a whole. Situating Lacoue-Labarthe's reading of Conrad in a wider intellectual community to which both Jacques Derrida and Jean-Luc Nancy belong, Martine Hennard Dutheil de la Rochère both confirms and supplements Lacoue-Labarthe's account of the horror of *techne* by considering Conrad's fascination for the technique of X-Rays. Drawing on both textual and contextual evidence that shows the importance of this other *technique de la mort* in Conrad's tale allows Hennard Dutheil to 'sound the hollowness' at the heart of male, colonial bodies and, by extension, of the Western body politics at large. I conclude this section by considering the innovative *mimetic* line of inquiry in Conrad studies Lacoue-Labarthe opens up. Extending Lacoue-Labarthe's Platonic/anti-Platonic take on the question of affective mimesis to the multiple 'enthusiastic outbreak[s]' that structure the tale, I argue that the controversy concerning gender, race and ideology in *Heart of Darkness* must be reconsidered in light of the politics of mimesis vastly amplified in our contemporary, mass-mediatized world. Together, these essays provide three different readings of the horror that counter supplement, and echo, in their own singular voices, lines of inquiry opened up by 'The Horror of the West'.

After revisiting *Heart of Darkness* in the stimulating company of 'The Horror of the West', the book concludes with an interview with the American philosopher, feminist theorist and literary critic Avtial Ronell about Lacoue-Labarthe. As a former colleague and close personal friend of Lacoue-Labarthe, Ronell is ideally placed to step back and delineate the general importance of this increasingly influential thinker for literary studies and contemporary thought. Echoing Miller's 'Prologue', Ronell's 'Postface' not only casts precious light on the importance of Lacoue-Labarthe the philosopher but also adds a deeply felt reminiscence of the 'emotion of thought' that ties her to Lacoue-Labarthe the man. In so doing, Ronell offers precious guidance as to how to learn to 'listen' to the singularity of his voice, evaluates the timbre of Lacoue-Labarthe's rhetoric, including the 'rigorous hesitations' that distinguish him from other contemporary thinkers, while at the same time discussing the philosopher's sense of 'mission', 'struggle' and 'task' that, in his view, is constitutive of the experience of thought.

In sum, the centrepiece of this volume and the diversified theoretical halo that surrounds it function as a reminder that if *Heart of Darkness* continues to be an 'event of thought' it is not simply because this mythic text is now integral part of the Western imagination; it is also because it lifts the veil on Western horrors we often do not want to see, let along acknowledge. Above all, it reveals an ongoing difficulty for the West to face the horrors we continue to generate, in the name of the myth of humanism – for others. If the manifestations of the horror change historically, and the horror of *the* West constantly transgresses the boundaries of one single nation, country or continent, this does not mean that contemporary readers are not supposed to interrogate the aesthetic, psychological, ethical, political, religious, material and ontological causes of such horrors. In fact, despite their variety of perspectives and insights, the contributors to this volume agree in thinking that it is only if we inquire about the 'emotion of thought' *Heart of Darkness* generates for us today that we can have a chance to approach that 'glimpse of truth' Conrad attempts to make us see. This is, indeed, the challenge that the contributors to this volume were ready to pick up, in the illuminating company of 'The Horror of the West'.

Finally, before we begin, let us recall that if Lacoue-Labarthe's name may sound new to many ears, the fast-growing number of studies that are now beginning to be written on him only confirms what his friends and colleagues were quick to recognize during his lifetime. As Jacques Derrida puts it, his is a voice that addresses the questions that 'will have to be thought tomorrow'.[12] 'The Horror of the West' is one of those untimely philosophical arrows aimed towards the future Lacoue-Labarthe did not get to see. Luckily, however, his arrow arrived – and he is now addressing us. His voice, not unlike Marlow's, is a voice that cannot be silenced. The task to respond to it, as adequately as we can, is now left open to that future to which, *volens nolens*, we belong.

Notes

1 *Philippe Lacoue-Labarthe, Lignes* 22 (mai 2007).

2 Philippe Lacoue-Labarthe, *L'imitation des modernes* (*Typographies 2*) (Paris: Galilée, 1986). Unless specified otherwise, translations of works by Lacoue-Labarthe unavailable in English are the editor's.

3 Joseph Conrad, *A Personal Record* (New York: Doubleday, 1924), xx.

4 Joseph Conrad, 'Preface', *The Nigger of the Narcissus* (New York: Doubleday, 1924), xi–xvi, xiv.

5 Plato called vision 'the most sunlike of all the instruments of sense' (Plato. *Republic*, in *The Collected Dialogues of Plato*, ed. E. Hamilton & H. Cairns, trans. P. Shorey [New York: Bollingen Series, 1963], 575–844, 6.508b, 743) and, of course, theory comes from Greek, *theorein,* to look.

6 Conrad, 'Preface', xiv.

7   Joseph Conrad, *Heart of Darkness*. In *Youth: A Narrative and Two Other Stories* (London: J. M. Dent & Sons Ltd., 1923), 45–162, 151. Henceforth all quotations to *Heart of Darkness* in this volume are from this edition.

8   Lacoue-Labarthe (with Heidegger) liked to speak of 'thinking poetry' [*poésie pensante*] or, better, thinking *prose*, because (with Benjamin) he was fascinated by 'the Idea of poetry as prose' (*Heidegger: La politique du poème* [Paris: Galilée, 2002], 50).

9   Harold Bloom, in his critical evaluation of Conrad's tale, also admits that '*Heart of Darkness* has taken on some of the power of myth' ('Introduction', *Joseph Conrad's Heart of Darkness*, ed. Harold Bloom (New York: Infobase, 2008), 7–11, 10.

10 As Derrida reminds us this mimetic practice, while being but a precondition for true reading to take place, 'is not easy', especially if its aim is not so much to 'protect' but to 'open' a critical reading. Jacques Derrida, *De la grammatologie* (Paris: Editions de Minuit, 1967), 227.

11 Jacques Derrida, 'Introduction: Desistance', in Philippe Lacoue-Labarthe, *Typography: Mimesis, Philosophy, Politics* (Cambridge, MA: Harvard University Press, 1989), 29.

12 Derrida, 'Desistance', 6.

Prologue: Revisiting *'Heart of Darkness Revisited'* (in the company of Philippe Lacoue-Labarthe)

J. HILLIS MILLER

The contributors to this volume have been asked to say something about Philippe Lacoue-Labarthe's superb essay on *Heart of Darkness*, 'L'horreur occidentale, translated now as 'The Horror of the West'. I hope the phrase in my title, 'in the company of', does not seem disrespectful of Lacoue-Labarthe's memory. I mean to call attention by that phrase to the strong presence in his essay of the author's voice speaking to his auditors, as when he says, 'This evening, in front of you, I would like to try to justify myself, [*essayer de me justifier*]. . . . This type of exercise, as we know, is dangerous. I therefore ask you, in advance, to forgive me [*Je vous demande à l'avance de bien vouloir m'en excuser*] if my remarks will be a little experimental' (111–112). When I read his essay, Lacoue-Labarthe seems to be speaking to me too, as well as to his original auditors. He exhorts me to see his reading of *Heart of Darkness* as a bearing witness that may need excusing or that may be an act of self-justification.

Excusing and self-justifying, we know, are speech acts. They are performative, not constative, utterances, as is the act of bearing witness through speech, through a voice. Both Lacoue-Labarthe and I have a lot to say in our essays about voice as testimony in *Heart of Darkness*. Conrad's novel, we both say, is made of a relay of testifying voices, one nested inside the next like Russian dolls, each bearing witness for the one before, back (or forward) to the most inside voice, Kurtz's. His voice speaks the ultimate testifying words. Of these words Marlow says, 'He had summed up—he had judged. "The horror!"' (151). A critical essay too, Lacoue-Labarthe's or mine, is a bearing witness, a speech act. It does not so much say, 'This is the truth about this work', as 'I swear to you that I believe this is the truth about this work, though you may need to excuse me for what I say'.

It is an important event to have Lacoue-Labarthe's essay now available in English. 'L'horreur occidentale' is a major essay on Conrad's novel, one of the best ever written. About it one can say what Lacoue-Labarthe says about *Heart of Darkness* itself that it is an 'event of thought' [*événement de pensée*] (112) or, in his even more striking phrase, something that 'prompts an emotion of thought' [*provoque une émotion de la pensée*] (111). I shall return to this latter phrase. 'The Horror of the West' should be in the top group of any list of essential essays on *Heart of Darkness*.

Philippe Lacoue-Labarthe was an extremely learned, original and distinguished philosopher. He had a special interest in the philosophy of art, as in his two essential books, *Typographie* and *L'imitation des modernes*.[1] He might not have been expected, nevertheless, ever to turn his attention to *Heart of Darkness*, even in its French translation, which has such an odd sound to English-speaking ears: *Au coeur des ténèbres*. We are fortunate that he did so. One important feature of his reading is the way he makes a strongly persuasive case for seeing Kurtz as a hyperbolic example of the West's idea of the artist, from Plato through Diderot down to Nietzsche and Rimbaud. The Western artist, he argues, is, like Kurtz, nothing because able to be everything. The Western artist is totally *disponible*. Therefore, he or she is 'hollow at the core' (*HD* 131). As a consequence, the artist is vulnerable to invasion by the darkness, the horror. That is a strikingly original and provocative perspective. It is an issue on which my own essay does not touch. Was Joseph Conrad also hollow at the core and so vulnerable to the darkness? I think not. He defended himself by various strategies, especially by irony.

Reading 'The Horror of the West' has given me occasion to reread my old essay of 1983 and to juxtapose Lacoue-Labarthe's essay with mine. For the most part, I agree whole-heartedly with

Lacoue-Labarthe's reading. I have learnt much from it. We agree, for example, as I have said, in stressing the importance of *voice* in Conrad's story. We agree that voices are used in the story as a series of transmissions that bear witness to Kurtz's experience and to a truth that can only be expressed indirectly. We agree in seeing *Heart of Darkness* as one of the most important indictments of Western imperialism, and even in seeing it as 'one of the greatest texts of Western literature' (111). Everyone seriously interested in Conrad should read Lacoue-Labarthe's essay.

*

Now I shall bear witness, mildly and hesitantly, hoping you will excuse me for my temerity, to some small points of difference. It would not be worth doing this if questions of general importance were not at stake.

First difference: I would not assert, as Lacoue-Labarthe does, that the story fundamentally says: 'the West *is* the horror'. I would rather say that *Heart of Darkness* says Western imperialism is one aspect of a more ubiquitous and pervasive underlying horror. Lacoue-Labarthe's discussion of the horror and of its embodiment in the Western will to power is subtle and persuasive. Nevertheless, the phrase 'Horror of the West' invites the reader to think of Conrad's horror as specifically political and as peculiar to the West and to its destructive 'technics of death' [*technique de la mort*] (119).

The words of *Heart of Darkness*, however, especially its figures of speech, indicate rather that what is named by Kurtz as 'the horror' is a universal quasi-metaphysical entity, not a limited political one. The horror is something present deep within every man and woman, everywhere, at all times. It is also present at all times behind every aspect of nature everywhere. Lacoue-Labarthe says the first of these by way of his reference to Lacan's *la Chose*, to Heidegger's *das Ding*, the Thing and to Augustine's *extime*, his *interior intimo meo* (117), something inside me but unattainably beyond me. Lacan, Heidegger and Augustine provide three other names for the horror. After all, Lacoue-Labarthe's essay was given as a lecture before an on-going seminar of 1995–6 called *Psychiatre, Psychothérapie et Culture(s)*. Some reference to the psychiatric aspects of Conrad's presentation of Kurtz was in order, though Lacoue-Labarthe does not follow-up on Conrad's assertion that Kurtz, to speak plainly, has been driven mad by the wilderness. If so, he is deeply in need of psychotherapy. At one moment Marlow says, 'I wasn't arguing with a lunatic either' (144), but the next moment he says, 'But his soul was mad. Being alone in the wilderness, it had looked within itself, and, by heavens! I tell you, it had gone mad' (145).

It would be a mistake, however, to identify the horror exclusively with something in the depths of every human psyche. Many passages in the novel affirm that the horror is also within or behind non-human nature, as for example when Marlow says, in a striking extended prosopopoeia, that the superb native woman who comes down to the shore is the image of the personified wilderness:

> And in the hush that had fallen suddenly upon the whole sorrowful land, the immense wilderness, the colossal body of the fecund and mysterious life seemed to look at her, pensive, as though it had been looking at the image of its own tenebrous and passionate soul (136).

I agree with Lacoue-Labarthe, however, that what the West has done in its centuries-long world-conquering imperialisms is perhaps a major embodiment of this ubiquitous horror as it secretly motivates apparently idealistic action for example in causing in the name of enlightenment the deaths of so many Africans in the Congo during the Belgian occupation and exploitation at the end of the nineteenth century ('bringing the torch of civilization to darkest Africa', as we used to say). Another example is the way the United States has, much more recently, brought about so many deaths during the invasion of Iraq – perhaps as many as a million civilians by some counts and the displacement of many millions more. I would differ from Lacoue-Labarthe's emphasis on Western imperialism; however, by claiming that Conrad's horror is perhaps best identified, as I say in my essay, with death as universal, that is, with a heart of darkness that beats everywhere, absolutely everywhere, not just in the West. This is the horror that Kurtz glimpses and then passes over into at the climax of the story:

> Since I had peeped over the edge myself [says Marlow, speaking of his near-fatal illness during his return from meeting Kurtz], I understand better the meaning of his stare, that could not see the flame of the candle, but was wide enough to embrace the whole

universe, piercing enough to penetrate all the hearts that beat in the darkness. He had summed up—he had judged. 'The horror!' . . . It is his extremity that I seem to have lived through. True, he had made that last stride, while I had been permitted to draw back my hesitating foot. And perhaps this is the whole difference: perhaps all the wisdom, and all truth, and all sincerity, are just compressed into that inappreciable moment of time in which we step over the threshold of the invisible. Perhaps! (151)

This climactic passage equates the horror with death. Death, however, is no more than another name, like 'horror', for something that remains invisible and unnameable, though underlying everything. The word 'death' is a catachresis, that is, it is a displaced name for something that has no proper name, but can be named only in tropes. That is what Paul de Man meant when he said 'death is a displaced name for a linguistic predicament',[2] and what Conrad means when he says that you can only know death when you die. Dead men, as we know, tell no tales, though survivors can in a way speak for them, as Marlow speaks for Kurtz. His speaking, however, is indirect, not based on his own experience. In this, it is subject to Paul Celan's interdict against secondary bearing witness, for example, to the Holocaust: 'No one bears witness for the witness'.[3] What Giorgio Agamben calls 'Levi's paradox' applies to Kurtz's knowledge in *Heart of Darkness* too.[4] The only direct witness to the horrors of the gas chambers would be by someone who had experienced them first hand. But no one survived that experience. Similarly, Kurtz witnessed the horror directly, but only at the moment he stepped over the threshold into death. Other catachrestic figures for what Conrad names by the word 'horror' pervade *Heart of Darkness*, figures of the jungle wilderness, or of London, or of England when the Romans invaded it, or of African 'savagery,'or of those heads on stakes Marlow glimpses through his 'glass' (130–1), or, in the famous passage that Lacoue-Labarthe comments on, as I do at length in my essay, of the halo around the moon on a foggy night. This multiplicity of images indicates that none is adequate. Conrad has to keep trying, unsuccessfully, to get it right to find just the right figure, just the right form of words for what Kurtz calls 'the horror'.

The final scene of *Heart of Darkness* confirms the horror's ubiquity. When Marlow visits Kurtz's 'Intended' back in Europe

and lies to her about Kurtz's last words (he says they were her name
rather than 'The horror! The horror!'), he wonders why she cannot
hear Kurtz's true words spoken everywhere in the dusk, even back
home in Europe:

> I was on the point of crying at her, 'Don't you hear them?' The
> dusk was repeating them in a persistent whisper all around us, in
> a whisper that seemed to swell menacingly like the first whisper
> of a rising wind. 'The horror! the horror!' (161).

*

A second mild demurrer has to do with the way Lacoue-Labarthe
accepts perhaps a little too easily the explanatory power of an
autobiographical reading of *Heart of Darkness*. He says in so many
words, 'This narrative is, in large part, autobiographical (written
in 1899, it narrates a voyage Conrad undertook between spring and
winter 1890)' (112). Lacoue-Labarthe assumes that the first speaker
in the tale, the one who reports Marlow's storytelling on the deck of
the yacht named the *Nellie*, is straightforwardly Conrad himself. This
is already a little confusing, as it is Marlow who is delegated to tell in
the first person the 'autobiographical' story of Conrad's voyage. I do
not deny that *Heart of Darkness* has an autobiographical basis, the
details of Conrad's voyage of 1890, what the Congo was like at that
time and so on.[5] Nevertheless, seeing the text as so straightforwardly
referential allows a reader a little too easily to say, 'I see. It's just a
disguised autobiography. The sources are wholly explanatory, and
we need think no more about it'.

Lacoue-Labarthe does, of course, a lot more thinking about it,
but his reading is still basically a referential, representational or
realistic one. His reading is validated by its truth of correspondence
to things outside the text, for example, Belgium's perfidy in the
Congo or Conrad's trip there in 1890. Even Lacoue-Labarthe's
use of Plato, about which I shall say more below, supports this
referentiality. I should prefer to put the autobiographical facts
in brackets and to see *Heart of Darkness* as a radically fictional
transposition of historical and biographical facts that can by
no means be fully explained by them, formally, thematically or
rhetorically. We must read the text with close attention, for itself,
for example, by seeing that first narrator as a fictional invention

like all the other 'voices' that speak in this story. The story would be perfectly readable by someone who had no knowledge of its autobiographical basis, no matter how interesting these autobiographical details are.

*

This leads me to my third observation about the difference between our two essays. This is perhaps the most important difference, though it is not so much a disagreement as a recognition that our essays exemplify two substantially different methodologies of reading. These yield, not surprisingly, rather different results. These differences can be identified in two different ways, ways that nevertheless converge or that come to more or less the same thing. One way is to say that Lacoue-Labarthe's methodology is to a large degree what many people today would call narratological, whereas mine is more what would be called 'rhetorical'. Rhetorical refers, in this case, not to persuasion so much as to the deployment of tropes, as in what I have already said in this prologue about catachresis. The other way to specify the methodological difference between us is to say that Lacoue-Labarthe's approach is more Greek or Hellenic, whereas mine is more Biblical, with some overlapping, of course.

Let me explain what these methodological differences mean. Plato is the great grandfather of narratology, as Lacoue-Labarthe affirms when he says 'if you allow me to use Plato's categories (in reality, they are the only ones we have)' (113). Though Lacoue-Labarthe does not refer to the complex narratological terms and distinctions that were being developed by Gérard Genette, Wayne Booth, James Phelan and many others (implied author as against real author, reliable as against unreliable narrators, use of prolepsis, analepsis, multiple forms of diegesis and so on, in inexhaustible proliferation),[6] he is right to say that Plato in Book 3 of the *Republic* had already made the distinctions that are essential to narratological thinking. *Diegesis*, in Plato's usage, is a narrative that tells a tale in the voice of the author. *Mimesis* is a tale told by someone who assumes the voice of another, as Homer pretends to speak as Ulysses in the *Odyssey*. Conrad, according to Lacoue-Labarthe, speaks as himself, in *diegesis*, in the opening pages of the story (though Conrad, as Lacoue-Labarthe observes, usually says 'we', meaning all those on the deck of the *Nellie* hearing Marlow tell his story). Marlow's story is a *mimesis*, Conrad pretending to speak as Marlow. The whole story is a myth (*muthos*), meaning any story, not necessarily one about the gods, though Lacoue-Labarthe gives myth, in a splendid formulation, a specific (and still Platonic) definition, 'Myth means here:' he says,

> a spoken word [*parole*] which offers itself, by means of some *testimony*, as a bearer of truth. An unverifiable truth, prior to any demonstration or any logical protocol. [There speaks the professional philosopher! A philosophical truth ought to be demonstrable and follow an accepted logical protocol. (JHM)] A truth too difficult to enunciate directly, too heavy or too painful, above all, too obscure (113).

A Greek example would be the Oedipus myth that says human beings, especially those in high places, are cursed by the gods, who never forget a slight, and that all men want to kill their fathers and sleep with their mothers. Marlow's story and its indirect testimony to the truth of the horror are put by Lacoue-Labarthe under the aegis of the Greek or Platonic concept of myth:

> Conrad's entire undertaking consists in trying to find a witness for that which he wants to bear witness to. The Ancients invoked the gods; Conrad invents Marlow. But they do so in order to convey the same truth, a truth of the same order (114).

I suppose, to make the formulations strictly parallel, he might have to say, 'The Ancients invented Oedipus; Conrad invents Marlow'.

Lacoue-Labarthe, you can see, stresses narrative complexities in his reading, and as for Plato, these complexities of *mimesis* are grounded in a realistic or referential *diegesis*. Homer was a real person who at times in the *Odyssey* pretended to speak as Ulysses. Conrad was a real person, the basic 'I' of the story, who pretends to speak as Marlow. The authenticating ground of the story is 'realistic' – referential or representational, autobiographical in Conrad's case. This means that figures of speech used in the telling are ornamental or illustrative as in Lacoue-Labarthe's way of reading the tropes of the cracked nut and the halo around the moon as more or less transparent figures for two different kinds of stories.

It is not surprising, therefore, that Lacoue-Labarthe follows Heidegger (though without mentioning this specific link) in having relatively little interest in the rhetoric of tropes, nor surprising that he sees Conrad's story as modelled on the Greek descent into the underworld (with those knitting women at the beginning as the Fates). He even sees the savage clamour that Marlow hears on the shore as he approaches Kurtz as a species of chorus, such as that used in Greek tragedy. The only non-Greek narratological context Lacoue-Labarthe gives is an odd claim that *Heart of Darkness* can be seen as an oratorio, with the savage clamour as chorus and the characters' speeches as arias. Lacoue-Labarthe's citation of Schelling at the end of his essay to deny that *Heart of Darkness* is an allegory is in harmony with his Hellenizing, literalizing and representational approach. For him, *Heart of Darkness* just means what it says, literally:

> Schelling says that 'myths' are not 'allegorical'. They say nothing other than what they say; they do not have a different meaning from the meaning they enunciate. They are *tautegorical* (a category Schelling borrows from Coleridge). *Heart of Darkness* is no exception to this rule. It is not an allegory—say, a metaphysico-political allegory—at all. It is the tautegory of the West—that is, of art (of *techne*) (120).

If Lacoue-Labarthe's presuppositions for reading are narratological and Greek, mine follow the other stem of the West's divided lineage. My reading is Biblical and tropological. It is therefore not surprising that we come to somewhat different conclusions, though I hereby testify that I think my approach gets closer to the truth at the heart of darkness. The key terms in my reading are Biblical ones: parable, apocalypse and allegory. All of these words are Greek in origin, of course, but they were appropriated by the Christian Bible and by Biblical exegesis for non-Greek purposes. The Gospels transmit the parables of Jesus. The *Book of Revelation*, the last book of the New Testament, is the greatest and most influential example of the apocalypse genre.[7] The English word derives from a Greek word meaning 'unveiling' or 'revelation'. Though 'allegory' is a word in Greek rhetoric and its descendants, meaning, literally, 'saying something otherwise in the town square', the word was appropriated in Biblical exegesis, as in Dante's notorious distinction, in his *Letter to Can Grande*, between 'allegory of the poets' and 'allegory of the theologians', or in Walter Benjamin's use of the term 'allegory' in his book on German seventeenth-century *Trauerspielen*, mourning plays. Paul de Man in his influential distinction between allegory and symbol later picked up on Benjamin's use of the term.[8] I claim in '*Heart of Darkness* Revisited', contra Lacoue-Labarthe, that *Heart of Darkness* is parabolic, that it is an allegory, and following Derrida's essay on apocalypses,[9] that it is a quasi-apocalypse or a parodic apocalypse, an apocalypse that unveils the impossibility of an ultimate unveiling.

Though the difference between our two essays is a matter of nuance, my Biblical orientation means that I pay more attention than Lacoue-Labarthe does to small-scale tropes that work as catachresis, such as that halo around the moon bringing the fog into view by the spectral illumination of moonshine. For me the word 'horror' is a catachresis, not a literal naming. Though Lacoue-Labarthe, like me, speaks of indirect knowledge, he also follows Schelling's concept of 'tautegory' when he says 'the horror' *is* 'the truth of the West', as though the word 'horror'were a literal name. As opposed to that, I see the narrative of *Heart of Darkness* as a way of indirectly speaking about, and bearing witness to, something that cannot be spoken of literally or directly but only in parable or allegory and that can be borne witness to only in a sequence of voices, each speaking for the one before. As Marlow says, you can only confront what the word 'horror' indirectly names by stepping over the last threshold to enter that 'undiscovered country, from whose bourn/No traveller returns', as Shakespeare's Hamlet puts it.[10]

*

Now a word or two about affect, to conclude. I begin by saying that I have been a little suspicious of the turn to affect in recent theory, in cultural studies and in literary studies, in spite of my respect for the strong affective commitment of those who have made this turn. Like the recent vogue of 'the body', the turn to affect may be a way to avoid looking directly at language and other sign systems used by literature and cultural artefacts generally in order to ask just what this language or this collection of signs means or does. Body and its emotions seem so solid and tangible, as opposed to the abstractions of language and of language-based theory! Just as I agree with Jean-Luc Nancy, however, that 'there is no such thing as *the* body',[11] so that body is a deep and vexing philosophical problem, not something that can be taken for granted as an entity everyone knows and understands, *a priori*, so I have problems with the empirical study of emotions, though the problems are different in the case of affects. Though I have no doubt that reading *Heart of Darkness* generates affects in readers, me included, and though I am much struck by Lacoue-Labarthe's phrase asserting that reading *Heart of Darkness* or hearing it performed by a gifted reader, 'provokes an emotion of thought' (111), my problems begin when I try to think how one could be precise about just what those emotions are.

English, for example, has a great many affect words: 'anger', 'joy', 'happiness', 'love', 'affection', 'fear', 'anxiety', exaltation', 'exultation', 'enthusiasm', 'grief', 'melancholy', 'mourning', 'dismay', 'uneasiness', 'terror', 'horror'and the like. The list could be extended indefinitely. We have, no doubt, many more different affect words even more than the names Inuits have for different kinds of snow. They are all feelings, but feelings differ from one another. It is all snow, but there are many different kinds of snow. Even a single one of these affect words names many different feelings. As George Eliot says in *Middlemarch*, 'there are many wonderful mixtures in the world which are all alike called love, and claim the privileges of a sublime rage which is an apology for everything (in literature and the drama)'.[12] The difficulty is that though our affect words discriminate among different subjective feelings, and though we all know more or less what these discriminations are, such words nevertheless remain rather coarse sieves. Though we know how anger differs from joy, 'anger' still names an indefinitely wide range of feelings. Just how do I know that my friend means the same thing I would mean when he or she says, 'I am angry' or 'I am afraid'. As Edmund Husserl long ago recognized, to his lifelong chagrin, we do not have direct phenomenological access to other people's minds, including their feelings but only an indirect 'analogical apperception' of them, an 'appresentation'.[13] We must assume that what other people call anger is analogous to what I call anger, but we have no way to prove that assumption.

Nor, I am sorry to say, do recent brain studies help all that much. We can show what part of the brain lights up when a person seems

to be angry, joyful or afraid, but those brain scans do not tell us
what that person feels like when he or she says, 'I am really angry
now'. Surely, affect is a matter of subjective feeling, not of activity
in a certain part of the brain. Or is it? One might say, 'Anger *is* an
increased activity in a certain part of the brain. That is its essence,
its being'. We could then have people read *Heart of Darkness* and
see what parts of their brains light up. Many people, however,
me included, would not be entirely enthusiastic about this sort
of empirical approach, though much interest exists these days in
cognitive science as a basis for literary study. Some literary scholars
see it as the solution to all our problems. I, however, cannot quite
be satisfied by the vision of literary studies happily reduced to the
study of brain scans.

I have mentioned anger as one of my affect words because I
have had in mind two brilliant essays by J. L. Austin, 'Other Minds'
and 'Pretending'. In both these essays, the question of how I can
know that another person is angry comes up as an example of
the general problem of 'other minds'.[14] Discussing these essays
would be a long business, but I cite one passage from 'Pretending'
as exemplary of the problem with 'affect' I find most perplexing,
as does Austin. The passage is also wonderfully ironic and funny,
as Austin often is. Austin is discussing a paper by Errol Bedford.
The question is, 'How can we know a person is *really* angry and
not just pretending?'

> Our man (sic), then, is 'behaving as if he were angry'. He scowls,
> let us say, and stamps his foot on the carpet. So far we may
> (or perhaps must?) still say 'He is not really angry: he is (only)
> pretending to be angry'. But now he goes further, let us say he
> bites the carpet: and we will picture the scene with sympathy—
> the carpet innocent, the bite untentative and vicious, the damage
> grave. Now he has gone too far, overstepped the limit between
> pretence and reality, and we cannot any longer say 'He is
> pretending to be angry' but must say 'He is really angry'.[15]

You see the problem. Perhaps the man is still pretending and only
trying to convince us that he is really angry by the theatrical gesture
of viciously biting the innocent carpet. Or perhaps, anger is best
defined as angry behaviour, without any attempt to get at what the
angry person is feeling. The problem with this out, as Austin goes

on to say, is that being angry, in ordinary language, means feeling angry. In criticism of Bedford, Austin says,

> we are still not told what really being angry, for which this [biting the carpet] is only the *evidence*, *is*, not therefore shown that it does not involve, or even reside in, the feeling of a feeling—the evidence *might* be evidence that he is feeling a certain feeling.[16]

This problematic of 'the feeling of a feeling' might be followed interminably and tautegorically, but I do not think we would ever get beyond the limitations of not having direct access to the feelings of another person, even the feelings of imaginary persons in works of fiction, and of not having a clear and precise definition of just what anger, or any other affect, 'really *is*'. Echoing Nancy, I would say, 'There is no "the" anger, no "the" horror', in spite of Kurtz's use of the latter locution. 'The' horror is a diffuse and multitudinous terror.

I conclude with a word or two more about 'horror'. Horror is certainly an affect. The word 'horror' is at the centre of the complex verbal integument that is woven in *Heart of Darkness*. Lacoue-Labarthe and I agree about that, though in somewhat different ways. Why did Conrad choose just the word 'horror'? It has a good many valences, including many trivializing ones. 'I encountered a huge lion in the bush. I was horrified.' 'Belgian genocide in the Congo is horrifying to learn about.' '"*Horreurs!*," she said, when she found the tea was already cold.' 'Her dress and makeup were, as usual, horrors'. I suppose the literary pretexts for *Heart of Darkness* are so-called horror stories, but *Heart of Darkness* is certainly an odd or anomalous example of the genre. This is the case not least because the object of horror is never specified as such, only given in endless figurative substitutions for something that cannot be literally named, whereas horror stories usually embody the horror. You might argue that this makes *Heart of Darkness* the ideal or paradigmatic horror story. Horror stories are often tales about zombies, were wolves, vampires and other uncanny apparitions. These give the reader something concrete to be horrified by. It is easy to find such stories laughable, as Jane Austin did in *Northanger Abbey*, or as do college students when they laugh delightedly at horror movies they have seen dozens of times. The vogue of horror stories precedes *Heart of Darkness*. It goes back at least to late eighteenth century Gothic tales. *Horror Stories* was the name of a pulp magazine of the

1930s. I googled 'horror stories' and got 4,690,000 results in 0.09 seconds.[17] That rapidity makes me more than a little uneasy. Conrad appropriates the word to name something invisible and intangible that only Kurtz sees. Marlow's evidence that the horror exists is that he hears Kurtz utter the word as a name for something he sees at his moment of death. Marlow also hears the word whispered in the dusk when he goes to visit Kurtz's Intended back in Europe. What is odd about Conrad's usage is that he hypostatizes an affect word and uses it as the name for something external and universal, '*the* horror', not as the name of an internal affect, as when one might say, 'I am horrified by this', or 'I feel horror'.

Does reading *Heart of Darkness* generate horror in me, I mean horror at '"the" horror'? Not really, I must admit, though that may make me seem cold-hearted. Reading *Heart of Darkness* does generate in me anger (I dare to use that word) and grief (more inconsolable melancholy than appeaseable mourning, to remember Freud's distinction) about what the Belgians did in the Congo and, by displacement, about all the other genocides down to those of the present day. I would even say that I am horrified at the thought of them. How could human beings be so inhuman? I can testify to feeling those affects.

Conrad's masterwork, however, generates in me, in addition to anger and grief, what Marlow says the manager of the Central Station generated in him: 'He inspired uneasiness. That was it! Not a definite mistrust—just uneasiness—nothing more. You have no idea how effective such a . . . a . . . faculty can be' (73). That's it! Reading *Heart of Darkness* inspires in me the affect we call 'uneasiness'. Conrad's story has that faculty. One uneasiness is my uncertainty about whether *Heart of Darkness* proves that Conrad was, as Chinua Achebe famously asserts, 'a thoroughgoing racist'.[18] I want to believe, as many other critics do believe, that Conrad was not a racist and that he was in *Heart of Darkness* attacking the racist side of imperialism, partly by embodying it ironically in Marlow. Nevertheless, the novel employs many racist stereotypes as well as racist clichés from journalism and popular literature of the time: the idea of 'darkest Africa' implicit in the title; the 'savage clamour' on the shore; native dances ('They howled and leaped, and spun, and made horrid faces; but what thrilled you was just the thought of their humanity—like yours—the thought of your remote kinship with this wild and passionate uproar' [96]); distant tom-toms in the jungle (drums *were* used for communication at the time, but it is still a cliché); notions about African primitivism ('Going up that river was like travelling back to the earliest beginnings of the world' [92]) and so on. These require some explaining.

My affective response to reading *Heart of Darkness* is an 'emotion of thought' in the sense that my feeling of uneasiness prompts me to read the novel again and again in an attempt to think out just what it means and just how I should pass judgement on it. I want to understand just what it means that the entire novel's episodes echo one another, one behind the other, each like a curtain opened to expose another curtain. Emotion and thought are to some degree opposing movements of the mind. An 'emotion of thought' is an oxymoron, as Lacoue-Labarthe was doubtless aware. All my thinking about *Heart of Darkness* may be unconsciously apotropaic. It may be a not wholly successful attempt, like Conrad's (or Marlow's) pervasive irony, to ward off a feeling of horror. This might be a horror of thought, in another sense, objective genitive rather than subjective genitive, in which case it would name a resistance to emotive thinking. This horror at the thought of thinking about *Heart of Darkness* might render me speechless with terror at where my feeling-thoughts are taking me.

*

The essays that make up this volume are distinguished in their originality, learning and insight as well as in the diversity of their responses to *Heart of Darkness* and to Lacoue-Labarthe's essay. One might have thought that everything of importance that *could* be said about *Heart of Darkness has* been said, but these essays show that this is by no means the case. These admirable essays show that a great masterpiece like *Heart of Darkness* is always inexhaustibly open to further illuminating commentary. Why is this? I think the source of this inexhaustibility is the extreme complexity of rhetorical, narratological, conceptual and figurative language in a work like *Heart of Darkness*, though no other work has just this specific complexity. The specificity of each work means that as a reader of literary texts you are always pretty much on your own. Generalizations about 'literary language' plus tons of narratological or tropological sophistication are not of much help in a given case. Blanchot eloquently expressed in *The Writing of the Disaster* this excess of literature over literary theory: 'all theories, however different they may be, constantly change places with one another, distinct each from the next only because of the writing which supports them and which thus escapes the very theories purporting to judge it'.[19] The authors of the essays in this volume have responded aggressively to this impasse by returning to the text of *Heart of Darkness* itself as it is illuminated by the new radiance shed on it by Lacoue-Labarthe's distinguished essay. This happens just as the glow of moonlight brings out a haze, to borrow Conrad's own figure.

What strikes me most about these essays is not only their high quality and originality but also their diversity. Who would have thought that Lacoue-Labarthe's instigation would produce so many new ways of reading *Heart of Darkness*, sometimes indeed in opposition to what Lacoue-Labarthe says. From Michael Bell's placement of *Heart of Darkness* in the context of modernist thinking about myth and ideological *Weltanschauungen* from Nietzsche through Heidegger down to Lacoue-Labarthe himself; to Nidesh Lawtoo's reading of *Heart of Darkness* in the context of Lacoue-Labarthe's theories about mimetic contamination or 'enthusiasm'; to Martine Hennard Dutheil de la Rochère's demonstration that Conrad was influenced in his presentation of Kurtz and other characters in *Heart of Darkness* by the then new technique of X-rays, a technique that turns bodies into visible skeletons, as if they were dead already; to Henry Staten's focus on the complex ideas about masculinity in Conrad's novel, including its assumptions about what emotions manly men can legitimately feel and acknowledge (as opposed to a more common focus on Marlow's deplorable ideas about women) – but I pause here. I could go on through a complete inventory of these remarkable essays. These examples, however, will make my point about their diversity and originality. I have learnt much from them. I shall never read *Heart of Darkness* again in the same way. That is meant as high praise.

Notes

1   Philippe Lacoue-Labarthe, *Typographies 1: Le sujet de la philosophie* (Paris: Galilée, 1979); Lacoue-Labarthe, *Typography: Mimesis, Philosophy, Politics,* ed. Christopher Fynsk and Linda M. Brooks (Cambridge, London: Harvard University Press, 1989);

Lacoue-Labarthe, *L'imitation des modernes (Typograhies 2)* (Paris: Galilée, 1986).

2 Paul de Man, 'Autobiography as De-Facement', in *The Rhetoric of Romanticism* (New York: Columbia University Press, 1984), 81.

3 '*Niemand/zeugt für den/Zeugen*'; Paul Celan, 'Aschenglorie', in *Breathturn*, bilingual ed., trans. Pierre Joris (Los Angeles: Sun & Moon Press, 1995), 179, 178.

4 Giorgio Agamben, 'The *Muselman*', in *Remnants of Auschwitz: The Witness and the Archive*, trans. Daniel Heller-Roazen (New York: Zone Books, 2002), 41–86; Primo Levi, *The Drowned and the Saved*, trans. Raymond Rosenthal (New York: Vintage, 1989), 83–4.

5 For a summary, see Ross Murfin, 'Introduction: Biographical and Historical Contexts', in *Joseph Conrad, Heart of Darkness: Complete, Authoritative Text with Biography and Historical Contexts*, ed. Ross Murfin (Boston: Bedford Books of St. Martin's Press, 1996), 3–16.

6 Gérard Genette, 'Discours du récit', in *Figures III* (Paris: Seuil, 1972), 65–282; Genette, *Narrative Discourse: An Essay in Method*, trans. Jane E. Lewin (Ithaca, NY: Cornell University Press, 1980); Wayne C. Booth, *The Rhetoric of Fiction* (Chicago, IL: University of Chicago Press, 1961); James Phelan, *Living to Tell about It: A Rhetoric and Ethics of Character Narration* (Ithaca, NY: Cornell University Press, 2005). These books are only the tip of a huge iceberg. Other distinguished narratologists would include Gerald Prince, Seymour Chatman, Shlomith Rimmon-Kenan, Shen Dan, Dorrit Cohn, Mieke Bal, Robert Scholes, Robert Kellogg, Wallace Martin, Jakob Lothe and many others. An attempt to do for *Heart of Darkness* what Genette did for *À la recherche du temps perdu* might repay the effort, since the narrative structure of Conrad's novel is extremely complex. I say 'might' because narratology may become merely descriptive rather than revelatory of meaning. One says, 'Yes, I see that is an analepsis, but so what?'

7 Nidesh Lawtoo has helpfully informed me that Lacoue-Labarthe uses the word apocalypse apropos of the Holocaust in an essay on Heidegger and Nazism: 'In the apocalypse at Auschwitz, it is no more or less than the essence of the West that is revealed' (Philippe Lacoue-Labarthe, 'Neither an Accident nor a Mistake', trans. Paula Wissing, *Critical Inquiry* 15.2 [1989], 484). The word 'apocalypse' is used a little figuratively here, as it is in the title of the film modelled on *Heart of Darkness, Apocalypse Now*. The word 'apocalypse', strictly speaking, names the unveiling of what is going to be revealed at the end of the world, not the uncovering of anything that can be revealed

in any 'now' during the course of history. Saint John of Patmos, the putative author of *The Book of Revelation*, thought the end of the world was at hand, as writers of apocalypses generally do. Saying the Holocaust reveals the essence of the West is, of course, analogous to saying 'the West is the horror'. 'Essence' and 'is' are totalizing words. They are even metaphysical, logocentric or essentialist words when used in the way Lacoue-Labarthe uses them. Indeed, it is hard to use them otherwise.

8   Dante Alighieri, 'Letter to Can Grande', *http://www.english.udel.edu/ dean/cangrand.html*, accessed 23 April 2011. This gives Dante's Latin, with an English translation by James Marchand. Walter Benjamin, *Ursprung des deutschen Trauerspiels* (Berlin: 1928; reissued in Frankfurt: Suhrkamp, 1963); Benjamin, *The Origin of German Tragic Drama*, trans. John Osborne (London: New Left Books, 1977); Paul de Man, 'Allegory and Symbol', in 'The Rhetoric of Temporality', in *Blindness and Insight* (Minneapolis, MN: University of Minnesota Press, 1983), 187–208.

9   Jacques Derrida, *D'un ton apocalyptique adopté naguère en philosophie* (Paris: Galilée, 1983); Derrida, 'Of an Apocalyptic Tone Recently Adopted in Philosophy', trans. John P. Leavey, Jr., *The Oxford Literary Review* 6.2 (1984), 3–37.

10 William Shakespeare, *Hamlet*, III, i, 79–80.

11 Jean-Luc Nancy, *Corpus,* trans. Richard A. Rand (New York: Fordham University Press, 2008), 119; Nancy, *Corpus* (Paris: Métailié, 2006), 104.

12 George Eliot, *Middlemarch* (Oxford: Oxford University Press, 1999), ch. 31, 333–4.

13 Edmund Husserl, 'Fifth Meditation: Uncovering the Sphere of Transcendental Being as Monadological Intersubjectivity', in *Cartesian Meditations: An Introduction to Phenomenology*, trans. Dorion Cairns (The Hague: Martinus Nijhoff, 1960), 89–151. See especially paragraph 50, 'The mediate intentionality of experiencing someone else, as "appresentation" (analogical apperception)', 108–11.

14 J. L. Austin, 'Other Minds' and 'Pretending', in *Philosophical Papers*, ed. J. O. Urmson and G. J. Warnock (Oxford: Oxford University Press, 1979), 76–116; 253–71.

15 Austin, 'Pretending', 254.

16 Austin, 'Pretending', 255.

17 *http://www.google.com/search?client=safari&rls=en&q=horror+st ories&ie=UTF-8&oe=UTF-8*, accessed 21 April 2011.

18 Chinua Achebe, 'An Image of Africa: Racism in Conrad's *Heart of Darkness*', in Joseph Conrad, *Heart of Darkness*, 4th ed., ed. Paul B. Armstrong (New York: W. W. Norton, 2006), 336–49. Also available at: *http://kirbyk.net/hod/image.of.africa.html*, accessed 22 April 2011.

19 Maurice Blanchot, *The Writing of the Disaster*, trans. Ann Smock. (Lincoln and London: University of Nebraska Press, 1995), 80; Blanchot, *L'Écriture du désastre* (Paris: Gallimard, 1980), 128.

PART ONE

Mythic Darkness

1

Heart of Darkness revisited

J. HILLIS MILLER

I begin with three questions: Is it a senseless accident, a result of the
crude misinterpretation or gross transformation of the mass media
that the cinematic version of *Heart of Darkness* is called *Apocalypse
Now*, or is there already something apocalyptic about Conrad's
novel in itself? What are the distinctive features of an apocalyptic
text? How would we know when we had one in hand?

I shall approach an answer to these questions by the somewhat
roundabout way of an assertion that if *Heart of Darkness* is perhaps
only problematically apocalyptic, there can be no doubt that it is
parabolic. The distinctive feature of a parable, whether sacred or
secular, is the use of realistic story, a story in one way or another
based firmly on what Marx calls man's 'real conditions of life, and
his relations with his kind', to express another reality or truth not
otherwise expressible.[1] When the disciples ask Jesus why he speaks
to the multitudes in parables, he answers, 'Therefore speak I to them
in parables: because they seeing see not; and hearing they hear not,
neither do they understand'.[2] A little later Matthew tells the reader
that 'without a parable spake he not unto them: That it might be
fulfilled which was spoken by the prophet, saying, I will open my
mouth in parables; I will utter things which have been kept secret
from the foundation of the world'.[3] Those things which have been
kept secret from the foundation of the world will not be revealed
until they have been spoken in parable, that is, in terms which the
multitude who lack spiritual seeing and hearing nevertheless see and

hear, namely, the everyday details of their lives of fishing, farming and domestic economy.

Conrad's story is a parable, in part, because it is grounded firmly in the details of real experience. Biographers such as Ian Watt, Frederick Karl and Norman Sherry tell us all that is likely to be learnt of Conrad's actual experience in the Congo as well as of the historical originals of Kurtz, the parti-coloured harlequin-garbed Russian and other characters in the novel. If parables are characteristically grounded in representations of realistic or historical truth, *Heart of Darkness* admirably fulfils this requirement of parable. But it fills another requirement too. Conrad's novel is a parable because, although it is based on what Marx called 'real conditions', its narrator attempts through his tale to reveal some as-yet-unseen reality.

Unlike allegory, which tries to shed light on the past or even on our origins, parable tends to be oriented toward the future, toward last things, toward the mysteries of the kingdom of heaven and how to get there. Parable tends to express what Paul at the end of Romans, in echo of Matthew, calls 'the revelation of the mystery, which was kept secret since the world began, but now is made manifest'.[4] Parable, as we can now see, has at least one thing in common with apocalypse: it too is an act of unveiling that which has never been seen or known before. Apocalypse *means* unveiling; an apocalypse is a narrative unveiling or revelation. The last book of the Bible is the paradigmatic example of apocalypse in our tradition, though it is by no means the only example. The *Book of Revelation* seeks to unveil a mystery of the future, namely, what will happen at time's ending.

My contention, then, is that *Heart of Darkness* fits, in its own way, the definitions of both parable and apocalypse and that much illumination is shed on it by interpreting it in the light of these generic classifications. As Marlow says of his experience in the heart of darkness: 'It was sombre enough too—. . . not very clear either. No, not very clear. And yet it seemed to throw a kind of light' (51). A narrative that sheds light, that penetrates darkness, that clarifies and illuminates – this is one definition of that mode of discourse called 'parabolic or apocalyptic', but it might also serve to define the work of criticism or interpretation. All criticism claims to be enlightenment or *Aufklärung*.

How, though, does a story enlighten or clarify: in what ways may narratives illuminate or unveil? Conrad's narrator distinguishes

between two different ways in which a narrative may be related to
its meaning:

> The yarns of seamen have a direct simplicity, the whole meaning
> of which lies within the shell of a cracked nut. But Marlow was
> not typical (if his propensity to spin yarns be excepted), and to
> him the meaning of an episode was not inside like a kernel but
> outside [Ms: outside in the unseen], enveloping the tale which
> brought it out only as a glow brings out a haze, in the likeness of
> one of these misty halos that sometimes are made visible by the
> spectral illumination of moonshine. (48)

The narrator here employs two figures to describe two kinds
of stories: simple tales and parables. Through the two figures,
moreover, Conrad attempts to present the different ways in which
these two kinds of narration relate to their meanings.

The meanings of the stories of most seamen, says the narrator,
are inside the narration like the kernel of a cracked nut. I take it the
narrator means the meanings of such stories are easily expressed,
detachable from the stories and open to paraphrase in other terms, as
when one draws an obvious moral: 'Crime doesn't pay' or 'Honesty
is the best policy' or 'The truth will out' or 'Love conquers all'. The
figure of the cracked nut suggests that the story itself, its characters
and narrative details, are the inedible shell which must be removed
and discarded so the meaning of the story may be assimilated.
This relation of the story to its meaning is a particular version of
the relation of container to thing contained. The substitution of
contained for container, in this case meaning for story, is one version
of that figure called in classical rhetoric *synecdoche*, but this is a
metonymic rather than a metaphorical synecdoche.[5] The meaning
is adjacent to the story, contained within it as nut within shell, but
the meaning has no intrinsic similarity or kinship to the story. Its
relation to the story that contains it is purely contingent. The one
happens to touch the other, as shell surrounds nut, as bottle its liquid
contents or as shrine-case its iconic image.

It is far otherwise with Marlow's stories. Their meaning – like
the meaning of a parable – is outside, not in. It envelops the tale
rather than being enveloped by it. The relation of container and
thing contained is reversed. The meaning now contains the tale.
Moreover, perhaps because of that enveloping containment, or

perhaps for more obscure reasons, the relation of the tale to its meaning is no longer that of dissimilarity and contingency. The tale is the necessary agency of the bringing into the open or revelation of that particular meaning. It is not so much that the meaning is like the tale. It is not. But the tale is in preordained correspondence to or in resonance with the meaning. The tale magically brings the 'unseen' meaning out and makes it visible.

Conrad has the narrator express this subtle concept of parabolic narration according to the parabolic 'likeness' of a certain atmospheric phenomenon. 'Likeness' is a homonym of the German *Gleichnis*, which is a term for parable. The meaning of a parable appears in the 'spectral' likeness of the story that reveals it or, rather, it appears in the likeness of an exterior light surrounding the story, just as the narrator's theory of parable appears not as such but in the 'likeness' of the figure he proposes. Thus, the figure does double duty, both as a figure for the way Marlow's stories express their meaning and as a figure for itself, so to speak; that is, as a figure for its own mode of working. This is according to a mind-twisting torsion of the figure back on itself that is a regular feature of such figuration, parables of parable, or stories about storytelling. The figure both illuminates its own workings and at the same time obscures or undermines it, since a figure of a figure is an absurdity or, as Wallace Stevens puts it, there is no such thing as a metaphor of a metaphor. What was the figurative vehicle of the first metaphor automatically becomes the literal tenor of the second metaphor.[6]

Let us look more closely at the exact terms of the metaphor Conrad's narrator proposes. To Marlow, the narrator says, 'the meaning of an episode was not inside like a kernel but outside, enveloping the tale which brought it out only as a glow brings out a haze, in the likeness of one of these spectral illuminations of moonshine'. The first simile here ('as a glow') is doubled by a second, similitude of a similitude ('in the likeness of. . .'). The 'haze' is there all around on a dark night, but, like the meaning of one of Marlow's tales, it is invisible, inaudible, intangible in itself, like the darkness, or like that 'something great and invincible' Marlow is aware of in the African wilderness, something 'like evil or truth, waiting patiently for the passing away off this fantastic invasion' (76). The haze, too, is like the climactic name for that truth, the enveloping meaning of the tale: 'the horror', those last words of Kurtz that seem all around in the gathering darkness when Marlow makes his visit to Kurtz's Intended and tells his lie. 'The dusk', Marlow says, 'was repeating them in a persistent whisper all around us, in a whisper that seemed to swell menacingly like the first whisper of a rising wind. "The horror! The horror!"' (149).

The workings of Conrad's figure is much more complex than perhaps it at first appears, both in itself and in the context of the fine grain of the texture of language in *Heart of Darkness* as a whole, as well as in the context of the traditional complex figures, narrative motifs and concepts to which it somewhat obscurely alludes. The atmospheric phenomenon that Conrad uses as the vehicle of this parabolic metaphor is a perfectly real one, universally experienced. It is as referential and as widely known as the facts of farming Jesus uses in the parable of the sower. If you sow your seed on stony ground, it will not be likely to sprout. An otherwise invisible mist or haze at night will show up as a halo around the moon. As in the case of Jesus' parable of the sower, Conrad uses his realistic and almost universally known facts as the means of expressing indirectly another truth less visible and less widely known, just as the narrative of *Heart of Darkness* as a whole is based on the facts of history and on the facts of Conrad's life but uses these to express something trans-historical and trans-personal, the evasive and elusive 'truth' underlying both historical and personal experience.

Both Jesus' parable of the sower and Conrad's parable of the moonshine in the mist, curiously enough, have to do with their own efficacy – that is, with the efficacy of parable. Both are posited on their own necessary failure. Jesus' parable of the sower will give more only to those who already have and will take away from those who have not even what they have. If you can understand the parable, you do not need it. If you need it, you cannot possibly understand it. You are stony ground on which the seed of the word falls unavailing. Your eyes and ears are closed, even though the function of parables is to open the eyes and ears of the multitude to the mysteries of the kingdom of heaven. In the same way, Conrad, in a famous passage in the preface to *The Nigger of the 'Narcissus'*, tells his readers, 'My task which I am trying to achieve is, by the power of the written word, to make you hear, to make you feel—it is, before all, to make you *see*'. No reader of Conrad can doubt that he means to make the reader see not only the vivid facts of the story he tells but the evasive truth behind them, of which they are the obscure revelation, what Conrad calls, a bit beyond the famous phrase from the preface just quoted, 'that glimpse of truth for which you have forgotten to ask'. To see the facts, out there in the sunlight, is also to see the dark truth that lies behind them. All Conrad's work turns on this double paradox: first the paradox of the two senses of seeing, seeing as physical vision and seeing as seeing through, as penetrating to or unveiling the hidden invisible truth, and second the paradox of seeing the darkness in terms of the light. Nor can the careful reader of Conrad doubt that in Conrad's case too, as in the case of the Jesus of the parable of the sower, the goal of tearing the veil of familiarity from the world and making us *see* cannot be accomplished. If we see the darkness already, we do not need *Heart of Darkness*. If we do not see it, reading *Heart of Darkness* or even hearing Marlow tell it will not help us. We shall remain among those who 'seeing see not; and hearing they hear not, neither do they understand'. Marlow makes this clear in an extraordinary passage in *Heart of Darkness*, one of those places in which the reader is returned to the primary scene of narration on board the *Nellie*. Marlow is explaining the first lie he told for Kurtz, his prevarication misleading the bricklayer at the Central Station into believing he (Marlow) has great power back home:

> I became in an instant as much of a pretence as the rest of the bewitched pilgrims. This simply because I had a notion it somehow would be of help to that Kurtz whom at the time I did not see—you understand. He was just a word for me. I did not see the man in the name any more than you do. Do you see him? Do you see the story? Do you see anything? It seems to me I am trying to tell you a dream—making a vain attempt, because no relation of a dream can convey the dream-sensation, that commingling of absurdity, surprise, and bewilderment in a tremor of struggling revolt, that notion of being captured by the incredible which is of the very essence of dreams. . . .
>
> He was silent for a while.
>
> No, it is impossible; it is impossible to convey the life-sensation of any given epoch of one's existence—that which makes its truth, its meaning—its subtle and penetrating essence. It is impossible. We live, as we dream—alone. . . .

He paused again as if reflecting, then added:
Of course in this you fellows see more than I could then. You see me, whom you know. . . .
It had become so pitch dark that we listeners could hardly see one another. For a long time already he, sitting apart, had been no more to us than a voice. There was not a word from anybody. The others might have been asleep, but I was awake. I listened, I listened on the watch for the sentence, for the word, that would give me the clue to the faint uneasiness inspired by this narrative that seemed to shape itself without human lips in the heavy night-air of the river. (82–3)

The denial of the possibility of making the reader see by means of literature is made here through a series of moves, each one ironically going beyond and undermining the one before. When this passage is set against the one about the moonshine, the two together bring out into the open, like a halo in the mist, the way *Heart of Darkness* is posited on the impossibility of achieving its goal of revelation, or to put this another way, the way it is a revelation of the impossibility of revelation.

In Conrad's parable of the moonshine, the moon shines already with reflected and secondary light. Its light is reflected from the primary light of that sun which is almost never mentioned as such in *Heart of Darkness*. The sun is only present in the glitter of its reflection from this or that object, for example, the surface of that river which, like the white place of the unexplored Congo on the map, fascinates Marlow like a snake. In one passage it is moonlight, already reflected light, which is reflected again from the river: 'The moon had spread over everything a thin layer of silver—over the rank grass, over the mud, upon the wall of matted vegetation standing higher than the wall of a temple, over the great river I could see through a sombre gap glittering, glittering, as it flowed broadly by without a murmur' (81). In the case of the parable of the moonshine too that halo brought out in the mist is twice-reflected light. The story, according to Conrad's analogy, the facts that may be named and seen, is the moonlight, while the halo brought out around the moon by the reflection of the moonlight from the diffused, otherwise invisible, droplets of the mist, is the meaning of the tale, or rather, the meaning of the tale is the darkness that is made visible by that halo of twice-reflected light. But of course the halo does nothing of the sort. It only makes visible more light. What can be seen is only what can be seen. In the end, this is always only more light, direct or reflected. The darkness is in principle invisible and remains invisible. All that can be said is that the halo gives the spectator indirect knowledge that the darkness is there. The glow brings out the haze, the story brings out its meaning, by magically generating knowledge that something is there, the haze in one case, the meaning of the story, inarticulate and impossible to be articulated, in any direct way at least, in the other. The expression of the meaning of the story is never the plain statement of that meaning but is always no more than a parabolic 'likeness' of the meaning, as the haze is brought out 'in the likeness of one of those misty halos that sometimes are made visible by the spectral illumination of moonshine'.

In the passage in which Marlow makes explicit his sense of the impossibility of his enterprise, he says to his auditors on the *Nellie* first that he did not see Kurtz in his name any more than they do. The auditors of any story are forced to see everything of the story 'in its name', since a story is made of nothing but names and their adjacent words. There is nothing to see literally in any story except the words on the page, the movement of the lips of the teller. Unlike Marlow, his listeners never have a chance to see or experience directly the man behind the name. The reader, if he or she happens at this moment to think of it (and the passage is clearly an invitation to such thinking, an invocation of it), is in exactly the same situation as that of Marlow's auditors, only worse. When Marlow appeals to his auditors, Conrad is by a kind of ventriloquism appealing to his readers: 'Do you see him? Do you see the story? Do you see anything? It seems to me I am trying to tell you a dream—making a vain attempt'. Conrad speaks through Marlow to us. The reader too can reach the truth behind the story only through names, never through any direct perception or experience. In the reader's case, it is not even names proffered by a living man before him only names coldly and impersonally printed on the pages of the book he holds in his hand. Even if the reader goes behind the fiction to the historical reality on which it is based, as Ian Watt and others have done, he or she will only confront more words on more pages – Conrad's letters or the historical records of the conquest and exploitation of the Congo. The situation of the auditors, even of a living speaker, Marlow says, is scarcely better, since what a story must convey through names and other words is not the fact but the 'life-sensation' behind the fact 'which makes its truth, its meaning—its subtle and penetrating essence'. This is once more the halo around the moon, the meaning enveloping the tale. This meaning is as impossible to convey by way of the life-facts that may be named as the 'dream-sensation' is able to be conveyed through a relation of the bare facts of the dream. Anyone knows this. who has ever tried to tell another person his dream and has found how lame and flat, or how laughable, it sounds, since 'no relation of a dream can convey the dream-sensation'. According to Marlow's metaphor or proportional analogy, as the facts of a dream are to the dream-sensation, so the facts of a life are to the life-sensation. Conrad makes an absolute distinction between experience and the interpretation of written or spoken signs. The sensation may only be experienced directly and may by no means, oral or written, be communicated to another: 'We live, as we dream, alone'.

Nevertheless, Marlow tells his auditors, they have one direct or experiential access to the truth enveloping the story: 'You fellows see more than I could then. You see me, whom you know'. There is a double irony in this. To see the man who has had the experience is to have an avenue to the experience for which the man speaks, to which he bears witness. Marlow's auditors see more than he could then – that is, before his actual encounter with Kurtz. Ironically, the witness cannot bear witness for himself. He cannot see himself or cannot see through himself or by means of himself, in spite of, or in contradiction of, Conrad's (or Marlow's) assertion a few paragraphs later that work is 'the chance to find yourself. Your own reality—for yourself, not for others—what no other man can ever know. They can only see the mere show, and never can tell what it really means' (85). Though each man can only experience his own reality, his own truth, the paradox involved here seems to run, he can only experience it through another or by means of another as witness to a truth deeper in, behind the other. Marlow's auditors can only learn indirectly, through Marlow, whom they see. They therefore know more than he did. Marlow could only learn through Kurtz, when he finally encountered him face to face. The reader of *Heart of Darkness* learns through the relation of the primary narrator, who learnt through Marlow, who learnt through Kurtz. This proliferating relay of witnesses, one behind another, each revealing another truth further in which turns out to be only another witness, corresponds to the narrative form of *Heart of Darkness*. The novel is a sequence of episodes, each structured according to the model of appearances and signs, which are also obstacles or veils. Each veil must be lifted to reveal a truth behind, which always turns out to be another episode, another witness and another veil to be lifted in its turn. Each such episode is a 'fact dazzling, to be seen, like the foam on the depths of the sea, like a ripple on an unfathomable enigma' (105), the fact that though cannibal Africans on Marlow's steamer were starving, they did not eat the white men. But behind each enigmatic fact is only another fact. The relay of witness behind witness behind witness, voice behind voice behind voice, each speaking in ventriloquism through the one next farther out, is a characteristic of the genre of the apocalypse. In the *Book of Revelation*, God speaks through Jesus, who speaks through a messenger angel, who speaks through John of Patmos, who speaks to us.

There is another reason beyond the necessities of revelation for this structure. The truth behind the last witness, behind Kurtz, for example, in *Heart of Darkness*, is no one can doubt it, death, 'the horror'; or, to put this another way, 'death' is another name for what Kurtz names 'the horror'. No man can confront that truth face to face and survive. Death or the horror can only be experienced indirectly, by way of the face and voice of another. The relay of witnesses both reveals death and, luckily, hides it. As Marlow says, 'the inner truth is hidden—luckily, luckily' (93). This is another regular feature of the genre of the apocalypse. The word 'apocalypse' means 'unveiling', 'revelation', but what the apocalypse unveils is not the truth of the end of the world it announces but the act of unveiling. The unveiling unveils unveiling. It leaves its readers, auditors and witnesses, as far as ever from the always 'not quite yet' of the imminent revelation – luckily. Marlow says it was not his own near-death on the way home down the river, 'not my own extremity I remember best', but Kurtz's 'extremity that I seem to have lived through'. Then he adds, 'True, he had made that last stride, he had stepped over the edge, while I had been permitted to draw back my hesitating foot. And perhaps in this is the whole difference; perhaps all the wisdom, and all truth, and all sincerity, are just compressed into that inappreciable moment of time in which we step over the threshold of the invisible. Perhaps!' (151). Marlow, like Orpheus returning without Eurydice from the land of the dead, comes back to civilization with nothing, nothing to bear witness to, nothing to reveal by the process of unveiling that makes up the whole of the narration of *Heart of Darkness*. Marlow did not go far enough into the darkness, but if he had, like Kurtz, he could not have come back. All the reader gets is Marlow's report of Kurtz's last words and a description of the look on Kurtz's face: 'It was as though a veil had been rent. I saw on that ivory face the expression of sombre pride, of ruthless power, of craven terror — of an intense and hopeless despair' (149).

I have suggested that there are two ironies in what Marlow says when he breaks his narration to address his auditors directly. The first irony is the fact that the auditors see more than Marlow did because they see Marlow, whom they know; the second is that we readers of the novel see no living witness. (By Marlow's own account that is not enough. Seeing only happens by direct experience, and no act of reading is direct experience. The book's claim to give the reader access to the dark truth behind appearance is withdrawn by the terms in which it is proffered.) But there is, in fact, a third irony in this relay of ironies behind ironies in that Marlow's auditors, of course, do not see Marlow either. It is too dark. They hear only his disembodied voice. 'It had become so pitch dark', says the narrator, 'that we listeners could hardly see one another. For a long time already he, sitting apart, had been no more to us than a voice'. Marlow's narrative does not seem to be spoken by a living incarnate witness, there before his auditors in the flesh. It is a 'narrative that seemed to shape itself without human lips in the heavy night-air of the river'. This voice can be linked to no individual speaker or writer as the ultimate source of its messages, not to Marlow, nor to Kurtz, nor to the first narrator, nor even to Conrad himself. The voice is spoken by no one to no one. It always comes from another, from the other of any identifiable speaker or writer. It traverses all these voices as what speaks through them. It gives them authority and at the same time dispossesses them, deprives them of authority, since they only speak with the delegated authority of another. As Marlow of the voice of Kurtz and of all the other voices, they are what remain as a dying unanimous and anonymous drone or clang that exceeds any single identifiable voice and in the end is spoken by no one:

> A voice. He was very little more than a voice. And I heard him—it—this voice—other voices—all of them were so little more than voices—and the memory of that time itself lingers around me, impalpable, like a dying vibration of one immense jabber, silly, atrocious, sordid, savage, or simply mean, without any kind of sense. Voices, voices—. . . (115)

For the reader, too, *Heart of Darkness* lingers in the mind or memory chiefly as a cacophony of dissonant voices. It is as though the story were spoken or written not by an identifiable narrator but directly by the darkness itself, just as Kurtz's last words seem whispered by the circumambient dusky air when Marlow makes his visit to Kurtz's Intended, and just as Kurtz presents himself to Marlow as a voice, a voice which exceeds Kurtz and seems to speak from beyond him: 'Kurtz discoursed. A voice! a voice! It rang deep to the very last. It survived his strength to hide in the magnificent folds of eloquence the barren darkness of his heart' (147). Kurtz has 'the gift of expression, the bewildering, the illuminating, the most exalted and the most contemptible, the pulsating stream of light, or the deceitful flow from the heart of an impenetrable darkness' (113–4). Kurtz has intended to use his eloquence as a means of 'wringing the heart of the wilderness', but 'the wilderness had found him out early, and had taken on him a terrible vengeance for the fantastic invasion' (131). The direction of the flow of language reverses. It flows from the darkness instead of towards it. Kurtz is 'hollow at the core' (131), and so the wilderness can speak through him, use him so to speak as a ventriloquist's dummy through which its terrible messages may be broadcasted to the world: 'Exterminate all the brutes!' 'The horror!' (118, 149). The speaker too is spoken through. Kurtz's disembodied voice, or the voice behind voice behind voice of the narrators, or that 'roaring chorus of articulated, rapid, breathless utterance' (146) shouted by the natives on the bank, when Kurtz is taken on board the steamer – these are in the end no more direct a testimony of the truth than the words on the page as Conrad wrote them. The absence of a visible speaker of Marlow's words and the emphasis on the way Kurtz is a disembodied voice function as indirect expressions of the fact that *Heart of Darkness* is words without person, words which cannot be traced back to any single personality. This is once more confirmation of my claim that *Heart of Darkness* belongs to the genre of the parabolic apocalypse. The apocalypse is after all a written not an oral genre, and as Jacques Derrida has pointed out, one characteristic of an apocalypse is that it turns on the invitation or 'Come' spoken or written always by someone other than the one who seems to utter or write it.[7]

A full exploration of the way *Heart of Darkness* is an apocalypse would need to be put under the multiple aegis of the converging figures of irony, antithesis, catachresis, synecdoche, aletheia and personification. Irony is a name for the pervasive tone of Marlow's narration, which undercuts as it affirms. Antithesis identifies the division of what is presented in the story in terms of seemingly firm oppositions that always ultimately break down. Catachresis is the proper name for a parabolic revelation of the darkness by means of visible figures that do not substitute for any possible literal expression of that darkness. Synecdoche is the name for the questionable relation of similarity between the visible sign, the skin of the surface, the foam on the sea and what lies behind it, the pulsating heart of darkness, the black depths of the sea. Unveiling or *aletheia* labels that endless process of apocalyptic revelation that never quite comes off. The revelation is always future. Personification, finally, is a name for the consistent presentation of the darkness as some kind of living creature with a heart, ultimately as a woman who unmans all those male questors who try to dominate her. This pervasive personification is most dramatically embodied in the native woman, Kurtz's mistress: 'the immense wilderness, the colossal body of the fecund and mysterious life seemed to look at her, pensive, as though it had been looking at the image of its own tenebrous and passionate soul' (136).

Heart of Darkness is perhaps most explicitly apocalyptic in announcing the end, the end of Western civilization, or of Western imperialism, the reversal of idealism into savagery. As is always the case with apocalypses, the end is announced as something always imminent, never quite yet. Apocalypse is never now. The novel sets women, who are out of it, against men, who can live with the facts and have a belief to protect them against the darkness. Men can breathe dead hippo and not be contaminated. Male practicality and idealism reverse, however. They turn into their opposites because they are hollow at the core. They are vulnerable to the horror.

They *are* the horror. The idealistic suppression of savage customs becomes, 'Exterminate all the brutes!' Male idealism is the same thing as the extermination of the brutes. The suppression of savage customs is the extermination of the brutes. This is not just word play but actual fact, as the history of the white man's conquest of the world has abundantly demonstrated. This conquest means the end of the brutes, but it means also, in Conrad's view of history, the end of Western civilization, with its ideals of progress, enlightenment and reason, its goal of carrying the torch of civilization into the wilderness and wringing the heart of the darkness. Or, it is the imminence of that end which has never quite come as long as there is someone to speak or write of it.

I claim to have demonstrated that *Heart of Darkness* is not only parabolic but also apocalyptic. It fits that strange genre of the apocalyptic text, the sort of text that promises an ultimate revelation without giving it and says always 'Come' and 'Wait'. But there is an extra twist given to the paradigmatic form of the apocalypse in *Heart of Darkness*. The *Aufklärung* or enlightenment in this case is of the fact that the darkness can never be enlightened. The darkness enters into every gesture of enlightenment to enfeeble it, to hollow it out, to corrupt it and thereby to turn its reason into unreason, its pretence of shedding light into more darkness. Marlow as narrator is in complicity with this reversal in the act of identifying it in others. He too claims, like the characteristic writer of an apocalypse, to know something no one else knows and to be qualified on that basis to judge and enlighten them. 'I found myself back in the sepulchral city', says Marlow of his return from the Congo,

> resenting the sight of people hurrying through the streets to filch a little money from each other, to devour their infamous cookery, to gulp their unwholesome beer, to dream their insignificant and silly dreams. They trespassed upon my thoughts. They were intruders whose knowledge of life was to me an irritating pretence, because I felt so sure they could not possibly know the things I knew. (152)

The consistent tone of Marlow's narration is ironical. Irony is truth-telling or a means of truth-telling, of unveiling. At the same time, it is a defence against the truth. This doubleness makes it, though it seems so coolly reasonable, another mode of unreason, the unreason of a fundamental undecidability. If irony is a defence, it is also inadvertently a means of participation. Though Marlow says, 'I have a voice too, and for good or evil mine is the speech that cannot be silenced' (97), as though his speaking were a cloak against the darkness, he too, in speaking ironically, becomes, like Kurtz, one of those speaking tubes or relay stations through whom the darkness speaks. As theorists of irony from Friedrich Schlegel and Soren Kierkegaard to Paul de Man have argued, irony is the one trope that cannot be mastered or used as an instrument of mastery. An ironic statement is essentially indeterminate or undecidable in meaning. The man who attempts to say one thing while clearly meaning another ends up by saying the first thing too, in spite of himself. One irony leads to another. The ironies proliferate into a great crowd of little conflicting ironies. It is impossible to know in just what tone of voice one should read one of Marlow's sardonic ironies. Each is uttered simultaneously in innumerable conflicting tones going all the way from the lightest and most comical to the darkest, most sombre and tragic. It is impossible to decide exactly which quality of voice should be allowed to predominate over the others. Try reading aloud the passage cited above and you will see this. Marlow's tone and meaning are indeterminate; his description of the clamour of native voices on the shore or of the murmur of all those voices he remembers from that times in his life also functions as an appropriate displaced description of his own discourse. Marlow's irony makes his speech in its own way another version of that multiple cacophonous and deceitful voice flowing from the heart of darkness, 'a complaining clamour, modulated in savage discords', or a 'tumultuous and mournful uproar', another version of that 'one immense jabber, silly, atrocious, sordid, savage, or simply mean, without any kind of sense', not a voice but voices (102, 115). In this inextricable tangle of voices and voices speaking within voices, Marlow's narration fulfils, no doubt without deliberate intent on Conrad's part, one of the primary laws of the genre of the apocalypse.

The final fold in this folding in of complicities in these ambiguous acts of unveiling is my own complicity as demystifying commentator. Behind or before Marlow is Conrad and before or behind him stands the reader or critic. My commentary unveils a lack of decisive unveiling in *Heart of Darkness*. I have attempted to perform an act of generic classification, with all the covert violence and unreason of that act, since no work is wholly commensurate with the boundaries of any genre. By unveiling the lack of unveiling in *Heart of Darkness*, I have become another witness in my turn, as much guilty as any other in the line of witnesses of covering over while claiming to illuminate. My *Aufklärung* too has been the continuing impenetrability of Conrad's *Heart of Darkness*.

Notes

1   Marx, Karl, "Manifesto of the Communist Party," in *The Marx-Engels Reader*, ed. Robert C. Tucker (New York: Norton, 1978), 476.

2   Matthew 13:13

3   Matthew 13:34–35

4   Romans 16:25–26

5   In metaphorical synecdoche, a part of something is used to signify the whole: 'I see a sail' means 'I see a ship'. A metonymic synecdoche is one in which the signifying part is really only something contiguous with the thing signified, not intrinsic to it; 'the bottle' is a metonymic synecdoche for liquor, since glass cannot really be part of liquor in the way a sail is part of a ship.

6   The 'vehicle' of a figurative expression is the term used to refer to something else; the 'tenor' is the person, thing or concept referred to by the vehicle. In the metaphorical synecdoche used as an example in footnote 5, 'sail' is the vehicle and 'ship' is the tenor; in the metonymic synecdoche, 'bottle' is the vehicle and 'liquor' the tenor. If you say you feel blue to mean you feel sad, 'blue' is the vehicle and 'sadness' the tenor.

7   See Jacques Derrida, 'D'un ton apocalyptique adopté naguère en philosophie', in *Les Fins de l'homme*, ed. Philippe Lacoue-Labarthe and Jean-Luc Nancy (Paris: Flammarion, 1981), 445–79, especially p. 468ff. The essay has been translated by John P. Learey, Jr., and published in the 1982 number of *Seineia* (62–97).

2

Modernism, myth and *Heart of Darkness*

MICHAEL BELL

Philippe Lacoue-Labarthe's highly suggestive essay on *Heart of Darkness* records his fresh rediscovery of the familiar text, his sense of the immensity of its theme as that now sounds in the echo chamber of twentieth-century history and thought. I believe he is drawn into some over-reading of the tale but can readily endorse his perception that something enormous is at stake within it. His admiration, not just for but, in the older sense of the word, at, Conrad's story is the appropriate, and welcome, starting point. At the same time, his reference to 'the myth of the West' (112), which the story exposes, affirms its moral and historical scope at the expense of precision and the significance of this can be usefully focused by reflecting on some of the multiple myths, and indeed different senses of the word 'myth', in modern literature and culture. I believe the myth at work in *Heart of Darkness* is more specific than what Lacoue-Labarthe's account implies as can be seen by relating it to an important counter-myth. In a jointly written essay he has spoken similarly of 'The Nazi Myth' (written with Jean-Luc Nancy) and the following remarks also have a bearing on the ambivalence emphasized in that more specific construction as it arises from a deeper history of German thought.[1]

The Nazi instance may serve as a reminder that in the present case the import of myth is historical as well as intrinsic. Since myths live and die, or at least rise and fall, in history, the precise placing of Conrad's story in relation to modernism and modernity is important. Although we have good reason to count him among the modernists, the Conrad of this tale was writing not just literally but culturally within the Victorian era. In its original magazine appearance, it could be read as a tale of British imperial adventure in which the corruption and cruelty of rival powers, such as the Russians, would be a standard feature. And the narrative framing through secondary narrators was also familiar in popular tales of the supernatural or the uncanny. In this respect, it is hard to know to what extent Conrad was simply of his time or artfully simulating. And that, of course, is intrinsic to the tale's power: initially conceived as a controlled explosion within the moral order of colonialism it proved to be an early intimation of the critical process whereby the whole structure would be brought down. It is hard to read it now without investing it with the full weight of this later knowledge.

But the imminent generation of European modernist writers such as Joyce, Lawrence, Thomas Mann or the later Yeats were to take up these themes in new ways, and despite their great mutual differences, they had a significant feature in common. This was their self-reflective use of myth. In other words, these writers did not just employ mythic figures, themes and structures but recognized the mythopoeic bases of human life at all times. Whereas the study of myth in the nineteenth century had typically focused on ancient or 'primitive' people, or on literary uses, these writers saw that man continues to be an inescapably mythopoeic animal. Moreover, with this came the recognition that myth is not merely a superstitious element to be dispelled by Enlightenment reason but may be a healthful condition when properly lived and acknowledged. In other words, there is all the difference in the world between unconscious or naïve myth, which is likely to act as superstition or literal belief and the self-conscious mythopoeia of modernity. Such an inner awareness may properly pervade the daily consciousness of modern man but it is especially enshrined in the creative self-consciousness of the modernist work of literature. The aesthetic is the modern form of myth. The philosophical articulation of this recognition stemmed above all from Friedrich Nietzsche who was a potent presence for all the writers just mentioned. Apart from any particular conception of the world, or of man, that might be drawn from Nietzsche's work, a crucial aspect of his legacy was his consciousness of living within a worldview.

This development puts an abyssal distance between Conrad and these only slightly later writers, yet the recognition to which I am adverting was not evident in these terms even to many of the most sympathetic and sophisticated readers of modernist literature. Hence quite different, and sometimes opposed, understandings of myth were entertained simultaneously. And more importantly again, mythopoeic world-creation occurs at different levels. Behind any conscious myth that might be an object of study or critique, there is frequently a less conscious one at the level of *Weltanschauung*, a general view of the world. Specific myths may illuminate the worldview as they did for the Victorian and early twentieth-century anthropologists who sought to reconstruct the worldview of primitive man from the study of his mythic thinking. But a worldview is dispositional as well as perceptual and is likely to be too fundamental, intuitive and habitual to be brought fully into consciousness by those who inhabit it. Hence, even if one of the crucial lessons of modern literature was that all human beings inhabit their worlds mythopoeically, it remains almost impossible to turn the eye upon itself and identify the features of one's own worldview. Wittgenstein's comments on James Frazer's *The Golden Bough* provide a case in point: Frazer, Wittgenstein observed, could not really understand his primitive people because he could only think of them within his own worldview as superstitious and misled.[2]

It must, at the same time, be mentioned here that, in their essay on 'The Nazi Myth', Lacoue-Labarthe and Nancy stress the use made by Nazi ideologues precisely of their self-conscious *Weltanschauung*. And indeed it is true that such a self-consciousness is an ontological recognition that can be invested with quite varied and opposed moral qualities. It is no necessary reflection on philosophical truths that they can be politically co-opted. Margaret Thatcher's declaration that there is 'no such thing as society' has a perfectly proper meaning, yet her use of it was felt by many to be a shameful derogation from social responsibility. As a matter of moral and intellectual quality, the Nazi hijacking of this philosophical heritage for the apodictic propounding, and enforcing, of their own *Weltanschauung* is reminiscent of the reply made by Richard Nixon's one-time running mate, Spiro Agnew, when asked by journalists how he, a man of notorious stupidity, could run for the office of Vice-President. 'Well', he replied, 'What about all the stupid people, don't they have a right to be represented?' His riposte, worthy of Sancho Panza, is unanswerable in its sublimely stultifying absurdity.

Worldviews, then, are not beyond discussion but they are beyond argument and the implicit worldview that underwrites *Heart of Darkness* is one of two opposed dispositions which governed, and continue to govern, modern conceptions of man and civilization. These may be called the Freudian and the Nietzschean. In *Totem and Taboo* (1913) and *Civilization and Its Discontents* (1930), particularly, Freud defined his tragic view that there was a primordial aggressive instinct and that civilization depends on the repression and sublimation of instincts. By contrast, Nietzsche's conception of the tragic origins of civilization was affirmative of instinctual life. Although the power celebrated by the ancient Greeks as Dionysos has long since dwindled to a repressed, residual and dishonoured condition, Nietzsche sought to restore it to honour.

His argument in *The Birth of Tragedy* (1872) constituted a double affirmation, both philosophical and psychological. Philosophically, it affirmed the enduring significance of mythopoeic thought as Nietzsche insisted that the gods were not allegorical, or otherwise reducible to an idea. Psychologically, it affirmed a trust in the instincts; a motif that was to be made explicit in *The Gay Science*:

> I find those people disagreeable in whom every natural inclination immediately becomes a sickness, something that disfigures them or is downright infamous: it is *they* that have seduced us to hold that man's inclinations and instincts are evil. *They* are the cause of our great injustice against our nature, against all nature. There are enough people who *might well* entrust themselves to their instincts with grace and without care; but they do not, from fear of this imagined 'evil character' of nature. That is why we find so little nobility among men; for it is always the mark of nobility that one feels no fear of oneself.[3]

In Nietzsche's account, the birth of tragedy was one with the origins of culture. It was the extended moment in which the primordial, naïve, participatory experience of myth was transposed into an aesthetic modality. Whereas the Apollonian power has eventually overcome and repressed the Dionysian, for Nietzsche the proper role of the Apollonian is to enable the encounter with the Dionysian within aesthetic conditions. For although the Dionysian as such is an impossible or destructive return to oneness with the all, it is nonetheless the basis of human existence and should be honoured.

Honouring Dionysos, for Nietzsche, would not be a matter of scholarly recovery but a different mode of being in the present. As the passage from *The Gay Science* makes clear, the ancient myth does not just refer to a necessary moment in remote antiquity. It bears upon the present, if it is not indeed to be seen as an interpretative image projected from the present. And the same applies to Freud's conception of cultural origins. His foundational myth of parricide in *Totem and Taboo* represents a view of the instincts which is evident throughout his *oeuvre*.

In so far as these two views were classically instantiated in Nietzsche and Freud, they did not directly confront each other. Freud kept a wary distance from Nietzsche who had clearly anticipated some of his own insights. And Nietzsche's view of Freud, had he lived to know his work, would be a matter of rich speculation. But they were each aware of the counter case. Freud understood very well that instinctual life was damaged by repression. This recognition provided, after all, the premise and the goal of psychoanalysis. And just as Nietzsche's Dionysos was intrinsically destructive of the moral ego, so, in the passage quoted, he acknowledges that justifiable trust in the instincts is to be found only in the rare and noble individual. Nonetheless, there is a radical dispositional difference between them. It is the early twentieth-century version of the irresolvable conflict between Jean-Jacques Rousseau and the traditional doctrine of original sin. Argument across this abyss is rarely profitable if it is even possible. For what is at stake for each side is not so much a conviction that could be identified and changed as the familiar experience of a long-inhabited world. There is no Archimedean point on which to weigh incommensurable life experiences against each other.

That, indeed, is one of the reasons that imaginative literature is necessary, and why modernist literature in particular had the monumental ambition, and very largely the achievement, which is still acknowledged today. More especially again, it points to the importance of the formal consciousness that characterizes modernist writing so much. For, although formal consciousness has often dwindled to cliché or empty self-regard, it had a truly philosophical significance in the greatest modernist writers. It brought into focus the underlying condition of all great literature: that it does not merely rest on pre-existing beliefs *about* the world but embeds them in an independent experience *of* the world. And it is in most fully recognizing the personal nature of conviction that the writer is most likely to impersonalize it as an independent world. The mythic signature of modern works, such as *Ulysses*, *The Rainbow* or *Joseph and his Brothers*, is the indicator of this awareness in the texts; an awareness of the responsibility of world creation. Conrad's fiction does not have that kind of modernist formal consciousness; yet, his persistent technique of narrative indirection performed a comparable function. It enabled the act of story-telling, as Lacoue-Labarthe observes, to be identified as an exploratory, sense-making activity within the text.

Published at the very turn of the century, the transitional nature of *Heart of Darkness*, both formally and historically, can be seen by comparison with D. H. Lawrence's *The Rainbow* which appeared some 15 years later. The comparison turns not just on difference of worldview but on differing orders of self-consciousness about the worldview.

Heart of Darkness is the classic expression of what, as a convenient short-hand, I am calling the Freudian view and it exemplifies the radical, pervasive and self-fulfilling nature of such conviction. In the mental world of the turn of the century, the model of necessary control in Freud's *superego* and *id* was readily extrapolated into an elite view of social order and into the responsibilities of imperialism. It was almost universally accepted at this time that tribal peoples around the world represented earlier phases of development that European man had passed through in the remote past. In *Primitive Mentality* (1922), Lucien Lévy-Bruhl still assumed this to be the case albeit he placed a newly positive value on the 'primitive'. And the final monumental version of Sir James Frazer's *The Golden Bough* appeared in the same year. Although Freud was alert to the fact that contemporary tribal people were themselves at some unknown distance from their origins, he did not question this underlying assumption. Indeed, he drew on such anthropological material as evidence of the persistence of earlier developmental layers within the modern psyche. The consonance between these different orders of authority in the individual, the social order and the empire, gives them a mutual reinforcement. Indeed, it might be hard to say which, if any, should be seen as the originating model.

Heart of Darkness inhabits this mental world. Africa is a place of darkness comparable to the ancient Britain that was once colonized. Africa is the deep layer of the modern psyche whose exposure constitutes the true discovery at the heart of the story. The colonial enterprise is justified by an idea of its civilizing mission and by the exercise, in the meantime, of a dutiful protectorate. The present evil in the Congo, for both Marlow and Conrad, lies precisely in the dereliction of this double duty. So also, Marlow is struck by the quasi-civilized 'restraint' (105) of the African crewmen, under threat of starvation, in not killing and eating their European passengers. Although Conrad's immediate irony here bears upon the moral superiority of the African crew to their passengers, it is nested within contemporary anthropological understanding. As Freud suggests in *Totem and Taboo*, during the early stages of moral development, instinctual restraint requires the absolute and arbitrary power of taboo. So the African stoker performs his duty with a superstitious terror of the hungry demon in the furnace.

Some 15 years later, D. H. Lawrence's *The Rainbow* (1915) includes a remarkable episode which reads like a corrective allusion to *Heart of Darkness*. Anton Skrebensky, who as it happens was, like Conrad, from an émigré Polish family of patrician descent, serves as an officer in the British army. Ursula Brangwen has already come to detach herself from him as she recognizes that he is what T. S. Eliot, in a poem which also makes direct allusion to *Heart of Darkness*, was later to call a hollow man. But when Skrebensky returns from service in Africa she is briefly fascinated by him again as he tells her of the African darkness:

> Then in a low, vibrating voice he told her about Africa, the strange darkness, the strange, blood fear.
>
> 'I am not afraid of the darkness in England', he said, 'It is soft and natural to me, it is my medium, especially when you are here. But in Africa it seems massive and fluid with terror—not fear of anything—just fear. One breathes it, like the smell of blood. The blacks know it. They worship it really, the darkness. One almost likes it—the fear—something sensual.'
>
> She thrilled again to him. He was to her a voice out of the darkness.[4]

The episode continues at some length. As with Kurtz, and then with Marlow, the experience of the African darkness is mediated above all by a voice; a voice which touches the psyche of the listener with an uncanny directness. Ursula thrills to him during the episode because

he is, for once, exposing some real emotional interiority to her; and
an emotion, moreover, which appeals to her own exotic proclivities
arising from her now intense frustration. But the attraction does
not last because the emotion is essentially inauthentic; or more
precisely, it arises from Skrebensky's inauthenticity. He is horrified
by the African darkness because it represents a repressed self which
he can only dimly allow himself to feel in so far as it is invested in
an image of complete otherness. At the same time, he is fascinated
by it because it is his repressed and alienated self. Lawrence's
episode encapsulates with extraordinary precision and inwardness
the central recognition of later post-colonial critique. Skrebensky's
'Africa' is not to do with Africa but is the exoticized projection of
his own condition. Appropriately, after the final breakdown of the
relationship with Ursula, he goes off to colonial service in India.

Lawrence's episode also throws light on the early critical
reception of *Heart of Darkness*. It is not so much what Skrebensky
says that affects Ursula as the quality of his voice. His words cannot
convey the significance to which she intuitively responds. And as
so often in Lawrence, the words themselves come over as a murky
rhetoric that casual or hostile readers have constantly seen as simply
authorial. But Lawrence has framed the experience in such a way
as to make its obscurity to the participants an important part of
its meaning as self-mystification. Marlow's rhetoric was also seen
as obfuscatory, and was similarly laid at the door of the author. It
was *à propos Heart of Darkness* that F. R. Leavis endorsed, with his
own discriminations, E. M. Forster's comment that Conrad is 'misty
in the middle as well as at the edges, that the secret casket of his
genius contains a vapor rather than a jewel'.[5] But in the well-known
passage quoted by Lacoue-Labarthe, the primary narrator of *Heart
of Darkness* describes Marlow's rhetoric for the reader in an image
that is very close to these terms:

> to him the meaning of an episode was not inside like a kernel
> but outside, enveloping the tale which brought it out only as a
> glow brings out a haze, in the likeness of one of those misty halos
> that, sometimes, are made visible by the spectral illumination of
> moonshine. (48)

Forster, of course, is still entitled to his judgement and may indeed
have been recollecting this description of Marlow's story-telling
as pre-emptive justification on Conrad's part. But in so far as the

primary narrator alerts us to some obscurity, and even perhaps some illusion, in Marlow's rhetoric it may be taken as significantly dramatized. The drama of the Marlow novels lies partly in his own internal struggle as, for example, with the temptation to excessive identification with the central character; a character who is partly his own speculative creation. The play of Marlow's language, therefore, is not just the vehicle but an essential part of the action; as it is more evident, perhaps, in the case of Skrebensky who is not also the principal narrator of the novel in which he occurs. The experience at the heart of the tale is vertiginous and, as Lacoue-Labarthe puts it, Conrad's originality was that 'he makes this giddiness the object of the work' (119). His further thought that Conrad's tale could be made into an 'oratorio' (114) has some purchase here: music might well convey ambivalent feelings which are not acknowledged or understood by the speaking character.

Lawrence's complex, inward treatment of this psychological structure is more remarkable, perhaps, for its parenthetical nature: the book is not 'about' colonialism and it handles this subtheme with such remarkable aplomb precisely as an aspect of its internal study of European modernity. Fundamental to Lawrence's novelistic/philosophical genius was his understanding of how his characters create their own worlds or inhabit their own worldviews. Along with his psychological belief in the damaging nature of instinctual repression, this philosophical recognition was his crucial affinity with Nietzsche; the two aspects being, of course, completely intertwined and self-reinforcing as the Skrebensky episode shows. In an argument between Rupert Birkin and Gerald Crich about 'spontaneity' towards the beginning of *Women in Love*, Birkin rehearses a very similar case to that quoted above from *The Gay Science*.[6] In general terms, then, the Skrebensky episode reads as a diagnostic exposure of the colonial and 'Freudian' assumptions underlying *Heart of Darkness*. And likewise, of course, Lawrence's interest in 'primitive' people was directly opposite to this. His account of the Etruscan form of life in *Etruscan Places* (1932) might be taken as the counter model to *Civilization and Its Discontents*. So rather than '*the* myth of the West' (p. 112; italics added), it would be more appropriate to think of a struggle of rival myths. The modern version of Jean-Jacques Rousseau's challenge to the myth of original sin has taken on new historical and anthropological dimensions within the unfolding of what we now think of as modernism.

I have emphasized the opposition between the Freudian worldview and that of Nietzsche and Lawrence. But, of course, the Freudian genius was devoted to understanding precisely such psychic mechanisms as Skrebensky's, and Lawrence's analysis of him is within a mode of understanding that later generations have derived, above all, from the Freudian tradition. Skrebensky's African darkness is a text book instance of the Freudian 'uncanny' as a return of the repressed. So also, the increasingly linguistic turn in the Freudian tradition allows later generations to read Kurtz's 'Exterminate all the brutes' (118) with a further edge. In Conrad's context, it represents Kurtz's collapse into barbarism, his discovery of the savagery lurking beneath his missionary idealism. But for a post-Freudian reader, alert to linguistic slippage and ambivalence, it may suggest the more intrinsic subtext of the civilizing mission itself: even in its supposedly benign forms, this mission will indeed exterminate these people as people.

It is evident here why Joyce and Lawrence, respectively, kept an ironic and a critical distance from Freud. They were all working in the same territory with common intuitions but Lawrence particularly opposed the Oedipal view of civilization as a necessary authority over the instincts. Of course, he was equally far from the reductive caricatures with which he has been saddled: the naïve espousal of instinct and return to the supposedly primitive. His positive mode of thought may perhaps be approached through his opposition to Freud's scientism which invoked the culture's most prestigiously impersonal, external mode of authority to support, in the relation of the *superego* and *id*, a model of necessary internal authority. In contrast to Freud, both Joyce and Lawrence relativized the truth claims of natural science within the human world and saw that world as sustained in an essentially aesthetic spirit. The word 'aesthetic' here, of course, does not refer to the languid connoisseurship of nineteenth-century legend but invokes the aesthetic as the primordial basis of human culture in the tradition stemming from Friedrich Schiller and articulated for the modernist generation by Nietzsche. Hence, the centrality in modernist literature of artist figures who focus its aesthetic mythopoeia, its conscious world creation.

I have dwelt on the transitional nature of *Heart of Darkness*, its distinctness from the moment of Joyce and Lawrence, as Lacoue-Labarthe's retrospective account tends to compress these different moments into one. And for the same reason I remain unpersuaded by his reading of Kurtz as an artist figure. Kurtz is, to be sure, the bearer of the central revelation because of his spiritual ambition and rhetorical power. And the comparison with Rimbaud's post-creative life is apt and suggestive. Yet Conrad, still on the brink of modernism, does not seem to me to deal in the kind of aesthetic self-consciousness that is being attributed to him here. Indeed, the power of the story rather lies in its creation of so much suggestion out of a figure whose *proprium* is that he lacks that kind of awareness. If Kurtz is indeed a 'the *figure* of this myth' (114), as Lacoue-Labarthe puts it, his meaning is engendered in the space between Marlow and Kurtz, rather than in Kurtz himself. This is perhaps the clue to the primary narrator's comment on Marlow's story-telling for, although its drift is plain enough in general, the image of the 'kernel' and the 'misty halo' is otherwise obscure in its detailed reference. It is as much as to say that Kurtz himself is the central locus, but not necessarily the conscious bearer, of the tale's recognitions. Indeed, it is possible that if Conrad had had such a characteristically modernist relation to his art, he might have been spared some of his agonies of writer's block.

The tradition of aesthetic self-consciousness coming from Schiller, and passing through Goethe and Nietzsche, is strongly associated with a sense of the human spirit's essential liberation from its compulsions, internal and external; albeit, this is often in a mode, not of escape, but of acceptance. There may be no necessary connection here, and there is of course another tradition of aestheticism in the nineteenth century, but the wing of later modernists mentioned here had a confidence in their aesthetic postures, and the world-changing potential these implied, which gave their work an affirmative lift distinct from the dark brooding of both Conrad and Thomas Hardy. Indeed, it is difficult to separate what is known of Conrad's creative struggle from the thematic struggles dramatized within the work itself. For the same reason, Conrad's dutiful relation to his craft as a form of truth-telling accomplished through professional obligation and honour seems different from the Heideggerian notion of *techne* as artistic means which Lacoue-Labarthe also invokes.

This latter claim also seems to run against the grain of Conrad's characteristic mode of moral thinking as a novelist. His critique of modernity bears upon the corruption of economic and political power, while moral sanity is preserved within the technical disciplines of professional pursuits. In *Heart of Darkness*, the physical preservation and functioning of the steamboat provide a moral focus for Marlow and such a commitment is necessarily sustained by a whole form of life. The navigation manual surely represents something more than what Lacoue-Labarthe calls 'manipulating objects' (117). Of course, this cannot answer the savagery and nihilism which it stands over against but that is part of the point: the stoical performance against the odds, such as Albert Camus honoured in *La Peste*. By contrast, it was in their mode of writing that Joyce, Lawrence, Proust, the later Thomas Mann and later Yeats would all make consciously aesthetic, Nietzschean affirmations addressed to contemporary nihilism. Undoubtedly, *techne* in *Heart of Darkness* has a major moral and philosophical resonance but it is of a deliberately humbler kind which only in that way provides the model of Conrad's art.

In sum, Conrad's internal drama of the civilized and the primitive in *Heart of Darkness* is 'Freudian' in its assumptions: the civilized ego is locked into a repressive relation to its instinctual and ancestral self. But where Freud sought liberation through rational understanding and acknowledgement, Conrad contemplated the dark truth of the civilized self with horror. The spirit of his art here was stoical rather than liberational and its sombre power arises from the moral pressure chamber in which its understanding of the psyche was enclosed.

Notes

1 Philippe Lacoue-Labarthe and Jean-Luc Nancy, 'The Nazi Myth', trans. Brian Holmes, *Critical Inquiry*, 16.2 (1990): 291–312. For an extended, and different, discussion of the German tradition of thought on myth in relation to modernism, see Michael Bell, *Literature, Modernism and Myth Belief and Responsibility in the Twentieth Century* (Cambridge: Cambridge University Press, 1997).

2 Ludwig Wittgenstein, *Remarks on Frazer's 'Golden Bough'*, ed. Rush Rees, trans. A. C. Miles (Hereford: Brynmill Press, 1979).

3 Friedrich Nietzsche, *The Gay Science*, trans. Walter Kaufmann, (New York: Random House, 1974), 236.

4 D. H. Lawrence, *The Rainbow*, ed. Mark Kinkead-Weekes (Cambridge: Cambridge University Press, 1989), 413.

5 F. R. Leavis, *The Great Tradition* (London: Chatto and Windus, 1948), 173.

6 D. H. Lawrence, *Women in Love*, ed. David Farmer, Lindeth Vasey and John Worthen (Cambridge: Cambridge University Press, 1987), 32–3.

3

Civilization and its darkness

JONATHAN DOLLIMORE

*May we not be justified in reaching the diagnosis that . . .
some civilizations, or some epochs of civilization – possibly
the whole of mankind – have become 'neurotic'?*

SIGMUND FREUD, *Civilization and Its Discontents*

When Lacoue-Labarthe says 'the West is the *horror*' (112), we probably
find ourselves readily assenting and somewhat relieved at the double
exoneration which the remark implies: of Africa, and by implication
of Conrad, whose reputation has in recent times been tarnished by
Achebe's notorious charge of racism in relation to Africa.

But we might also pause to realize that something rather
remarkable lies behind this, perhaps now, unremarkable claim
that the horror is intrinsic to the West rather than to Africa. It is
something not much older than the anxiety about racism in the
canonical literature of the West. I am referring to that momentous,
discursive, historical reversal which has been at once and inseparably
social, psychic, philosophical and political: over time, through
struggle, often at great cost, the negativity hitherto projected onto
the demonized other has been returned to its source: as the 'other'
was gradually, haltingly, 'redeemed' in discourse, so, conversely, has
the demonizer become pathologized.

It is true that simplistic political versions of this process have come to prevail in recent times – for example, the too easy claim that the homophobe is 'really' a repressed homosexual; likewise that the misogynist and the racist are really just 'screwed up' – deficient, insecure, perhaps also unconsciously desiring those they despise even as they project their own fears and inadequacies onto them. But these simplistic appropriations – in which, anyway, there was always a germ of truth – cannot detract from the immense importance of this historical process of change; indeed, in retrospect, and as appropriations, they actually attest to its importance.

Even so, to understand this process in its full complexity, we need to bring the psychic back into greater tension with the social and the political. Some of the last century's most significant thinkers realized that Marx and Freud 'needed each other'. The idea here was not a facile synthesis but a commitment to thinking across division, of pushing thought to the point of breakdown and susceptibility to something beyond itself. While Marxists and psychoanalysts denounced each other and erected intellectual barriers to prevent this, history was proving their endeavour futile, while literature, of course, had already done so.

Ironically – and it is a deeply significant irony – we find the beginnings of the process of return in the very discourses which pathologized otherness. In this regard, and especially relevant to Conrad's *Heart of Darkness*, is the theory of degeneration.

Degeneration

Kurtz is possessed of a supremely civilized intelligence; we're told, for example, that '[a]ll Europe' contributed to his making, and that his achievements range from being a great musician, and a poet, to being entrusted to report to 'the International Society for the Suppression of Savage Customs' (117). Yet, when Kurtz deviates into the barbaric, it is because of, not in spite of, being so civilized. In *Heart of Darkness*, the over-civilized is seen to have an affinity with the excesses of the primitive. Kurtz embodies the terrible paradox that contemporary degeneration theorists like Max Nordau tried to explain but only exacerbated, namely that civilization and progress seem to engender their own regression and ruin. The very logic of progress evolves civilization into what it had supposedly left behind – into what it is the essence of civilization not to be.

Following the pioneering degeneracy theorist Benedict Morel, Nordau defines degeneration as a morbid deviation from an original type or normal form, transmissible through heredity. All versions of degeneracy originate in a 'bio-chemical and bio-mechanical derangement of the nerve-cell'.[1] But major causes of degeneration also came from outside the organism. Modern environmental changes were especially dangerous. Thus, Nordau believed that a major cause of degeneracy was the accelerating pace of modern life and the growth of urban centres – 'the excessive organic wear and tear suffered by the nations through the immense demands of their activity, and through the rank growth of large towns'.[2] Such theories are often dismissed as pseudo-scientific ranting. They were much more than that; there's a line of descent from these theories through to the Holocaust of World War II and the racist rhetoric which both enabled and survived it. Degeneration is a powerful idea still, if by other names: it is that which threatens contagion, the loss of immunity and ultimately the threat of social death and even extinction of species. Max Nordau was only one of the most famous exponents of the idea. His book *Degeneration* (1892) was immensely popular throughout Europe, its English version going through seven editions in six months.

The 'alienist' who examines Marlow before his departure, asking him about mental illness in the family, and admitting to a 'theory' (58) he is out to prove, recalls the doctors of degeneration, while Kurtz resembles what Nordau and others called a 'higher degenerate', someone who is excessively, dangerously, brilliant because he is endowed with an intelligence which has evolved *too far* and at the expense of the other faculties, especially the ethical ones, which have become correspondingly atrophied. According to Nordau, the higher degenerate is a genius who is inclined to scepticism, brooding, 'a rage for contradiction' and, of course, atavism: he 'renews intellectually the type of the primitive man of the most remote Stone Age'.[3] Higher degenerates have something in common with other agents of cultural subversion including Satan, the pervert, the dissident and the insurgent; all threaten from within; all threaten to disintegrate internally what are regarded as arduously created, indispensable yet vulnerable social orders.

Nordau seemed to fear that evolution was going into reverse; worse still that evolution was simultaneously accelerating and regressing, and equally out of control in both respects; a terrifying backward *and* forward unbinding of the arduously achieved higher forms of civilization and biology. Nordau tirelessly identifies hundreds of symptoms of degeneration with the intention of isolating, quarantining and combating them: 'We stand now in the midst of a severe mental epidemic; of a sort of black death of degeneration'.[4] But the more he does this the more we sense an underlying fear that degeneration is not just an isolatable aberration of evolution but somehow its logic and destiny. It is as if there is an unconscious, teleological drive in evolution which leads to decline, exhaustion, disintegration and self-destruction. Instinct and the unconscious, far from being the forces which might guarantee evolutionary progress, become prime carriers of degeneracy. Nordau had nothing to do with psychoanalysis but, as we will see, there are notions in his book which anticipate Freud's theory of the death drive – especially the idea of degeneration as a force which internally unbinds civilization's arduously achieved and always precarious unities. In Conrad's story, the death drive becomes even more disturbing than degeneration; it leads the reader ineluctably into the Dionysian ecstasy, and, inseparably, into the metaphysics of oblivion. It is these, rather than a specific political culpability, which make Conrad's story a controversial text. The socio-political needs to be understood in a larger perspective which is philosophical, mythological and, ultimately, theological in origin. Politics and metaphysics prove to be inseparable.

Perversion

In the pre-sexological sense of the word – that is the theological sense – Kurtz is also the archetypal pervert[5]: He accelerates civilization into decadence (the over-civilized), but also, at the same moment – almost as the same process – regresses it back to the primitive (the pre-civilized). The desire of the pervert is characterized by this aberrant movement which both progresses and regresses towards death. Put another way, Kurtz makes a fatal, perverse deviation from the normative trajectory of an 'advanced' culture whose essence is within him, embracing in the process what that culture defines itself over and against – whose essence is also within him. Crucially, this deviation is not an accident, nor entirely a consequence of the inherent instability of the solitary genius/pervert; he has deviated because of, and not in spite of, following one of his culture's most advanced trajectories. Perverts are the agents of degeneration but they embody the paradoxes which render unstable the very theory which creates and deploys them. The theory cannot contain the paradoxical dynamic which perversion attests to, that contradictory double movement, a regression into primitive origins, and a progression, even an acceleration, into decadent decline such that civilization is doubly beleaguered: before (i.e. behind) is the scandal of its origins, while before (i.e. ahead) is the scandal of its destiny, *to become everything which it is not yet, yet always was.* Nordau castigates the artists of his time because they endanger and disintegrate the arduously achieved and precarious unities of civilization. In a certain sense, Nordau is right; what we find in writers like Joseph Conrad is what Nordau knew and fights fiercely against, including the seductiveness of dissolution.

Both Kurtz and the narrator of the tale, Marlow, are described as wanderers (48, 127, 143). But it is Kurtz who wanders perversely, deviating from his assigned task; Marlow only follows, seeing and understanding a great deal more than most, but never as much as Kurtz, whose deviation becomes the focus for a radically paradoxical narrative full of dangerous knowledge. In the process, there emerges this desolate affinity between the primitive and the civilized, suggesting that the survival of civilization depends upon the rest of us not wandering (deviating) even as far as Marlow, let alone Kurtz.

'Going up that river', says Marlow 'was like travelling back to the earliest beginnings of the world. . . . we penetrated deeper and deeper into the heart of darkness' (92, 95). Discovered there are not so much the distant, obscure origins of civilization, as its identity now: 'all the past' is still in 'the mind of man' (96). Culture and civilization are merely a 'surface truth' (97), involving a necessary disavowal of this other always-present truth of present origins. But this other truth, though compelling, is deeply obscure. Marlow discovers a deserted hut, inexplicably vacated and (equally inexplicably) containing a remnant of its one-time civilized inhabitant, a tattered book called *An Inquiry into Some Points of Seamanship*. The surface of things, including this hut and this book, does not confirm by contrast a deeper truth but, on the contrary, becomes itself increasingly undecipherable and disorienting. This *is* the truth, a kind of desublimation which eludes meaning, or which is swamped by too much meaning.

An Inquiry into Some Points of Seamanship, as its all too apt title proclaims, is necessarily blinkered in its purposefulness. It recalls the chief accountant Marlow met earlier, who, elegantly dressed and even slightly scented, works industriously at his desk: 'in the great demoralization of the land he kept up his appearance' (68). His books are in apple-pie order; Marlow encounters him in the middle of the colossal and dark jungle 'making correct entries of perfectly correct transactions' while 'fifty feet below the doorstep he could see the grove of death' (70). Like this accountant, the book on seamanship expresses 'a singleness of intention, an honest concern for the right way of going to work' (99); the obsessively narrow, undeviating civilized quest as it was supposed to cut through the jungle. Marlow half-subscribes to the same; to be preoccupied with the mundane tasks, to keep the ship going, is the wise person's wisely narrowed focus; attending to 'the mere incidents of the surface' keeps the 'reality', the 'truth' of the 'mysterious stillness', almost hidden: 'There was surface-truth enough in these things to save a wiser man' (97). Thus, there is the preoccupation with getting hold of some rivets to repair the ship – 'to stop the hole' (83). As he says at the opening of the story, 'what saves us is efficiency' (50). And yet nothing is more vulnerable to the darker side of human desire than human efficiency. More generally, civilization itself is only an intensity of concentration, a blinkered adherence to the straight and narrow, which is also therefore an inevitable and not an accidental blindness epitomized by the 'civilized' quest itself, the collecting of ivory: a brutal, industrious, determined operation executed by agents necessarily oblivious to all else.

Primeval density

So, there is a necessary shallowness to the 'civilized' which contrasts with a terrible, intense density in the primitive – or rather the primeval. The contrast I am after is elaborated succinctly and revealingly in John Buchan's *The Three Hostages* (1924). That novel has a character, Dr Greenslade, who recalls some of Conrad's.

He has been a ship's doctor and is widely travelled, especially beyond the Western world. He also has an 'insatiable curiosity' about everything. He believes that the recent World War has left in its wake madness and crime, such that – and here he recalls the 'alienist' doctor who examines Marlow – 'every doctor nowadays has got to be a bit of a mental pathologist'. He goes on:

> the barriers between the conscious and the sub-conscious . . . are growing shaky and the two worlds are getting mixed . . . The result is confusion . . . You can't any longer take the clear psychology of most human beings for granted. Something is welling up from the primeval deeps to muddy it.[6]

The book's main hero, Dick Hannay, replies that he finds this agreeable: 'We've overdone civilization, and personally I'm all for a little barbarism. I want a simpler world'. Greenslade, in a blunt repudiation of Hannay's Rousseauian naivety, replies:

> Then you won't get it . . . The civilized is far simpler than the primeval. All history has been an effort to make definitions, clear rules of thought, clear rules of conduct, solid sanctions . . . these are the work of the conscious self. The sub-conscious is an elementary and lawless thing . . .[7]

Here then is the idea of civilization not as a superior complexity but rather as a superior simplification, a necessary yet vulnerable simplification. The density, the complexity, is in the primeval – that which has necessarily been repressed in the evolution of the civilized;[8] repressed, not eliminated: for Greenslade, the primeval persists in the sub-conscious. And I think this is exactly the idea embodied in that image of the impeccably dressed accountant making precise entries into his books and which is articulated in that other book with its 'right way of going to work', and even in Marlow preoccupied with his rivets. Civilization is, at some level, profoundly and necessarily limited, focused and exclusionary, built on repressions which remain constitutive.

Kurtz's fatal swerve into knowledge is in the first instance a realization of the falsity of what 'counts' as knowledge, and of the assumed difference between the civilized and the primitive upon which the effort of discrimination depends. This is the sense in which the land 'demoralizes': it saps purposeful but limited energy of those civilized subjects entering it and fatally blurs their narrowness of focus. What they thought was the self-sustaining core of their being dissolves away, leaving an emptiness that fills up with otherness. Similarly, civilization's frenzied, blind expression of its own acquisitive dynamic (the quest for ivory) is halted and becomes disorganized, unravelled and confused; in the very process of defining itself over and against the primitive, the civilized is invaded by the other whose history and proximity it requires yet disavows. Kurtz deviates from the necessary 'singleness of intention' into the obliterating silence which that singleness also disavows, a wilderness which whispers to him things he did not know, which 'echoed within him because he was hollow at the core . . .' (131).

Lacoue-Labarthe is surely right to see this inner emptiness as crucial, but I cannot share his Lacanian/Heideggerian linking of this to the nothingness of being. On the contrary, the horror is very much about the terrifying, conflicted and repressed density of being. However, Lacoue-Labarthe adds '. . . if you prefer . . . the "heart of darkness" is the *extime* – the *interior intimo meo* of Augustine, God, but as internal exclusion' (117). I find that reference more persuasive, suggesting as it does the pressured intensity of repression which haunts Conrad's tale. It is after all from within this hollowness that 'forgotten and brutal instincts' are awakened: 'the memory of gratified and monstrous passions. This alone, I was convinced, had driven him out to the edge of the forest . . . had beguiled his unlawful soul beyond the bounds of permitted aspirations' (144). What is glimpsed here is the most terrifying paradox: the perverse frenzy of the 'primitive' is both the energetic antithesis of death and its intimate familiar, its prime mover. The 'rioting invasion of soundless life' echoes a familiar Western idea of death as a powerful, relentless force of unbinding at times inseparable from the life force itself – what one very different writer from several centuries earlier called 'the blast of death's incessant motion' (George Herbert). A Western obsession is displaced to, rediscovered within, Africa.

Lacoue-Labarthe says, in a summary of his own piece, that

> the West is defined as a gigantic colony—it was also the case with the Greeks, well before Rome—and that *beneath* this colony is the *horror*. But this horror is less the *de facto* horror of savagery than the power of fascination that savagery exerts

over the 'civilized' who suddenly recognize the 'void' upon which their will to ward off the horror rests—or fails to rest. It is its own horror that the West seeks to dispel. Hence its work of death and destruction, the evil it generates and spreads to the confines of the earth . . . (119)

This is surely a compelling account of the source of the horror. But is the 'death and destruction' wreaked by the West really generated from a void? Surely, the most cursory history of the West tells us otherwise. To which it might be replied that it is philosophy and myth rather than history which are Lacoue-Labarthe's main concern. Indeed, but here too, the truth seems to me to be otherwise. The discovery of the void is fashionable: where there was once spiritual substance, the grounds of Man (universal) and the Individual (the instantiation of the universal), the modernist now reveals only emptiness, absence and division.

The fact is that in 'his' theology, myth and philosophy, Western 'Man' has always been deeply and *densely* conflicted, from the myth of the Fall onwards. Haunted by loss, wounded by transience, riven with guilt, driven by a desire infected with death (the Fall again), he has always been inwardly tormented and driven forward by lack. The neurosis, anxiety and alienation which some see as deriving from a recent crisis in Western notions of Man were not only there at 'his' mythico-theological beginnings, but also actually imparted to him that restless driven-ness in all its expansionist, aggrandizing forms, of which empire and colonialism are just two manifestations. But because of this history, it is inevitable that there is a reverse pull – driven forward but always yearning to regress: 'Beneath it all, desire of oblivion runs' (Larkin). It is ironic that Freud's theory of the death drive – the notion that, as he put it in *Beyond the Pleasure Principle* (1920), 'the aim of all life is death' – is the one that has met the most resistance from within and beyond the psychoanalytic fraternity; ironic because this is one of the most traditional and derivative of Freud's ideas, and no less significant for being so.

I also find unconvincing Lacoue-Labarthe's related notion of Kurtz's 'hollowness' as somehow derivative from Western notions of the artist/genius. And here it is as much a question of style as that of argument. Lacoue-Labarthe tells us, at the beginning of the piece, how much he admired a reading of Conrad's tale by David Warrilow; especially memorable was the way this actor's 'exhausted voice' had a quality of 'sovereign *detachment*' (111 his italics). Later, he speaks of Kurtz as being 'absolutely *sovereign*. Being nothing, he is, indeed, everything. His *voice* is all-powerful' (116 again, his italics). I can't help feeling that, in his own narrative voice in this article, Lacoue-Labarthe is aiming for something similar – if not sovereign detachment, then a kind of philosophical omniscience. On the way to this claim about Kurtz, and in just a few lines, he has invoked in his support all of the following: Plato, Diderot, Nietzsche, 'the great Western tradition', the Greeks, Musil, the Russian anarchists and Ulysses. Stylistically, he resembles that other writer whom, on the next page, he also enlists in his support, namely Jacques Lacan. Lacan too was always keen to cite great thinkers in the Western tradition, and often did so in a similarly elliptical way, the implication being that they had anticipated something which could only now be fully understood properly through him, Lacan. It has always seemed to me that Lacan used psychoanalytic categories to fantasize himself into a position of omniscience.[9] It may even be a characteristic of French intellectual thought more generally. This is by way of an aside; it is the conflicted density of Western categories which concerns me here.

The metaphysics of oblivion

When Marlow returns to London he goes to visit Kurtz's 'Intended', to return to her some letters and a photograph (of her) which Kurtz had given him. He lies to her about Kurtz ('The last word he pronounced was – your name', 161), and he does so in order to protect her. The necessary simplifications of civilization, because rooted in repression, of course entail lying. What Marlow was unable or unwilling to speak to her is hardly revealed, or revealed only as that which confuses what we thought we knew. In the foreground is a mindless contemporary civilization scarcely removed from its origins in a frenzied primeval anarchy. And behind both the contemporary moment and the primeval past is something into which they fade indistinguishably – from it and from each other: the oblivion, the sea of inexorable time, the great solitude which dissolves all into an entropic oblivion, the darkness which Marlow senses even there, in the London drawing room of this woman and which the Romans encountered when they journeyed up the

Thames but 'yesterday' (49). What preoccupies Marlow is, perhaps less, the primitive forces resurfacing within the blind plundering energies of the civilized than the forces of oblivion inside both: the sea of inexorable time and the great solitude are not only what we eventually dissolve into, but also what pervade the present and the identity of the living, flooding it with a past which can be neither known nor escaped in the future – that *is* the heart of darkness:

> Nobody moved for a time. 'We have lost the first of the ebb', said the Director, suddenly. I raised my head. The offing was barred by a black bank of clouds, and the tranquil waterway leading to the uttermost ends of the earth flowed sombre under an overcast sky—seemed to lead into the heart of an immense darkness. (162)

Kurtz's existential angst cannot plausibly be read as an affirmation of authentic selfhood; it is much more like the appalled recognition of a subjectivity at once informed and rendered utterly insignificant by what has preceded, what surrounds and will survive it.[10] But nor is this merely regression, since the historical narrative which regression presupposes is also obliterated. It is rather a profoundly regressive encounter with the oblivion which is before time and before memory:

> We were cut off from the comprehension of our surroundings; we glided past like phantoms. . . . We could not understand because we were too far and could not remember, because we were travelling in the night of first ages, of those ages that are gone, leaving hardly a sign—and no memories. (96)

Marlow remains fascinated by it all, 'wondering and secretly appalled' (96). As for Kurtz's sense of the horror of it all, there can be no horror, only relief, in the silence which the death drive delivers us to. Even so, for Marlow and Kurtz, caught somewhere between degeneration and the death drive, there is residual terror in the seductive encounter with non-being.

Consider again Conrad's story in the light of the political question which has been asked with increasing urgency in recent times: is it a racist text?[11] In Conrad's defence, it has been said that he exposes, either directly or ironically, the brutality of imperialist exploitation in Africa. Also that he relentlessly undercuts the supposed superiority and difference of the civilized to the primitive even to the point of collapsing the one into the other. And that is important, especially at the time of the novel's appearance, when such assumptions of superiority were powerfully active in the ideological justification of exploitation. This merging or collapsing of the assumed differences between Africa and Europe, the civilized and the primitive, is, as we saw, intrinsic to the paradoxical nature of Kurtz. But the problem goes deeper.

At the end of the novel, when Marlow returns to London and lies to Kurtz's intended, it is to protect her from the darkness which he now perceives just behind the veneer of civilization, a darkness which, as dusk fell, seemed to be gathering even in her own drawing room (156–7). He has of course prepared us for this at the beginning of his story: moored on the Thames at Gravesend, east of London, he remarks 'this also . . . has been one of the dark places of the earth' (48). He reflects that, when the invading Romans struggled up the Thames their encounter with death, disease and the alien closely resembled that of the Europeans' later encounter with Africa and indeed his own journey up the Congo: 'I was thinking of very old times, when the Romans first came here, nineteen hundred years ago—the other day. . . . Darkness was here yesterday' (49). Marlow imagines 'a decent young [Roman] citizen' encountering the primitive life in England and feeling that same ambivalence: it is 'incomprehensible, detestable, but has a fascination, too. . . The fascination of the abomination. . .' (50). Here is the same ambivalence. The darkness seems to be both the oblivion and the primitive frenzy of life; the two things seem almost inseparable: the frenzy is death-driven, intent upon returning to the oblivion which it has emerged from. For me, this recalls Freud's death drive. As life flickered in inanimate substance, says Freud, 'it endeavored to cancel itself out. In this way the first instinct came into being: the instinct to return to the inanimate state. It was still an easy matter at that time for a living substance to die'.[12]

This is the origin of the death drive, that which seeks to 'dissolve' life back into its 'primaeval inorganic state';[13] an instinctual reaching towards that state in which there is the complete absence of excitation, a state of zero tension characteristic of the inorganic or the inanimate. We should be clear about what Freud is claiming here: the most basic instinctual drive for satisfaction is in fact a backward movement to death, to the absence of all tension: '*the aim of all life is death*'.[14] As he wrote to Albert Einstein in 1932, the death instinct is 'at work in every living creature and is striving to bring it to ruin and to reduce life to its original condition of inanimate matter'.[15]

Whereas Freud here imagines the fragile, mysterious emergence of life from inanimate matter – no more than a flicker – Conrad in *Heart of Darkness* repeatedly evokes primal life as frenzy; there is even a scandalous suggestion that this primal frenzy, with its 'forgotten and brutal instincts' (144) has a fuller intensity than anything known in civilization with its repressions and attenuations. Yet, if anything, Conrad's conception of primal life is even more death-driven than Freud's; life in its frenzy is driven to return to the immense silence which is its eternal backdrop. The death drive is integral to the life force and indistinguishable from it, hence those paradoxical metaphors like the 'rioting invasion of soundless life' (86). At one level, this is just the lush vegetation of the jungle, at another, it is the vital blindness of inanimate nature, at yet another, it is the terrifying realization of how completely the life force is indifferent to life itself, and ultimately of how the death drive inheres within the very principle of generation as that 'soundless[ness]' at the heart of a 'rioting invasion'. It is even suggested in Conrad's title: the heart, the beating source of life, is here also the darkness of death. Strangely perhaps, but to listen carefully to the pulsing (deadly) regularity of the heartbeat – your head on a lover's chest – is also to intimate within it the indifference of the life force: indifferent of course to the individual – and so to the principle of individuation upon which our civilization is built – but also, more deeply, life's indifference to itself.

How does the frenzy of civilization differ from that of the primeval? Certainly it is more muted, and the pull of oblivion more attenuated, at least at a conscious level. But the desire to 'surrender' (149) to it is still there, '[b]eneath it all'. Hence too perhaps the deeply dream-like aspect of the narrative, with sleep being the nearest intimation of oblivion available to consciousness. If dreams are where repressed desires resurface, they are also about loss, about what is irretrievably gone and so already half given up to oblivion.

A frenzy in which the life force and the death drive become indistinguishable: maybe this is the core of that density I have been referring too: something which must always be a scandal to a civilization based on the necessary repression and disavowal of such complex intensities. It might even be regarded as Dionysian or at least compared with the Dionysian orgy. I am thinking especially of Nietzsche's distinction between Christianity and Dionysus. 'Life itself', says Nietzsche, 'involves agony, destruction, the will to annihilation'. And whereas in Christianity, suffering 'is supposed to be the path to a sacred existence', in the Dionysian worldview, *'existence is considered sacred enough* to justify even a tremendous amount of suffering'. Thus, 'The God on the cross is a curse on life, a pointer to seek redemption from it'; whereas Dionysus cut to pieces is a *promise* of life: it is eternally reborn and comes back from destruction'.[16] Intentionally or not, Kurtz also resembles Nietzsche's exceptional man, someone with sufficient courage to quest beyond good and evil, who knows that there is a truth beyond the deceptions of morality. For Nietzsche, a courage of being leads to the truth of being. But for him too it was a terrible, even an unbearable truth, and certainly one bought at the expense of violating our humanity, whatever that is. This is important; even after having only 'glimpsed' the 'appalling . . . truth' (151), our humanity is thrown into crisis, and can never remain the same again. After such knowledge, what forgiveness? And while I am not concerned to exonerate Conrad, to consider his narrative in relation to Dionysus might at least pre-empt facile charges of racism. And yet there is a way in which the preoccupation with racism occludes something darker, deeper and longer; at the very least, my invocation of both Dionysus and Nietzsche should remind us that we must never underestimate the violent inhumaneness which pressures some of the theology, myth and philosophy of Western culture and of other cultures and civilizations.

But perhaps it is less the primitive frenzy and more the metaphysics of oblivion which invites the charge of racism. If oblivion's complete erasure of difference enables a kind of critique of imperial exploitation, it also invites the charge of dehumanizing Africa, of making the Congo the blank space onto which Europe maps its own 'spiritual' neurosis even as it materially plunders it. In short, where the primeval darkness is concerned, there is not much to distinguish Africa now from London then, or even now: it all dissolves into 'that oblivion which is the last word of our common fate' (155).

Edward Said says that Conrad's 'tragic limitation' was that, while being aware that imperialism involved brutal exploitation, he was so much a creature of his time that he 'could not then conclude that imperialism had to end. . . . Conrad could not grant the natives their freedom, despite his severe critique of the imperialism that enslaved them'. Similarly, his characters could not recognize 'that what they disablingly and disparagingly saw as a non-European "darkness" was in fact a non-European world *resisting* imperialism so as one day to regain sovereignty and independence'.[17] Said wants to exonerate Conrad to a degree by making him a creature of his time. But the fact is – and in humane-political terms, this may make him more not less culpable – Conrad claimed to see much more than Said allows. As with many writers before him, the metaphysics of oblivion renders questions of resistance virtually irrelevant; such things fall into insignificance because we are all 'reconciled' into this 'common fate'. It is the democracy of dust. Conrad himself put it like this, in a letter written in January 1898, the year before *Heart of Darkness* was published:

> The fate of a humanity condemned ultimately to perish from cold is not worth thinking about. If you take it to heart it becomes an unendurable tragedy. If you believe in improvement you must weep, for *the attained perfection must end in cold, darkness, and silence*. In a dispassionate view the ardour for reform, improvement for virtue, for knowledge, and even for beauty is only a vain sticking up for appearances as though one were anxious about the cut of one's clothes in a community of blind men. Life knows us not and we do not know life—we don't even know our own thoughts. . . . Faith is a myth and beliefs shift like mists on the shore; thoughts vanish; words, once pronounced, die; and the memory of yesterday is as shadowy as the hope of to-morrow.[18]

In such a world, the aspirations of a radical, reforming praxis would be the most radical deception of all. Africa dissolves the rationale not just for the exploitative quest for ivory, but also all other manifestations of praxis in the 'first' world along with any aspiration for change in the third. Not for the first time, the 'spiritual' obliteration of all difference leaves existing material differences intact. And if this is offensive to our modern commitment to an emancipatory politics, it is also true that this is a politics which cannot afford even to consider – must necessarily repress – any consideration of the metaphysics of oblivion. The progressive aspects of our culture, no less than the reactionary ones, have their constitutive repressions.

This underlying absorption in a metaphysics of oblivion which threatens or promises a radical erasure of all identity, and of all difference, was not new.[19] And nor had it yet found its most extreme modern form, which was, arguably, Freud's theory of the death drive, itself drawing on sources as recent as Schopenhauer and as old as Empedocles. And Freud of course, like Conrad, was deeply sceptical of 'the ardour for reform', believing, for example, that Marxism fatally ignored 'the untameable character of human nature'.[20] In *Beyond the Pleasure Principle*, he even suggests that the 'untiring impulsion towards further perfection' is at heart a frustrated displacement of the death drive itself.[21]

Civilization is built on repression and remains intrinsically unstable because of this, the repressions always threatening to return, with potentially devastating effect. If some of us are intensely ambivalent about the prospect of that return, it is partly because we know that if the ethical and humane basis of our culture is not to atrophy, it must be periodically confronted with its own vital exclusions – that is, it must be exposed to that which makes it possible in the first place; exposed, that is, to the repressed part of itself. Certain kinds of literature and philosophy have always done this. However, just as there is no prior guarantee that our culture survives unchanged or unchallenged by these encounters with its own vital exclusions, there is no guarantee that we as readers of this literature and philosophy remain immune to them; they are no less seductive for being encountered vicariously. The reader no less than the writer is potentially a higher degenerate. So to read sensitively, to think deeply, isn't necessarily to become a more humane person, as defenders of the humanities sometimes claim. Some artists and some philosophers have felt that our morality, even our humanity, obscures and even deceives us about the truth of our being, and to take art seriously is to recognize that it has the power to compromise both our morality and our humanity.

For sure, certain kinds of literature, including Conrad's story, are fascinated by the return of the repressed and those who are drawn to it, who want to seek out, explore, confront what is excluded; who are simultaneously appalled by and drawn to it – thus perhaps 'the strange commingling of desire and hate' which Marlow discerns in Kurtz's last words (151). Other seminal literary explorations of this theme, from around this time, include Robert Louis Stevenson's *Dr Jekyll and Mr Hyde* (1886), Oscar Wilde's *The Picture of Dorian Gray* (1890/91) and Thomas Mann's *Death in Venice* (1912).

These other fictions also confront the paradox at the heart of Conrad's story, which we have already considered but which I put slightly differently now (because in a larger philosophical-literary context): dramatized in Kurtz (as in Jekyll/Hyde, Dorian Gray and Aschenbach) is one of the enduring paradoxes of the literature which most interests me: only the most highly civilized can become truly daemonic. Thus 'the colossal scale of [Kurtz's] vile desires' (156). It is not a new realization; its origins are theological, and its history quite diverse: the fallen angel is capable of an evil always somehow pressured and intensified by his previous exaltation; Renaissance and Enlightenment sceptics observed that corrupted reason was capable of an intensity of evil unknown to the non- or irrational. Shakespeare, with a certain metaphoric succinctness, tells us 'Lilies that fester, smell far worse than weeds' (Sonnet 94). Freud remarked that the superego could be a gathering place for the death-instincts and, as such, 'as cruel as only the id can be'.[22] In a state of repression, this destruction and cruelty is masochistic and directed at the self; in sexual desublimation, it can find expression as a sadism which complements rather than replaces the masochism.

Finally, and from my point of view most importantly for giving a psychic and philosophical density to Lacoue-Labarthe's phrase, 'the West is the *horror*' (112): what is intimated in all of these fictions is that when the repressed returns it never does so in its 'original' form; one might say that it comes back *with a vengeance*: in other words, it comes back intensified by the very process of repression which it is breaking through.

Indeed, creations like Kurtz incarnate the realization which both invites and undermines a Freudian narrative; I mean the realization that there is a virulence in the return of the repressed which suggests that, after repression, we can never again access the pure drive prior to its repression, and so calls into question the very existence of such a drive, and more generally, of our related ideas of the primitive and the primeval.

But whether or not the drive exists in a primal, pre-civilized form – and *after all*, how would we ever know of its existence *as such*? – the fact remains that whatever is repressed returns with a virulence inseparable from the process of its repression: the repressed comes back mysteriously contaminated and intensified by its history – *which is also the history of civilization.*

Notes

1 Max Nordau, *Degeneration*, trans. from 2nd edition, (New York: Appleton and Co., 1895), 16, 254.

2 Nordau, *Degeneration*, 43.

3 Nordau, *Degeneration*, 166, 556; see also 23, 36, 161.

4 Nordau, *Degeneration*, 537.

5 Kurtz's 'unspeakable rites' (71) include the sexual but they cannot be explained exclusively, or even primarily, by it. There is a more inclusive dimension to his deviation, as befits a text which, though chronologically only just prior to Freud's first and major work on the sexual perversions (*Three Essays*, 1905), might be described as pre- or even non-Freudian in conception, at least with regard to the issue of sexual perversity. On the theological and philosophical history of perversion, and especially its Augustinian origins, see Jonathan Dollimore, *Sexual Dissidence: Augustine to Wilde, Freud to Foucault* (Oxford: Clarendon Press, 1991), parts 5 and 6.

6 Buchan, John, [1924] *The Three Hostages* (Ware: Wordsworth, 1995), 4.

7 Buchan, *Three Hostages*, 6–8.

8 Buchan's novel develops this idea in ways which certainly cannot be exonerated from the charge of racism. But what is especially relevant in this regard is the way his heroes lack the depth of their 'evil' and more primitive opponents. His heroes have great integrity and phenomenal courage, but these are qualities which exist not in spite of, but precisely because they also have a limited apprehension.

9 Nidesh Lawtoo has suggested to me, rightly I think, that my divergence from Lacoue-Labarthe's interpretation of the void is essentially due to my indebtedness to Freud, as distinct from Lacoue-Labarthe's to Lacan. I would add that I regard certain ideas of Freud – including that of the death drive – as in a crucial sense mythological – even theological – and none the worse for that: while

not being literally true, they are truthful to experience and history in ways which literal truth cannot be. So, in this regard, and for a sense of how Freud invests the human psyche with an unbearable degree of conflicted density, one need only glance at the diagram he offers – what he calls, with a rather wicked irony, his 'unassuming sketch' – of the 'mental personality' in *New Introductory Lectures on Psychoanalysis*, in *The Pelican Freud Library*, vol. 2 (Harmondsworth: Penguin, 1973), 111.

10 See the suicide of Decoud in Conrad's *Nostromo* [1904] (Harmondsworth: Penguin, 1963). Adrift in a boat on the ocean, doubting his own individuality, unable to differentiate it from the inanimate world around him and perceiving the universe as a 'succession of incomprehensible images', Decoud shoots himself. The sea into which he falls remains 'untroubled by the fall of his body'; he disappears 'without a trace, swallowed up by the immense indifference of things', the proverbial, quantifiably indistinct and indiscernible drop in the ocean (409, 411–12).

11 Chinua Achebe wrote: 'Conrad was a thorough going racist. . . . And the question is whether a novel which celebrates this dehumanization, which depersonalizes a portion of the human race, can be called a great work of art. My answer is: No, it cannot'. 'An Image of Africa: Racism in Conrad's *Heart of Darkness*', in Joseph Conrad, *Heart of Darkness*, 4th ed. Ed. Paul B. Armstrong (New York: W. W. Norton, 2006), 336–49, 344.

12 Sigmund Freud, *Beyond the Pleasure Principle* [1929/1930], in *The Pelican Freud Library*, vol. 11, *On Metapsychology: the Theory of Psychoanalysis*, trans. J. Strachey, ed. A. Richards (Harmondsworth: Penguin, 1984), 311.

13 Sigmund Freud, *Civilization and its Discontents*, [1929/1930], in *The Pelican Freud Library*, vol. 12, *Civilization, Society and Religion* (Harmondsworth: Penguin, 1985), 310. Compare Schopenhauer: 'Awakened to life out of the night of unconsciousness, the will finds itself as an individual in an endless and boundless world, among innumerable individuals, all striving, suffering, and erring; and, as if through a troubled dream, it hurries back to the old unconsciousness', Arthur Schopenhauer, *The World as Will and Idea* [1819/1844], 2 vols., trans. E. F. J. Payne (New York: Dover, 1966), II. 573.

14 Freud, *Beyond the Pleasure Principle*, 311; both the emphasis and the quotation marks are his.

15 Sigmund Freud, 'Why War?' [1932/33], in *The Pelican Freud Library*, vol. 12, *Civilization, Society and Religion* (Harmondsworth: Penguin, 1985), 357.

16 Friedrich Nietzsche, *The Portable Nietzsche*, ed. Walter Kaufmann, (Harmondsworth: Penguin, 1976), 459. On the relationship between Conrad and Nietzsche, see Nic Panagopoulos: '*Heart of Darkness*' and *The Birth of Tragedy: A Comparative Study* (Athens: Kardamitsa, 2002).

17 Edward Said, *Culture and Imperialism* (London: Chatto and Windus, 1993), 33–4.

18 Joseph Conrad, *Collected Letters*, vol. 2, 1898–1902, eds. F. R. Karl and L. Davies (Cambridge: Cambridge University Press, 1986), 17.

19 See *Death Desire and Loss in Western Culture* [1998] (New York: Routledge, 2001), parts 1–4.

20 Sigmund Freud, *New Introductory Lectures on Psychoanalysis*, in *The Pelican Freud Library*, vol. 2 (Harmondsworth: Penguin, 1973), 219.

21 Sigmund Freud, *Beyond the Pleasure Principle*, 314–5.

22 Sigmund Freud, *The Ego and the Id*, in *The Pelican Freud Library*, vol. 11, *On Metapsychology: the Theory of Psychoanalysis*, trans J. Strachey, ed. A. Richards (Harmondsworth: Penguin, 1984), 395.

PART TWO

Conrad *avec* Lacoue-Labarthe

4

A frame for 'The Horror of the West'

NIDESH LAWTOO

Pour Philippe, le rapport à la littérature—c'est-à-dire à la mimesis—était prégnant.[1]

JEAN-LUC NANCY, *'D'une "mimesis sans modèle"'*

Reading Lacoue-Labarthe is always a challenging experience, and this challenge is accentuated when the reader encounters his thought for the first time. Part of the difficulty emerges from an assumption not uncommon among contemporary French philosophers: when Lacoue-Labarthe approaches a specific problem, author, text or – as it is the case with 'The Horror of the West' – all of the above, the entirety of his thought is 'always already' *en jeu*. His reading of Conrad is thus not simply an interpretation among others, nor is it a way for the French philosopher to apply his 'approach' or 'method' to *Heart of Darkness*. Rather, Lacoue-Labarthe addresses the difficult 'truth' *about* the West Conrad wants his readers to 'see', and, in order to do so, he implicitly mobilizes the entirety of his own thought *on* the West. This also means that the textual economy of 'The Horror of the West' exposes the reader to the fundamental literary, philosophical and ethico-political concerns that traverse the entirety of Lacoue-Labarthe's *oeuvre*. For this reason alone, it can be a real challenge to gauge the stakes, implications and ramifications of his evaluation of *Heart of Darkness* as 'one of the greatest texts of Western literature' (111).

This is obviously not the place to attempt a general introduction to Lacoue-Labarthe's thought. Such introductions already exist and the reader will undoubtedly benefit from them.[2] At the same time, a brief and necessarily partial introductory frame (or preface) to his essay on *Heart of Darkness* could facilitate a first approach to what has already been called an 'event' for literary studies (Hillis Miller). The present essay joins arms with Hillis Miller's admirable 'Prologue' in order to help readers catch a preliminary glimpse of what Lacoue-Labarthe calls the 'truth of the West' (114) *Heart of Darkness* makes us see – and perhaps hear. The aim of this frame will be attained if it manages to clarify a few conceptual difficulties, indicate some theoretical signposts and, by doing so, amplify the chances to hear the contemporary relevance of Lacoue-Labarthe's untimely theoretical voice.

Philosopher-poet

I have mentioned in the 'Introduction' that Philippe Lacoue-Labarthe was an important French philosopher commonly associated with what goes under the rubric of 'theory' or 'poststructuralism', but this statement needs to be qualified. Like so many heterogeneous figures of his untimely generation, Lacoue-Labarthe's thought transgresses homogeneous definitions. Already during his lifetime his closest collaborators recognized in him a profound thinker who escaped easy identifications. Or, better, they recognized in him a thinker who problematized the very essence of identification. As Jacques Derrida puts it in 'Desistance': 'Assimilation or identificatory projection: these are what Lacoue-Labarthe constantly puts us on guard against'.[3] Hence, as we approach 'The Horror of the West', we should refrain from trying to 'identify' Lacoue-Labarthe's reading of Conrad within the boundaries of a given movement, school or approach – if only because this identificatory urge is precisely what his essay warns us against.

We should also be careful not to identify Lacoue-Labarthe uniquely with philosophy. If it is true that Lacoue-Labarthe was first and foremost a philosopher,[4] it is equally true that he tended to adopt this title with reluctance. He was always the first to acknowledge his fundamental debt to the Western philosophical tradition and to engage with the abyssal questions that emerged from it, and always the last to use the title of 'philosopher' in order to act as a figure of authority. Like Jacques Derrida, Gilles Deleuze, Michel Foucault, Jean-Luc Nancy and so many of his generation, Lacoue-Labarthe liked to situate himself at the 'margins' of philosophy. But if he treated this term with extreme precaution it is perhaps also because Lacoue-Labarthe was never *only* a philosopher. As his last name already suggests, his identity was at least double: A man of many sides, protean in his interests and approaches, Lacoue-Labarthe was a heterogeneous, mimetic thinker who worked at the *juncture* where literature and philosophy, emotion and thought, meet, challenge and confront each other. As his lifelong friend and colleague, Jean-Luc Nancy succinctly puts it: 'This is how he was a philosopher—against philosophy'.[5]

Lacoue-Labarthe's philosophical and literary interests spanned from the Greeks to the Romantics and beyond, into Modernism and Postmodernism. Fascinated by the Ancient problematic of mimesis – the conceptual *Leitmotif* of his thought – he did not hesitate to link Plato's and Aristotle's 'mimetology' to the Romantic take on 'genius', the psychoanalytical 'unconscious' to different forms of 'madness', aesthetic concerns with *techne* to political concerns with fascism and will to power. If 'The Horror of the West' is an 'event' for literary studies, it is also because all these problematics inform his reading of *Heart of Darkness* – and many others too. In fact, we should not forget that Lacoue-Labarthe was also a prolific translator (of Nietzsche, Benjamin, but especially Hölderlin), an acute interpreter of psychoanalysis (Freud and Lacan, but also Reik), *connaisseur* of music (from opera to jazz and blues),[6] a politically and ethically engaged thinker (most notably of the Holocaust) and, as critics are now beginning to recognize, a poet in his own right.[7]

Lacoue-Labarthe's literary interests were particularly focused on the Romantic tradition and culminate in his career-long engagement with Hölderlin but, for us, it is important to stress that Lacoue-Labarthe was equally fascinated by Anglo-American modernists. As Jean-Luc Nancy says, his friend was a passionate reader of 'Malcolm Lowry, Conrad, Faulkner, as well as T. S. Eliot'.[8] Conrad obviously occupied a special place in Lacoue-Labarthe's thought because he is the only British modernist he felt the need to write about. This is perhaps not surprising since, as we shall see, so many of his literary and philosophical interests find expression in *Heart of Darkness*. Lacoue-Labarthe's reading of Conrad can thus not be dissociated from the rest of his protean *oeuvre*, which, while not being a system, constantly returns to that juncture where literature and philosophy, emotion and thought, *pathos* and *logos*, meet, dialogue and, above all, affect and reflect (on) each other.

Framing the frame

Given the heterogeneous dimensions of Lacoue-Labarthe's investigations, one might wonder what, exactly, led him, towards the last decade of his life, to comment on *Heart of Darkness*. The reasons are undoubtedly manifold, obscure and cannot be easily explained. As Lacoue-Labarthe himself puts it, they belong to 'the realm of fascination' (112). This fascination for Conrad's tale was far from being new. It dated back to his youth, to a period when Lacoue-Labarthe's destiny was still suspended, as it were, between different possible trajectories. Not having chosen between the path of philosophy and the one of art (a choice which, strictly speaking, he will refuse to make), he considered filmmaking as a possible career. As he explains in an autobiographical essay, between the age of 20 and 25, under the spell of the seventh art, he 'thinks or, better, dreams, "cinema"'.[9] He even goes as far as writing scenarios for literary masterpieces he would like to see represented on the screen. Conrad's *Heart of Darkness* was second on his list of cinematic projects.

His script for *Heart of Darkness* was never finished, the film never made and Lacoue-Labarthe eventually took the path of philosophy. And yet, the fascination for Conrad continued to haunt him. Thus, much later in his career, upon seeing not a film, but a theatrical representation of *Heart of Darkness*, he fell, once again, under the spell of Conrad's tale. The play just over, the careful philosopher famous for his abundant use of quotation marks, dashes and interminable explanatory footnotes risked, in a moment of enthusiasm, the following evaluation: '*Heart of Darkness*', he said, 'is one of the greatest texts of Western literature' (111). 'The Horror of the West' is a philosophical explanation of the conceptual and affective motivations that inform this deeply felt aesthetic affirmation.

At first sight, Lacoue-Labarthe's opening does not seem ideal to inaugurate a new philosophical reading of *Heart of Darkness*. He comes at the text indirectly, speaking in what may appear to be an informal, even colloquial way. Originally delivered as a talk in the context of a seminar titled *Psychiatrie, Psychothérapie et Culture(s)* in 1995–6 (organized by the association *Parole sans frontière*), '*L'horreur occidentale*' is a text written, first of all, to be spoken.[10] And from its very first lines, it is clear that in the published version Lacoue-Labarthe did nothing to hide its original, oral dimension – a dimension Hannes Opelz and I did our best to preserve in the English version. Here is how Lacoue-Labarthe begins: 'The origin of these brief remarks lies in a rash phrase of mine [*une phrase imprudente*], the kind of declaration one cannot help but make on such occasions' (111). These opening remarks have an immediate ring. As Hillis Miller points out in his 'Prologue', readers feel personally addressed by what he calls the 'strong presence . . . of the author's voice',[11] a voice that adopts a confessional, autobiographical tone in order to share thoughts that are of the order of a lived, affective experience. Lacoue-Labarthe's implicit assumption that his listeners understand his allusive remarks to 'such occasions' and 'the kind of declarations' that ensue ('yes', one is tempted to reply, 'it happened to me too!') has the rhetorical function to create a bond, if not of intimacy, at least of shared complicity with his listeners. We already begin to see that such a beginning is not without echoes with the text under consideration (Marlow is addressing his listeners in intimate, familiar terms too), and the mimetic doublings, repetitions and echoes will unfold as we continue to frame Lacoue-Labarthe's framing of Conrad's tale.

At this stage, however, an academic suspicion may begin to arise. Such a mimetic, rhetorical strategy, one might say, may work for an audience tangentially interested in Conrad, but it might travel less well among an audience of readers who have turned *Heart of Darkness* into a privileged object of scholarly investigation. This suspicion is accentuated by the fact that, in this piece, Lacoue-Labarthe transgresses some of the most basic scholarly conventions: he does not position himself within the field; he does not rely on previous interpretations; he does not add a bibliography at the end. . . . Instead, he addresses his audience with what he calls, in all simplicity, some 'brief', 'inchoate' or as he also says, 'experimental remarks' (111, 112, 120) about *Heart of Darkness*. Furthermore, he makes clear that the original impulse for his reflection is not Conrad's text itself but, rather, 'a theatrical representation of this text' (111) – and a representation offered in French. Not only doesn't Lacoue-Labarthe refer to the original version of *Heart of Darkness*, but he also adds another layer of mediation by taking as its starting point a theatrical representation of a French translation of Conrad's text – that is, an interpretation of yet another interpretation.

'Brief', 'inchoate remarks' based on an emotional response generated by a theatrical representation of *Au coeur des ténèbres*, dramatized in a Parisian theatre: these may appear to be tentative initial steps, indeed. But as readers of Lacoue-Labarthe have learnt to recognize, such steps are often but initial 'steps back' that allow him to subsequently leap ahead, into uncharted theoretical territory. In fact, in a philosopher-translator-theatrical man-poet who spent his life rethinking the Platonic conception of mimesis, the choice of adding a *theatrical* frame around Conrad's already densely layered narrative is not deprived of *theoretical* meaning. As Lacoue-Labarthe is fond of reminding us, the origins of the word 'theory' and 'theatre' are, indeed, the same, and they refer to *theorein*, looking attentively in order to *see* – a term which, as we know, is also central to Conrad's poetics. Lacoue-Labarthe's theatrical redoubling of Conrad's narrative frame is thus not the accidental move it may initially appear to be. On the contrary, Lacoue-Labarthe is consciously introducing a theoretical/theatrical device in order to *reframe*, in an allusive, deceivingly informal way, the fundamental formal and theoretical assumptions that will guide him throughout his entire investigation, assumptions about the relation between literature and philosophy, emotion and thought, mimesis and politics, voice and truth, origin and copy.

Lacoue-Labarthe's philosophical insights into what he calls 'the horror of the West' emerge upon witnessing a theatrical adaptation of *Heart of Darkness*, that is, a visual representation (*mimesis*) of a text whereby a mimetic actor (*mimos*) gives voice, in dramatic speech (mimetic *lexis*), to Conrad's tale. Here is how Lacoue-Labarthe describes the theatrical scene which makes him hear an echo of the horror:

David Warrilow—the actor preferred by the later Beckett— drained by a serious illness and himself living his last moments, was telling Conrad's *tale*, in all simplicity, standing and leaning against the edge of the stage. The reading was in French, a language Conrad had nearly chosen as his own. It was overwhelming: suddenly one could hear this *tremendous* [*immense*] text as no other intimate or silent reading (even a painstaking one) could have allowed us to hear. We understood it—in all its breadth and depth. Warrilow's exhausted voice, in its sovereign *detachment*, prompted an emotion of thought [*émotion de la pensée*] which I daresay remains, to this day, incomparable (111).

Lacoue-Labarthe's reference to David Warrilow's theatrical voice and to the 'emotion of thought' that is conveyed through it may stray from conventional academic practices. And yet, it is perfectly in line with Conrad's/Marlow's communicative project to make their audience of listeners and readers both *feel* and *see* something which is of the order of the 'truth [they may] have forgotten to ask'.[12] Not unlike Conrad, Lacoue-Labarthe does not think it possible to access the traumatic experience of the horror directly. Thus, in his reading, he adds an additional frame to Conrad's tale, a theatrical, mimetic frame which, quite literally, *re*-presents (i.e. presents again, for a second time) *Heart of Darkness* on the theatrical scene. A mimetic representation of a text is thus at the source of a mimetic impersonation of a character/narrator and this impersonation gives voice to narrative events that may have taken place in the Congo. To use Plato's canonical terminology, we could say that the spectators in the theatre are not only twice but three times removed from the origin of this text.

We begin to see that Lacoue-Labarthe's apparently informal theoretical/theatrical frame allows him to implicitly engage with fundamental ontological assumptions concerning the inimical relation between philosophy and literature, art and reality, mimesis and truth. That Lacoue-Labarthe is operating within a Platonic conceptual universe is clear. A few paragraphs later, speaking of Plato's distinction of narrative modes, he says that Plato's categories are 'the only ones we have', and qualifies Conrad's narrative frame in terms of a '"mimetic" device [*dispositif "mimétique"*], something almost "theatrical"' (112). And what this medium reveals is that mimetic *distance* puts him, Lacoue-Labarthe, paradoxically, in a position to hear the text from an unprecedented degree of affective *proximity*. Thus, he says: 'one could hear this *tremendous* text as no other intimate or silent reading (even a painstaking one) could have allowed us to hear' (111). For Lacoue-Labarthe, then, it seems that the further removed the spectator appears from the original voice, the closer he or she actually is.

This is, indeed, one of those paradoxes which, for the French philosopher, informs the logic of mimesis in the modern tradition, a paradoxical logic (or 'hyperbologic') which could be formulated as follows: the more it is distant to the original, the closer it is to truth; the closer it seems, the more distant it actually is. In this case, the pathos of Warrilow's mimetic voice (i.e. the voice of a dying mime) is the very *medium* that puts the listeners in the theatre in a position to 'hear', if not the horror of death itself, at least the echo of the voice of another mimetic figure (i.e. the voice of dying Kurtz). This additional *theatrical* frame doubles Kurtz's 'voice', echoes 'the horror' this voice attempts to convey and, by doing so, communicates an 'emotion of thought' that would have been difficult to experience so intimately had the spectator had access only to the original words on the page. Many critics have recognized the oral qualities of *Heart of Darkness*. Lacoue-Labarthe dramatizes this critical point in order to make a larger claim concerning the complex relation between mimesis and truth and, by extension, literature and philosophy. In fact, for him, mimesis is not inimical to truth, literature not antithetical to philosophy. On the contrary, philosophical truth requires a form of literary mimesis to become, if not fully visible, at least partially audible. Elsewhere, Lacoue-Labarthe goes even as far as making voice the very condition for writing as such. As he claims in *Phrase*, 'the phrase – *literature* – is oral./It needs voice [*Il y faut la voix*]'.[13]

Does this mean that the voice of the dying actor renders the experience of the dying hero of Conrad's fiction fully present? Does Lacoue-Labarthe assume that without such a full speaking presence, Kurtz's original phrase, '"The horror! The horror"' (149), would have remained impossible to hear? It is not so simple. Lacoue-Labarthe, along with Derrida, is deeply sceptical of the metaphysics of presence which privileges immediacy over mediation, speech over writing, revelation of truth over its dislocation. It is thus no accident that he relies on a theoretical/theatrical device in order to call attention to the different levels of *mediation* that are 'always already' at work in Conrad's *narrative* frame: Kurtz's dying words are reported by Marlow, whose words are reported by the frame narrator; and all these layers of mediation are now given expression by an actor whose dying voice echoes, from an abyssal distance, the experience of the horror for a contemporary audience to hear. If we add to this that Lacoue-Labarthe is part of this theatrical audience and, in turn, feels compelled to theorize the 'emotion of thought' conveyed by Warrilow's voice by giving himself voice to a text written for yet another audience of listeners and, later, readers, we see the vertiginous degree of multi-layered formal mediation introduced by Lacoue-Labarthe's apparently informal frame.

How does Lacoue-Labarthe's mimetic frame relate to what it frames? How does this formal, mimetic device help us approach what the French philosopher calls, in a problematic phrase, 'the truth of the West', or the 'essence' of Kurtz (114, 115)? These are tricky questions. As Hillis Miller reminds us, words like 'essence' and 'truth' are 'totalizing', 'metaphysical' words, and it is 'hard to use them otherwise' (34). We should thus be careful with such concepts in order not to perpetuate what Nietzsche famously called 'The History of an Error'.[14] This said, another Nietzschean suspicion begins to emerge: Could it be that Lacoue-Labarthe's frame allows him to use these words otherwise, turning them against the totalizing metaphysical tradition from which they originate – in a playful, artistic way? Mimesis, as Lacoue-Labarthe understands it, is, indeed, linked both to presence and to absence, participation and observation, feeling and seeing, pathos and distance, revelation and dislocation. It is also a malleable, slippery and, above all, playful concept that constantly masks itself as it acts out its different roles on the theatrical scene. This mimetic play is tacitly but fundamentally at work in the initial pages of 'The Horror of the West'. These pages suggest that mimesis might get close to the 'truth', but never fully reveals it; it is a framing device which envelops such a revelation of 'truth' in multiple layers of quotation marks. In fact, if we take into consideration the carefully crafted theatrical frame whereby Lacoue-Labarthe starts, we begin to see or, better, hear or, better, read, that through Lacoue-Labarthe's account of Warrilow's voice, it is not the 'truth' itself that is revealed but, rather – to use a word that is central to Lacoue-Labarthe's understanding of mimesis – an 'echo' of the truth, 'a truth' which, as he himself reminds us, is 'too difficult to enunciate directly, to heavy or too painful – above all, too obscure' (114). Or, if you prefer Conrad's figure, we could say that Lacoue-Labarthe's frame creates a 'haze' around his metaphysical reading of 'the horror', a reading that renders visible a 'misty halo' that both brings out the illuminating power of his *logos*, while at the same time also bracketing off transparent notions of 'essence' and 'truth'.

As these preliminary remarks suggest, the problematic of mimesis, while not always explicitly identified, appears from the beginning of the essay in all its polymorphous manifestations and in-*forms* everything that follows. Mimesis is, indeed, at the heart of Lacoue-Labarthe's conception of 'truth'. But unlike a stable reflection, representation or figuration in a mirror, this mimetic truth is a vanishing, retreating truth – like an echo is a vanishing, retreating doubling of an original voice that has already disappeared. As Jean-Luc Nancy reminds us, the echo of a voice 'returns [*revient*], but in returning, loses itself'.[15] And it is this double-movement of appearance and disappearance, this 're(-)treat' [*retrait*] that Lacoue-Labarthe, in an impossible move characteristic of his thought as a whole, tries to capture.[16]

Perhaps, then, the theatrical frame which serves as the starting point for Lacoue-Labarthe's reading of *Heart of Darkness*, with its disconcerting doubling and redoubling of mimetic effects and affects, functions as an echo chamber where the actor's voice resonates and vanishes, becomes audible while disappearing and, by doing so, renders (in)visible the mimetic experience that, for Lacoue-Labarthe, is at the heart of Conrad's tale. As he puts it elsewhere, '[t]he theater is not mimesis, but the medium through which mimesis is revealed [*le révélateur de la* mimésis]'[17] – which does not mean that the theatre tells us what mimesis actually 'is,' but that it shows us something about what mimesis 'does'. In fact, what mimesis invites us to confront is what Lacoue-Labarthe calls – introducing another of his key philosophical-literary concepts – nothing less and nothing more than 'the myth of the West' (112).

Mythic mimesis

Lacoue-Labarthe's philosophical take on 'myth', like his take on 'mimesis', must be understood against the larger background of his philosophical *and* literary preoccupations. Lacoue-Labarthe tells us that he considers *Heart of Darkness* as a narrative that relies on the 'device of myth' in order to 'offer itself, by means of some *testimony*, as a bearer of truth' (113). What is at stake in this association between 'myth' and 'truth' is both a confrontation with, and an inversion of, what Jacques Derrida calls 'the most constraining Platonic tradition'.[18] This underlying philosophical *agon* directly informs Lacoue-Labarthe's striking claim that what *Heart of Darkness* attempts to account for is 'the myth of the West' or, alternatively, 'the truth of the West' (114). How, we may wonder, can a 'myth' reveal the 'truth'? Why is the affective power of *muthos* linked to the rational power of *logos*? These oxymoronic connections are, indeed, at the heart of the 'emotion of thought' Lacoue-Labarthe encourages us to think – as a philosopher-poet, writing with and against philosophy.

As it was also the case with Nietzsche before him, the French philosopher-poet thinks with Plato, contra Plato, in order to account for *both* the power of revelation *and* the danger of intoxication in the modern resurgence of myth. *Contra* Plato, Lacoue-Labarthe claims that mythic narratives are far from being antithetical to the register of philosophical truth. Here is the key claim upon which the entirety of his reading of Conrad's tale *qua* 'myth' hinges. 'When I say, "*Heart of Darkness* is one of the greatest texts of Western literature," I am thinking, simultaneously and inextricably, of two things: its *mythical* power and what constitutes it as an *event of thought*' (112). This is clearly an anti-Platonic claim. In fact, Plato in Books 2 and 3 of the *Republic* – two books that loom large in Lacoue-Labarthe's thought, from *Typography* to 'The Nazi Myth' and beyond – condemned myths recited via a mimetic narrative device (most notably tragedy) for not telling the truth about the gods. Lacoue-Labarthe, on the other hand, argues that the register of myth and the one of truth are far from being antithetical and cannot, strictly speaking, be dissociated. Thus he says: '[i]t is impossible, in theory, to dissociate these two aspects' (112). And, then, in a characteristic *tour de force* which sums up his thesis about *Heart of Darkness* in a nutshell, he adds: 'The myth of the West, which this narrative [*récit*] recapitulates (but only in order to signify that the West is a myth), *is*, literally, the thought of the West' (112). The entire essay is a rigorous attempt to unfold the implications of this striking philosophical-literary affirmation – along both Platonic and anti-Platonic lines.

We have seen that *contra* Plato, Lacoue-Labarthe associates 'myth' with 'truth' in order to reveal something 'essential' about the experience of thought, but we should not forget that *with* Plato he insists that the question of myth opens up a fundamental ethico-political question that is at the heart of the Western body politic.

What worries Plato, and in a different sense Lacoue-Labarthe, is that myths (like any stories or fables heard in childhood or, nowadays seen on TV, the internet, videogames and other new mimetic inventions) provide subjects with models to imitate, *exampla* or, as Lacoue-Labarthe says, following Plato, 'types' that have the power to impress, figure and disfigure the malleable character of subjects.[19] The fundamental Platonic worry is that through such initial impressive spectacles and dramatizations, through this process of typographic impression (or 'onto-typo-logy'), myths are endowed with the power to shape both the characters and opinions of the entire body politic. The logic of Plato's concern with myth could thus be summed up in the following Socratic interrogations: tell me which stories you have been told in childhood and I will tell you which opinions you will have in adulthood; tell me who are your mythic figures and I shall tell you who will be your leader figures; or, closer to our own 'democratic', mass-mediatized societies, tell me which actors you like and I will tell you who you will vote for.

Now, if the French philosopher says that *Heart of Darkness* is a fiction endowed with what he calls the 'mythic power' to reveal the 'truth of the West', it is both in its Platonic and anti-Platonic sense that he mobilizes the concept of 'myth': anti-Platonic because this fiction reveals something *true*, not false, about the West; and Platonic because this fiction reveals the potentially *damaging* formative power of myths over the political destiny of the West. We can thus better understand why Lacoue-Labarthe and Nancy, in a text that has tremendous resonance with 'The Horror of the West' titled 'The Nazi Myth', define myth no longer simply as a 'spoken word' but, rather, as 'an instrument of identification'. And they add that myth 'is in fact *the* mimetic instrument par excellence'.[20] For the two philosophers, then, it is very difficult to keep the category of myth apart from the one of mimesis – if only because myths are, by definitions, *mimetic* mechanisms. In sum, Lacoue-Labarthe's account of *Heart of Darkness* as a 'mythic' tale that reveals 'the horror of the West' suggests that *mythic mimesis* is both an instrument of obfuscation and of illumination; it is both the problem and the solution to the problem or, if you prefer Plato's terminology, a poison and a medicine, that is, a *pharmakon*.[21]

We are beginning to realize that if Lacoue-Labarthe considers Conrad's 'mythic' tale as an 'event of thought', it is not so much because this tale offers us magical metaphysical cures for all kinds of social pathologies. Nor because it offers us a stable, static and transparent sense of the 'truth' or 'essence' of the West that reflects (on) the horrors of colonialism and imperialism – no matter how important this reflection continues to be. But, rather, this text constitutes an 'event of thought' because in his view, *Heart of Darkness* offers us an illuminating and incisive diagnostic that unmasks, in a Nietzschean move that is not deprived of ironic masks, the metaphysical horror that lies 'beneath' the very *idea* of the West and continues, up to these days, to inform its darkest *praxis*. Put differently, Lacoue-Labarthe considers Conrad's mythic tale as a revelatory mimetic mechanism that diagnoses, according to a 'hyperbologic' whereby the poison is also the cure, the affective logic, the pathos and the logos, or if you prefer, the mimetic pathology, that informs these horrors – including the 'propensity for extermination'(119) which is constitutive of the West. What we must add now is that for Lacoue-Labarthe, these horrors, or better, 'the horror', is most clearly revealed in that apocalyptic event in Western history that, along with Nancy, he calls 'the Nazi myth'.[22]

Western barbarity

There are, of course, no easy, pre-packaged solutions to account for the horror that Lacoue-Labarthe, with Conrad, sees as constitutive of the West, from the darkness of its origins to the terror of its destiny. Yet, this *is* the fundamental problematic that Lacoue-Labarthe's reading of *Heart of Darkness* asks us to face. In order to conclude our mimetic account of the silent logic of 'The Horror of the West', we must keep in mind that when Lacoue-Labarthe speaks of Conrad's mythic text as an 'event of thought' that reveals – and here we should multiply quotation marks – the 'truth of the West' (114), he is aligning Conrad with an influential modern tradition which goes from Diderot to Nietzsche, Hölderlin to Heidegger and beyond.[23] And if Lacoue-Labarthe convokes this tradition, it is because he considers that Conrad not only fully belongs to it, but also successfully unmasks the metaphysical assumptions responsible for the ethico-political horrors of modernity.

Given the heterogeneous dimension of Lacoue-Labarthe's *corpus*, we should not be surprised to see that his culminating insights into 'the horror' cannot easily be contained within a neatly sealed theoretical frame but spill over to address the artistic, psychic, ethical, political as well as metaphysical implications of Conrad's tale. I will attempt not to spoil the reader's first encounter with the remarkable complexity of Lacoue-Labarthe's analysis with my summary remarks. Schematically put, however, we could say that these insights emerge from two different, yet, related mimetic/ mythic problematics: one concerning the identity of the 'mythic hero'; the other concerning the identity of 'the West'. These two levels may sound distinct (one psychological and interior, the other political and exterior), but they are both constitutive of Lacoue-Labarthe's single concern with the horror that haunts individual Western figures and the Western body politic as a whole.

Mr Kurtz, the tragic figure of Conrad's fiction, constitutes the driving *telos* of Marlow's narrative; he equally occupies a central place in Lacoue-Labarthe's analysis because he joins the two problematics the French philosopher has been developing from the first pages of his essay. Indeed, in Kurtz's voice – a 'universal genius' (154) who, we are told, is revered as a god and commits atrocities on a massive scale – the question of imitation (*mimesis*) and the one of fiction (*muthos*) join hands in order to make us hear a type of horror that, for Lacoue-Labarthe, is constitutive of the West in general and Western art (*techne*) in particular. Lacoue-Labarthe is particularly attentive to the tonality, caesuras and silences of Kurtz's affective 'voice' as it resonates throughout Conrad's tale (as well as through Warrilow's voice). He is equally aware that such a voice, and the horror it attempts to make us hear and see, cannot be confronted in a theoretical vacuum. Thus, he relies on his previous philosophical work (on mimesis, genius and *techne*, as well as on Plato, Diderot and Heidegger), using his philosophical references as a theoretical chorus to make the implications of Kurtz's artistic and political voice audible and visible. Drawing heavily on *L'imitation des modernes*, Lacoue-Labarthe argues that Kurtz's voice is characteristic of a mimetic 'artist' (or 'genius') as it emerges from the modern tradition. As he explains:

> the artist, or the genius, is he who is properly proper to everything [*proprement propre à tout*], or, if you prefer, having no property in himself [*propriété en lui-même*] (except this mysterious gift), he who is capable of appropriating them all for himself. (115)[24]

Kurtz, in other words, is nothing in himself, an empty, 'hollow' figure who is quite literally 'no one' (*personne*) (116). But according to a general law of mimesis whose 'hyperbologic' is now familiar to us, it is precisely because he is nobody that he can, paradoxically, become everybody; precisely because he has no proper gift that he can also re-produce the gift of different arts (from music to painting, political rhetoric to poetry), if not the gift of creation itself. As he puts it, this artistic figure (or *artiste maudit*) 'is perhaps the most decisive myth of the 19th century (and therefore also, in large part, of the 20th century)' (115).

So, the artist figure brings together the mimetic and mythic threads we have been following in our doubling, that is, mimetic commentary. But why should this mimetic being make us hear the horror at the heart of Conrad's 'myth' and, by so doing, reveal the 'truth' of the West itself? In order to gesture towards this realization, we must notice that the subject *of* this voice is *not*, strictly speaking, a subject, in the sense that he does not constitute a solid, unitary, substantial being, or *subjectum*. The modern subject, for Lacoue-Labarthe, might be moored close to the ground, yet its foundations rest on an abyssal ocean of darkness. There is thus an ontological void *beneath* the subject which, following Lacan, but thinking of a much older tradition that goes back to Augustine, Lacoue-Labarthe calls *la Chose*.[25] Lacoue-Labarthe is not primarily interested in psychologizing Kurtz or reading *Heart of Darkness* psychologically. If he reflects on Kurtz's interior void, as well as on the voice that resonates through him, it is because, in his view, this voice echoes a wider, exterior ethico-political horror that haunts modernity as a whole – and it is this interior/exterior horror that Lacoue-Labarthe, with Conrad, wants to make us hear and see.

Let us not forget that Conrad tells us that 'all Europe' contributed to the making of this figure with a German name, who is Kurtz. And according to a metonymical leap articulated most succinctly in 'The Nazi Myth'[26] and confirmed in Conrad's representation of Kurtz as a 'splendid leader of an extreme party' (154), Lacoue-Labarthe sees in this artistic/mythic character a wider Western vulnerability to the affective/conceptual will to the power of fascist leader figures.[27] This also means that the productive or 'general mimesis' that traverses Kurtz as an artist (*techne* as 'mimetic' art) has its counterpart in a passive or 'restricted mimesis' that Kurtz, as a leader figure, can put to use to subjugate others and enact massive forms of sacrificial horrors (*techne* as 'technique of death'). As Lacoue-Labarthe explains: 'in the domain of art proper, as in the domain of power (or of political art, if you will), he subdues and fascinates; he attracts and seduces (he even arouses love); he subjugates [*assujettit*]: he is absolutely *sovereign*' (116). And he adds: 'All the material details suggest that its stakes concern the revelation of a *technique of death*. And this is, after all, the best definition of the Western will to power that may be given' (119). In such passages, we see how Lacoue-Labarthe's double concern with the now audible problematic of mimesis and myth come together in order to address the devastating power of *techne* and the apocalyptic destiny for the West it entails.[28]

For Lacoue-Labarthe, then, the horror of the West has Greek origins and stretches from the Roman to the Colonial empire and beyond, into more contemporary horrors. It becomes most clearly visible as hollow leader figures with charismatic voices will rely on mimetic devices in order to subjugate the masses in the Europe of the 1930s and 1940s. 'We know what followed', says Lacoue-Labarthe, allusively. And then he adds: 'what is remarkable is that he [Conrad] saw this with such precision – through the example of colonization' (117). Lacoue-Labarthe does not only argue that Conrad, like Nietzsche, senses the horror of fascism and Nazism coming and warns the future against it. He also adds that Conrad's mythic tale is an 'event of thought' because it reveals the fundamental reasons that continue to be responsible for the unprecedented atrocities committed in the name of Western ideals.

*

Reading Conrad *avec* Lacoue-Labarthe is a way to make sure we do not forget to reflect on the horrors the West continues to generate – for others. And if it is tempting to neglect to ask for that 'glimpse of truth' Conrad struggles to make us see and hear, we should recall Lacoue-Labarthe's final, and perhaps most difficult-to-take, reflection on the horror of the West. Namely, that '[to] recoil from the horror is Western *barbarity* itself' (118).

As the reader is soon to find out, Lacoue-Labarthe's philosophical reading of *Heart of Darkness* is an impressively dense, often enigmatic, at times disputable, but always thought-provoking reading whose implications he leaves for the future to meditate.

As we are confronted with this difficult task, we should keep in mind that his claims about the horror of the West are but the tip of an iceberg formed by a lifelong reflection on the relation between mimesis and truth, myth and politics, literature and philosophy. Having now sketched this doubling frame, the only final piece of advice I can now offer is a doubling of what Jacques Derrida already says in 'Desistance': 'work at reading and rereading th[is] difficult text,' he writes. And then he adds, in a cautionary mood:

> If sometimes you have the feeling that you are dealing with a thinker who is panting or harried, don't kid yourself: you are reading someone who on the contrary is tracking—*polemos* without polemics—the most powerful thoughts of our tradition.[29]

Let us now allow this *polemos* to speak for himself. My hope is that this rather sketchy and – I am perfectly aware of it – incomplete theoretical frame will be of some help to keep up with a truly breathtaking reading experience.

Notes

1 'For Philippe, the relation with literature – that is to say, with mimesis – was pregnant with meaning' (my translation).

2 Jacques Derrida's seminal essay, 'Desistance' is, to my knowledge, still the most penetrating account of Lacoue-Labarthe's thought. For an English monograph on his thought, see also John Martis's *Philippe Lacoue-Labarthe: Representation and the Loss of the Subject* (New York: Fordham University Press, 2005). For French readers, other introductions are also available. See André Hirt, *Un homme littéral: Philippe Lacoue-Labarthe* (Paris: Kimé, 2011), and the special numbers devoted to Lacoue-Labarthe in journals such as *Europe*, *L'Animal* and *Lignes* where distinguished figures such as Jean-Luc Nancy, Alain Badiou, Avital Ronell and many others comment on the importance of Lacoue-Labarthe's thought in a relatively accessible, rigorous and thought-provoking way. Excellent starting points are Jean-Luc Nancy's meditations on Lacoue-Labarthe (see bibliography).

3 Jacques Derrida, 'Introduction: Desistance', in *Typography: Mimesis, Philosophy, Politics*, ed. and trans. Christopher Fynsk (Cambridge, London: Harvard University Press, 1989), 7.

4   Lacoue-Labarthe taught philosophy at the University of Strasbourg for most of his career, but he also occupied positions at the *ENS* and the *Collège de Philosophie* in Paris, as well as at Johns Hopkins and UC Berkeley.

5   Jean-Luc Nancy, 'Philippe Lacoue-Labarthe à Strasbourg', *Europe* 973 (2010): 13.

6   Given the text in question, it is perhaps not irrelevant to mention that 'blues' was also the last word of Philippe Lacoue-Labarthe. Avital Ronell reports the last exchange of Philippe with his wife, Claire Nancy: '"It's not going very well." – "What do you mean? Physically or psychically" – "A sort of blues" ["*une sorte de blues*"], he answered. . . .' Avital Ronell, 'L'indélicatesse d'un interminable fondu au noir', *Europe* 973 (2010): 21. [Translations of texts available only in French are mine.]

7   Lacoue-Labarthe's *Phrase* (2000) has already been called 'the greatest poem of our time'. Mehdi Belhaj Kacem, *Inesthétique et mimésis: Badiou, Lacoue-Labarthe et la question de l'art* (Paris: Lignes, 2010), 134. For a comprehensive list of Lacoue-Labarthe's publications, including his translations and articles, see 'Bibliographie', in *Lignes* 22 (mai 2007), 255–8.

8   Nancy, 'Mimesis', 112.

9   Philippe Lacoue-Labarthe, 'Bye bye Farewell', *L'Animal: Littératures, Arts & Philosophie* 19–20 (2008): 193.

10 The articles presented in the context of *Parole sans frontière*, including Lacoue-Labarthe's 'L'horreur occidentale', are now available online: *http://www.p-s-f.com/psf/spip.php?rubrique28*, accessed 20 October 2011.

11 Hillis Miller's 'Prologue' (17).

12 Joseph Conrad, 'Preface', in *The Nigger of the Narcissus* (New York: Doubleday, 1924), xiv.

13 Philippe Lacoue-Labarthe, *Phrase* (Paris: Bourgois, 2000), 17.

14 Friedrich Nietzsche, *Twilight of the Idols*, in *The Portable Nietzsche*, ed. and transl. Walter Kaufmann (New York: Penguin Books, 1982), 464–564, 485.

15 Jean-Luc Nancy, 'Philippe', in *Philippe Lacoue-Labarthe: La césure et l'impossible*, ed. Jacob Rogozinski (Paris: Lignes, 2010), 427.

16 On the concept of '*retrait*', see Philippe Lacoue-Labarthe, Jean-Luc Nancy, *Retreating the Political*, ed. Simon Sparks (London: Routledge, 1997), viii–ix. On the concept of 'echo', see Philippe Lacoue-Labarthe, 'The Echo of the Subject' in *Typography: Mimesis,*

Philosophy, Politics, ed. and trans. Christopher Fynsk (Cambridge, London: Harvard University Press, 1989), 139–207.

17 Lacoue-Labarthe, 'Bye', 196. See also 'Typography' in *Typography*, 43–138, 117.

18 Derrida, 'Desistance', 14.

19 See Plato, Book 2 of the *Republic*, trans. Paul Shorey, in *The Collected Dialogues of Plato*, eds. Edith Hamilton and Huntington Cairns (New York: Bollingen Series, 1963), 377a–8e, 623–5. On 'type' and 'figure', see also Lacoue-Labarthe, 'Typography', 54–55.

20 Philippe Lacoue-Labarthe and Jean-Luc Nancy, 'The Nazi Myth', trans. Brian Holmes, *Critical Inquiry* 16.2 (1990): 298.

21 In 'Plato's Pharmacy', Derrida writes that '*mimesis* is akin to the *pharmakon*', 'it has no nature, nothing properly its own' (139). And, indeed, many of the defining characteristics of the *pharmakon*, as Derrida understands it, are the same as the characteristics of *mimesis* as Lacoue-Labarthe understands it: 'The "essence" of the *pharmakon*' writes Derrida 'lies in the way in which, having no stable essence, no "proper" characteristics, it is not, in any sense (metaphysical, physical. . .) of the word, a *substance*. The *pharmakon* has no ideal identity'. Jacques Derrida, 'Plato's Pharmacy', in *Dissemination*, transl. Barbara Johnson (Chicago, IL: University of Chicago Press, 1981), 61–171, 125–6. Lacoue-Labarthe acknowledges this debt in 'Typography', 101.

22 As Lacoue-Labarthe puts it elsewhere, '[i]n the apocalypse of Auschwitz, it is nothing more and nothing less than the West, in its essence, that revealed itself – and that since, continues to reveal itself'. *La fiction du politique* (Paris: Bourgois, 1987), 59.

23 On this modern tradition, see *L'imitation des modernes (Typographies 2)* (Paris: Galilée, 1986). On the relation between 'tradition' and 'truth', see 'Tradition et vérité à partir de la philosophie' *Europe* 973 (2010): 61–7.

24 This thesis is developed on the basis of an engagement with Aristotle's conception of 'mimesis' in *L'imitation des modernes*, and is most clearly developed in his opening chapter on Diderot, 'Le paradoxe et la mimésis', 15–36.

25 Lacan calls *la Chose*, what he calls 'the absolute Other of the subject' (65) and is thus beyond 'representation' [*Vorstellung*] and 'signification' [*hors-signifié*] (67). In the chapter on 'Das Ding', in Seminar VII, Lacan reminds us that philosophers have reduced *Vorstellung* to what he calls, 'an empty body, a phantom, a pale nightmare of the relation to the world', a description which is not without analogies with

Kurtz. *Le séminare, livre VII. L'éthique de la psychanalyse (1959–60)* (Paris: Seuil, 1986), 75. On Lacoue-Labarthe's analysis of the Lacanian *la Chose*, see also 'De l'éthique: à propos d'Antigone', in *Lacan avec les philosphes* (Paris: Albin Michel, 1991), 33–5.

26   Lacoue-Labarthe and Nancy, 'Nazi Myth', 154.

27   As Lacoue-Labarthe and Nancy explain, one of the essential ingredients in fascism is *emotion*, collective, mass emotion'; and then they add: 'emotion always joins itself to *concepts*' ('Nazi Myth', 294). For a pioneering essay that addresses the question of the Holocaust, but from a different perspective, see Debra Romanick Baldwin, 'The Horror and the Human': the Politics of Dehumanization in *Heart of Darkness* and Primo Levi's *Se questo è un uomo*' *Conradiana* 37.3 (2005): 185–204.

28   Lacoue-Labarthe's career-long engagement with Heidegger's conception of '*techne*' involves a confrontation with the German philosopher's implication with the Nazi party, as well as his subsequent refusal to acknowledge this engagement. On Heidegger and Nazism, see esp. *La fiction du politique*, and 'Neither an Accident Nor a Mistake' *Critical Inquriy* 15.2 (1989): 481–4. On Heidegger, myth and politics, see *Heidegger: la politique du poème* (Paris: Galilée, 2002), esp. 22–38.

29   Derrida, 'Desistance', 15.

Je me demandais, je me demande encore en
quelle langue, sinon celle des morts,
cela l'avait-il traversé et s'était-il écrit.
Une langue, j'en suis convaincu, tout autant
étrangère, à traduire et traduire, sans répit,
que celle que je pense mienne.[1]

LACOUE-LABARTHE, *Phrase*

---

[1] Speaking of the concluding lines of/*Heart of Darkness*/Philippe Lacoue-Labarthe writes in/*Phrase*/:

I would ask myself, and I still ask myself in
which language, if not the one of the dead,
this had traversed him and had been written.
A language, I am convinced, as
foreign, to translate and re-translate, incessantly,
as the one that I think mine. (Editor's translation)

FIGURE 5.1[2]   Philippe Lacoue-Labarthe in his apartment in Strasbourg.

[2] Philippe Lacoue-Labarthe, Strasbourg, April 1995 (© Julien Daniel).

5

The horror of
the West

PHILIPPE LACOUE-LABARTHE

The origin of these brief remarks lies in a rash phrase of mine, the kind of declaration one cannot help but make on such occasions. And yet it is based on a real, long-standing and tenacious conviction: *Heart of Darkness* is one of the greatest texts of Western literature. The phrase is somewhat 'cut and dried.' Somewhat emphatic, too. All the same, there it is, just as I had used it, and this is not exactly the moment to regret it.

(The occasion which prompted my declaration was a theatrical representation of this text, or rather, given the extreme rigour of the sober means with which it was staged, a reading: David Warrilow – the actor preferred by the later Beckett – drained by a serious illness and himself living his last moments, was telling Conrad's *tale*,[1] in all simplicity, standing and leaning against the edge of the stage.[2] The reading was in French, a language Conrad had nearly chosen as his own. It was overwhelming: suddenly one could hear this *tremendous* text as no other intimate or silent reading (even a painstaking one) could have allowed us to hear. We understood it – in all its breadth and depth. Warrilow's exhausted voice, in its sovereign *detachment*, prompted an emotion of thought [*émotion de la pensée*] which I daresay remains, to this day, incomparable. At the end of the performance, I met Pierre Lagarde. We exchanged a few words. Still in the grip of this revelation, I made my rash declaration.)

This evening, in front of you, I would like to try and justify myself. I do not know to which extent what I will say will coincide with your preoccupations or will be inscribed in the general problematic that directly concerns you.[3] Nor do I know whether I will manage to explain myself on a subject that remains, for me, in the realm of fascination. This type of exercise, as we know, is a perilous one. I therefore ask you, in advance, to forgive me if my remarks will be a little experimental.

When I say, '*Heart of Darkness* is one of the greatest texts of Western literature', I am thinking, simultaneously and inextricably, of two things: its *mythical* power and what constitutes it as an *event of thought* [événement de pensée].[4] It is impossible, in theory, to dissociate these two aspects. The myth of the West, which this narrative [*récit*] recapitulates (but only in order to signify that the West is a myth), *is*, literally, the thought of the West, is that which the West 'narrates' about what it must necessarily think of itself, namely – though you know this already, you have read these pages – that the West is the *horror*.

For the purposes of exposition, I will have to dissociate these two aspects, nevertheless. I will do this in the most economical way possible.

What is most striking about this text, from the very first reading of it, is the economy of its enunciation. The 'narrative' proper (the ascent of the river Congo to the quarters of Kurtz, the enigmatic hero of the fable or *muthos*) is almost entirely a story told by Marlow, a character about whom we know practically nothing, except that he is or was, according to a law once formulated by Blanchot, the spokesman (the 'he') thanks to whom Conrad (the 'I') could enter into literature – and enter quite late, as we know. This narrative is in large part autobiographical (written in 1899, it narrates a voyage Conrad made between spring and winter 1890); Conrad never made a secret of it. We are therefore confronted, it would seem, with what one might describe, following Plato's canonical terminology, as a 'mimetic' device [*dispositif 'mimétique'*], something almost 'theatrical'[5] – and here I am thinking both of Jouanneau's stage production and of Warrilow's performance. The enunciator delegates his enunciation to someone else; the author does not speak in his own name but 'invents a fable' [*fabulise*]. And yet, it is not so simple. Before Marlow begins his narrative [*récit*], we are told, by an anonymous 'we', that it is during a conversation among friends – on the deck of a ship anchored in the Thames, waiting for the turn of the tide that will allow it to leave London – that

Marlow, reflecting on the Roman colonization of England, decides to give an account of his African adventure. The 'novel' [*roman*], if that is indeed what it is, will last as long as the tide – its ebb, which would have allowed, ultimately, for the ship's departure, will be missed because of Marlow's eloquence. The last, vertiginous lines, on the other hand, are pronounced by the narrative voice of Conrad himself (the real 'I', then), a voice we had barely heard before, and heard, very shortly and furtively, only twice[6]:

> I raised my head. The offing was barred by a black bank of clouds, and the tranquil waterway leading to the uttermost ends of the earth flowed sombre under an overcast sky—seemed to lead into the heart of an immense darkness. (162)[7]

If we add to this that Marlow's narrative is itself interrupted, at least once, by one of his listeners, we can see the degree of narrative complexity we are dealing with. This 'novel' [*roman*] is not a narrative [*récit*], nor is it simply the narrative of a narrative.[8] It is composed, if you allow me to use Plato's categories (in reality, they are the only ones we have) of a *diegesis* – a minimal *diegesis*, held together by the 'we' of the first three pages and by the rare instances of the 'I' (Conrad) which I have just indicated – taken over, in a mimetic mode, by a new *diegesis*, which is itself interrupted by mimetic passages.[9] And all of this recounts two or rather three things: a night watch in the harbour of London; an initiatory journey into the heart of Africa – and the entire destiny of the West.

I hope you will forgive me for having very hastily conformed to these formal considerations (one should, in truth, pursue a far more meticulous analysis). They are useful nonetheless, and for at least two reasons.

The first is that this device is the device of myth itself, at least in its Western version (let us say, once more: a Platonic version, since, for the sake of convenience and necessity, I have kept to this reference). Beyond the purely formal considerations mentioned earlier, here myth means a spoken word [*parole*] (neither simply a discourse nor simply a narrative) which offers itself, by means of some *testimony*, as a bearer of truth, an unverifiable truth, prior to any demonstration or any logical protocol, a truth too difficult to enunciate directly, too heavy or too painful – above all, too obscure. For Conrad, it is, of course, obscurity itself: the darkness, the horror.

And it is this truth, the truth of the West, to which he seeks to bear witness in such a complex way. Conrad's entire undertaking consists in trying to find a witness for that which he wants to bear witness to. The Ancients invoked the gods, Conrad invents Marlow. But they do so in order to convey the same truth, or at the very least, to convey a truth of the same order.

The second reason is the simple consequence of the first: Conrad's 'novel' does not rely on any characters (I am not saying any *figures*) but on *voices* only. It is evident that Marlow is only a voice, the voice of the 'narrator' [*récitant*]. On the other hand, his listeners, on the deck of the ship ('we', 'I'), are practically voiceless: they listen. The 'characters' Marlow says he has encountered (e.g. the Russian or, at the end of the narrative, Kurtz's 'Intended') are known only through what they said. In an oratorio (which is probably the true form of this work – but I cannot dwell on it here), their intervention would have given rise to two arias at most. In fact, everything is deliberately constructed around an opposition between two voices: that of the indistinct 'clamour' of the savages (the chorus) and that, obviously (and audibly) [*bien entendu*], of Kurtz – who is, surely, the *figure* of this myth or the hero of this *fiction*.

We must look at it more closely.

Even more so than Marlow, Kurtz is himself only a voice. For one, because it is in this way – and, so to speak, only in this way – that Marlow evokes him: 'The man presented himself as a voice'. 'A voice. He was very little more than a voice' (113, 115). This is what Marlow says before meeting Kurtz, and, what is more, at a time when he has almost given up all hope of ever meeting him. If Marlow admits that he always 'connect[ed] him with some sort of action' (113), if he recalls, without denying for a moment its truth, the legend that surrounds him (the adventurer, the ivory plunderer, the bloodthirsty despot or the mysterious 'king' who subjected a terrorized population, etc.), Marlow retains, of all his gifts, only his 'ability to talk, his words—the gift of expression, the bewildering, the illuminating, . . . the pulsating stream of light, or the deceitful flow from the heart of an impenetrable darkness' (113–4). And indeed, Kurtz will remain a voice throughout the entire narrative, from the moment of his long-expected (or prepared) apparition – the 'deep voice [reaching Marlow] faintly' (134) – until the moment of his death, in his last whisper where all is revealed: '"The horror! The horror!"' (149); or until the long work of mourning which, later on, governs Marlow's narrative ('the voice was gone' [150]) and rings out, at the end, the silent echo of the last – and henceforth forbidden – word (161–2).

However, if Kurtz is no more than a voice, it is because – and Marlow knows this full well – in his nature or his essence, Kurtz is but *a man of (his) word(s)* [homme de parole]. I mean by that a *mythic being* – purely mythic. And it is of course on purpose that I use these *equivocal* formulas.

On several occasions, Marlow insists on Kurtz's eloquence, his most obvious gift. He evokes, also, his talents as a writer. Not only does he mention the ('remarkable') report on colonization Kurtz wrote at the request of the 'International Society for the Suppression of Savage Customs' (the manuscript of which, you will recall, includes this terrible sentence, scribbled on the last page: '"Exterminate all the brutes!"' [118]); but he also alludes to his poems (140) – poems, besides, we shall know nothing about. In general, Marlow also speaks of him in terms of an artist; that is to say, as a genius: an extraordinarily gifted man, to the point of being gifted for the *'action'* (or adventure) which he eventually chose for himself. For that matter, it is difficult, when it comes to Kurtz's destiny, not to think of Rimbaud's destiny (as Conrad might have done): the renunciation of literature, the trafficking, the taste for money and power, the voluntary exile (without return), the conquered 'Royalty', the final status of a 'demigod' (i.e. strictly speaking, of a hero). All of this sums up the figure of an *artiste maudit*, which is perhaps the most decisive myth of the nineteenth century (and therefore also, in large part, of the twentieth century).

Who is an artist? Or who is a genius? As we learn from Plato, Diderot, Nietzsche, from the great Western tradition (I mean from the Western tradition which recognizes that the artist is the *figure* par excellence of the West), the artist, or the genius, is he whom nature (*physis*) has gifted with the innate gift (*ingenium*) to possess all the gifts that supplement his proper limitation (what the Greeks call *techne*) – starting with the gift of gifts: language.[10] This amounts to saying that the artist, or the genius, is he who is properly proper to everything [*proprement propre à tout*], or, if you prefer, having no property in himself [*propriété en lui-même*] (except this mysterious gift), he who is capable of appropriating them all for himself. Diderot has shown this, in a canonical way, via the example of the great actor.[11] The artist or the genius is 'the man without proper qualities' – the expression which provides Musil's masterpiece with its title.

This is exactly what Kurtz 'is'. He is presented not only as a kind of 'universal genius' (154), or even as an 'extremist' (154) – and as such, someone who will do anything, comparable in this to the Russian anarchists, that is, to the 'nihilists', but also as being *nothing himself*; or as being *no one* [personne], if we think of Ulysses. His eloquence is systematically linked to the 'barren darkness of his heart' (147), to his being 'hollow at the core' (131), to the void that is within him or, more exactly, the void that he 'is'. This is why he is only a voice. But this is also why, in the domain of art proper as in the domain of power (or of political art, if you will), he subdues and fascinates; he attracts and seduces (he even arouses love); he subjugates [*assujettit*]: he is absolutely *sovereign*. Being nothing, he is, indeed, everything. His *voice* is all-powerful.

Two consequences follow:

(1) The first involves the opposition or *agôn* between the two voices that structure Marlow's narrative: the savage, undifferentiated clamour and the voice of Kurtz. These are, purely and simply, the voice of nature (*physis*) and the voice of art (*techne*). One sentence puts them rigorously in relation to one another: the whisper of savagery 'echoed loudly within him because he was hollow at the core' (131). On the one hand, this is what explains the deep sadness of the clamour that lies behind its apparent savagery or violence and that resonates regularly throughout the entire narrative and punctuates it. It is a *lament* [*plainte*] – and, to tell the truth, more than of the suffering of exploitation and slavery which is nevertheless very present, I am thinking of Benjamin's celebrated phrase: if nature could speak, it would be in order to lament (colonial exploitation being, first and foremost, the exploitation of nature).[12] On the other hand, this explains, also, that the *horror*, the vertigo to which Kurtz falls victim, this horror about which we know basically nothing (What has he seen? What has he suffered? What is he talking about?) is less the 'savage' horror itself than the horror revealed by the echo of the clamour within him (in his 'intimate' void): it is his 'proper' horror, or better, it is the horror of his absence of any proper being [*être-propre*]. All that we can imagine in terms of savagery, of prehistory, of the reign of pure terror, of abomination and the incomprehensible, of a mystery without name, of cruelty, of the power of darkness; all that pulls him – and with him, all those who are fascinated by him – into the vertigo and leads him even to ecstasy,

this 'black hole', then, this 'heart of darkness', is 'him' – his void – as if outside himself [*comme hors de lui*]. If I may allow myself to use, in front of you, Lacan's terminology, when he speaks, precisely, of the tragic (I am thinking of his seminar on the *Ethics of Psychoanalysis*), I would say that the horror is *la Chose* – the *Thing* or *Ding* (another name for being, that is, for nothingness, the 'nothingness of being' [*le rien d'étant*], which Lacan borrows from Heidegger);[13] or, if you prefer, that the 'heart of darkness' is the *extime* – the *interior intimo meo* of Augustine, God, but as internal exclusion. Perhaps evil. . . I leave this question open, at least provisionally.

(2) To say that the horror is 'him' – Kurtz – is to say that the horror is *us*. You will have noticed that the fascination of the horror contaminates all those who, in one way or another, have approached him or *heard* him: Marlow, of course, but also the Russian (the fool, Kurtz's derisory double – a fool probably always accompanies a *figure*, whether this figure is called 'Don Quichotte, . . . Zarathustra' . . . and so on), and even Kurtz's 'Intended'. It is no accident that all these characters, trapped by the fascination for the Thing, defend themselves by manipulating *objects*: rivets and white lead, a navigation manual, knitting or a piano. The response to the vertigo of *techne* is *technical* agitation. And it is probably also in order to avert the horror (of art) that Kurtz tried to lose 'himself' in ivory trafficking and colonial royalty. Therein, precisely, is the *lure* par excellence, namely, the Western lure itself – that is, as long as the West (and Conrad, as the author of *Under Western Eyes*, knew what it meant) is understood as that which will have always shrunk from the dread of knowledge (another word to translate, in its full meaning, the Greek *techne*) by taking refuge in know-how [*savoir-faire*], and as that which will have always confused ability [*capacité*] (the gift) with power.

In modern philosophical thought, this is what revealed itself when Nietzsche called the gift (of art) 'will to power' and when, under this name, he conceived the essence of mankind as subject. He could not have prevented that 'power' as *puissance* (which means 'ability', or even, quite simply, 'genius'), when linked to will, would merge with 'power' as *pouvoir*: *potentia* with *potestas*. We know what followed (and Nietzsche, besides, was the first to fear it). I do not know whether Conrad had read Nietzsche (and this matters little), but what is remarkable is that he saw this with such precision – through the example of colonization. (I mention in passing that

Conrad's book caused a scandal and that Gide had great difficulties establishing its publication in France during the 1920s.) To recoil from the horror is Western *barbarity* itself, because it is the plain underside of the fascination with the Thing – a fascination that Kurtz, defying all *potentia* and all *potestas*, experiences as literally *impossible*. But when he dies of it, both sanctified and accursed (here a long analysis would be necessary), evil is done: Africa is destroyed – and Westerners (*we*) will not recover from it.

The implementation of this difficult thought no doubt explains the extraordinary work of writing to which Conrad devoted himself. And Conrad knew perfectly well that he was producing one of the most powerful *figurations* of the West. (Malraux, a nearly perfect anagram of Marlow, will recall this, at least from *La tentation de l'Occident* until *La voie royale*.) I cannot dwell on this here, but I would simply like to mention two, apparently enigmatic enunciations, where Conrad designates his *tale*,[14] that is to say, his *myth*, as being itself 'hollow' – much like its hero. Before attempting to conclude and get somewhat closer to your preoccupations, I will limit myself to quoting these lines:

> The yarns of seamen have a direct simplicity, the whole meaning of which lies within the shell of a cracked nut. But Marlow was not typical (if his propensity to spin yarns be excepted), and to him the meaning of an episode was not inside like a kernel but outside, enveloping the tale which brought it out only as a glow brings out a haze, in the likeness of one of these misty halos that, sometimes, are made visible by the spectral illumination of moonshine. (48)

> There was no sign on the face of nature of this amazing tale that was not so much told as suggested to me in desolate exclamations, completed by shrugs, in interrupted phrases, in hints ending in deep sighs. (129)

Ever since the appearance of the chapter, in Montaigne's *Essays*, devoted to the 'Cannibals', a long tradition of modern literature (one which leads up to at least Lévi-Strauss and Pierre Clastres) wonders what the West *is* through what the West *does* (to 'others') – a tradition turned giddy, at bottom (though this bottom is bottomless, is an abyss), with the *infinite* power of destruction that is its own, its propensity for extermination. Conrad is inscribed in this tradition – to this extent that he makes this giddiness the object of his work, and that is his originality.

From the very beginning of the narrative – that is, from the evocation of the Romans' encounter with the barbaric and savage 'darkness' of future England ('"And this also," said Marlow suddenly, "has been one of the dark places of the earth"' [48]), it is clear, one could say, that the West is defined as a gigantic colony – it was also the case with the Greeks, well before Rome – and that, *beneath* this colony is the *horror*. But this horror is less the *de facto* horror of savagery than the power of fascination that savagery exerts over the 'civilized' who suddenly recognize the 'void' upon which their will to ward off the horror rests – or fails to rest. It is its own horror that the West seeks to dispel. Hence its work of death and destruction, the evil it generates and spreads to the confines of the earth – up to those 'white' areas found on the maps of Africa, areas which, at the outset, irresistibly attract Marlow, that is to say, Kurtz. The West exports its intimate evil: it imposes its *extime*. Such is its curse, and such is the gloom it imposes on the whole world: pain, sadness, an endless lament, a mourning that no work will ever diminish.

Heart of Darkness is a kind of 'season in hell' or descent into the realm of the dead based on the model of the Homeric *nekyia*. When Marlow is welcomed by the knitting women at the Company's headquarters, the allusion to the Fates is transparent and deliberate. And the references to hell are innumerable. As excess or transgression, the Western *hybris* is the metaphysical will to pass through death. Marlow's journey is an initiatory journey. All the material details suggest that its stakes concern the revelation of a *technique of death*. And this is, after all, the best definition of the Western will to power that may be given – that is, if we keep to the ambiguity of the phrase (both the ambiguity affecting the term 'technique' and that resulting from the double genitive). Against the rites of the 'savages', which represent perhaps a *knowledge* of death, Kurtz, the artist (but the failed artist), only ever managed to oppose a technique – of death. As for the artist in-spite-of-himself or by proxy, namely, Marlow, the *mythomane* who was really horrified by Kurtz's fate (i.e. who really caught a glimpse of the horror), all he is left with, upon his return, is the artifice of a 'white lie'. He will not dare tell Kurtz's 'Intended' his last words; instead, he will leave it to love to cover up and disguise the fury of transgression, thus completing the work of sanctification that averts the Western gaze from its wickedness.

Schelling says that 'myths' are not 'allegorical'. They say nothing other than what they say; they do not have a different meaning from the meaning they enunciate. They are *tautegorical* (a category Schelling borrows from Coleridge).[15] *Heart of Darkness* is no exception to this rule. It is not an allegory – say, a metaphysico-political allegory – at all. It is the tautegory of the West – that is, of art (of *techne*). That this art, in this particular instance, is literature itself – in other words, the *mythical* usage of the original *techne* that is language – leaves open a question that the analytical outline I have just offered here cannot pretend to answer.

I will therefore leave it at that. My hope is that these brief and – I am perfectly aware of it – inchoate remarks will have afforded a glimpse of what is at stake in the horror, that is, the savagery in us.

Trans. Nidesh Lawtoo and Hannes Opelz

Notes

We would like to thank Anne Luyat for reading an early version of the translation and for sharing her feedback with us. Our translation greatly benefited from her helpful stylistic insights [trans. note].

1   In English in the original. Unless otherwise specified, endnotes to this essay are the translators'.

2   The performance, directed by Joël Jouanneau, was staged at the Théâtre de l'Athénée-Louis-Jouvet (Paris) in 1992.

3   This conference was held in the context of a seminar entitled *Psychiatrie, Psychothérapie et Culture(s)*, organized by the association *Parole sans frontière* in 1995–6. The essay was first published in the proceedings of this conference: *Au réel de la frontière*, ed. P.-S. Lagarde, B. Piret and K. Khelil (Strasbourg: Association Parole sans frontière & Conseil de l'Europe, 1996), 161–70 [note present in the original], now available online: *http://www.p-s-f.com/psf/spip. php?rubrique 28*, accessed 20 October 2011. It was subsequently reprinted in a special number of the Journal *Lignes* devoted to Lacoue-Labarthe, following his death: *Lignes* 22 (May 2007): 224–34. The present translation is based on the latter version.

4   Original in italics.

5 Lacoue-Labarthe is referring to Plato's discussion of theatrical
   mimesis in the *Republic*. In Book 3, Plato defines *mimesis* as a type
   of poetic speech whereby the poet/actor does not speak in his proper
   name but 'delivers a speech as if he were someone else'. Plato, *The
   Collected Dialogues of Plato*, ed. Edith Hamilton, Huntington Cairns,
   trans. Paul Shorey (New York: Pantheon Books, 1961), 575–844;
   3.393c, 638). For Lacoue-Labarthe's analysis of Plato's conception
   of theatrical mimesis, see Philippe Lacoue-Labarthe, 'Typography'
   (1975), in *Typography: Mimesis, Philosophy, Politics*, ed. and trans.
   Christopher Fynsk (Cambridge, MA: Harvard University Press,
   1989), 43–138.

6 Lacoue-Labarthe is assuming here that the frame narrator is Conrad
   himself, an assumption which is problematic from a narratological
   perspective.

7 Lacoue-Labarthe quotes from the French translation, relying on
   Jean-Jacques Mayoux's (bilingual) edition of *Heart of Darkness:
   Au cœur des ténèbres, Amy Foster, Le Compagnon secret* (Paris:
   Aubier-Montaigne, 1990). That Lacoue-Labarthe had access to the
   English version is confirmed by his poem, *Phrase*, where he cites
   the concluding lines of *Heart of Darkness* in English; see *Phrase*
   (Paris: Bourgois, 2000), XIV, II 87. The epigraph to this part is a
   commentary of these lines.

8 Lacoue-Labarthe is relying on Gérard Genette's narratological
   distinction between *récit* understood as narration (the fact of
   recounting) and *récit* understood as narrative (the discourse that
   recounts events in a fictional order) – as opposed to the sequence
   of events as they really happened (*histoire*). See, Gérard Genette,
   Narrative Discourse Revisited, trans. Jane E. Lewin (New York:
   Cornell University Press, 1988), 13–8.

9 In Book 3 of the *Republic*, Plato distinguishes three forms of poetic
   enunciation: 'pure narration' (*diegesis*),'narrative that is effected
   through imitation' (*mimesis*) and 'mixed style'. In diegetic speech,
   'the poet himself is the speaker and does not even attempt to suggest
   that anyone but himself is the speaker'; in mimetic speech, the poet
   'delivers a speech as if he were someone else' by impersonating his
   characters; mixed style combines both diegetic and mimetic speech.
   Plato, *Republic*, 3.392c–8b, 637–8.

10 Lacoue-Labarthe's definition of the artist/genius as a figure who
   supplements his/her limitations through art (*techne*) emerges from
   his deconstructive reading of the concept of *mimesis* as it appears
   in the works of Plato, Aristotle, Diderot, Nietzsche and other
   modern philosophers. See Philippe Lacoue-Labarthe, *L'imitation*

des modernes (Paris: Galilée, 1986). On the question of mimesis as 'supplement', see 24–9.

11 Lacoue-Labarthe is referring Diderot's claim, in *Le paradoxe sur le comédien*, that it is because the great actor 'is nothing [himself] that he can be everything par excellence'. 'The paradox is the following', explains Lacoue-Labarthe: 'in order to do everything, imitate everything. . . one needs to be *nothing* in oneself, have nothing *proper* to oneself'. Lacoue-Labarthe, *L'imitation des modernes*, 27 (his emphasis).

12 See Walter Benjamin, 'On Language as Such and on the Language of Man' (1916), in *Selected Writings*, vol. I, ed. Michael Jennings et al. (Cambridge, MA: Harvard University Press, 1996–2003), 62–74, 72.

13 See Jacques Lacan, *The Ethics of Psychoanalysis, 1959–60. The Seminars of Jacques Lacan, Book VII*, trans. Dennis Porter (London, New York: Routledge, 1992), 76.

14 In English in the original.

15 See F. W. J. Schelling, *Historical-Critical Introduction to the Philosophy of Mythology*, trans. Mason Richey and Markus Zisselsberger (Albany, NY: SUNY Press, 2007), 136, 187.

6

Philippe's lessons of darkness

FRANÇOIS WARIN

The African adventure I hereby set forth to relate had initially been told in the halo of Conrad's tale. First published in the Journal *Lignes*, *in memoriam* to Philippe Lacoue-Labarthe, this piece originally bore the Conradian title, 'Heart of Darkness'.[1] In the course of this African adventure, Philippe and I faced what for both of us proved to be an absolutely harrowing experience when, at the culminating point of our journey, we were given the opportunity to witness a Dagara funeral ceremony.[2] This ceremony, similar to those enacted by the Lobi people, testified to this knowledge of death [*savoir de la mort*] as Philippe called it, a knowledge to which, in our Western *hubris* and self-conceit we have now become fully foreign. Five years later, when I was confronted to the Rwandan Genocide, the discovery of Philippe's reading of Conrad, *L'horreur occidentale*, was particularly beneficial to helping me think through the emotional shock generated by this apparently African horror. 'The Horror of the West', then, allowed me to initiate, in the absence of Philippe this time, but in his textual company nonetheless, another reading of *Heart of Darkness*. It also enabled me to attempt a second, more subtle and more difficult navigation towards this unbearable outside whose *extimacy* has now become apparent and is there for all of us to face. It is at this stage that, for the occasion of this volume, I have added a philosophical *coda* to the first, more biographical and personal text.

The darkness of a sacrificial heart

> The true is hateful. We have art so as not to vanish through the
> bottom of things—foundered by truth.
>
> Friedrich Nietzsche, *Nachgelassene Fragmente*

This is the title that spontaneously comes to my mind as I attempt
to revise this essay in honour of Philippe Lacoue-Labarthe. First
of all, because it was Philippe who first advised me to read *Heart
of Darkness*, as I was just about to be embarked on a journey
to West Africa. Indeed, what better introduction to Africa than
Joseph Conrad's most celebrated tale? And what better guide than
this literary text to speak about Philippe, all the more so from an
experience I had been given the honour to partake in as a privileged
witness? It is, in fact, on the African continent that I have learnt to
really know and love Philippe. With Claire, his wife, he had come
to see us several times.[3] Every time, his coming was inscribed in
what was, for me, an entire horizon of theoretical and emotional
questions, questions that had long been on his mind and that were
centred around the question of myth. This question, undoubtedly
inherited from an old, twisted and conflicted Romanticism, often
led us to look in the same direction and to find ourselves on the
same ground, a ground that was, for both Philippe and myself, in
more than one sense, something like a native soil.

When I first met him in 1968, Philippe was already wrestling with
the brief and opaque *Remarques sur Oedipe et Antigone*[4] as well
as with the onset of modern atheism. For me, Philippe has always
remained the thinker who has attempted to respond to this work of
mourning (*Trauer*), to this categorical turning away from the divine,
that was, already for Hölderlin, tragedy as such (*Trauerspiel*). Or,
and this is practically the same thing, the thinker who, his body
notwithstanding, has given himself up during his entire life to a
severe and uncompromising critique of the *problematic of presence*
and, consequently, to a critique of every attempt to re-mythologize
Hölderlin. In a way, it is in contrast to his very protestant attitude
towards these Western questions that I understand Philippe's relation
to both Africa and Africans, a relation revealing of a tenacious force,
as well as of an abyssal obscurity against which he was set up hard.
From the moment he arrived on the African continent, however,

everything appeared to have been inverted. To speak like Schelling, the eternal 'yes' substituted itself to the eternal 'no', gentleness to force, understanding to sternness or love to anger.

And yet, in the case of Philippe, this had nothing to do with a return to a form of primary naïveté. He never fell into the trap of this kind of 'primitivism' or, as Sally Price would have called it, *hard* primitivism,[5] a primitivism that Conrad's *Heart of Darkness* contributed to constitute. Rather than denouncing the stereotypical representations of Africa still operating in Conrad's tale, as Chinua Achebe has famously done, it would be more productive to consider the tale from the more ambivalent angle of primitivism. As *Heart of Darkness* makes clear, primitivism assumes that the future of humanity is to be found in the past. It thus relies on an inversion of the ideology of progress and emphasizes at least two points. First, a generalized retroversion: from this perspective, the symbolic ascent up the river Congo is an ascent that is not only spatial but also temporal; it brings us back to what is most ancient and archaic, to the 'unconscious' and the 'prehistoric'. In a sense, this retroversion constitutes the structuring form of the novella as a whole. And second, the identification of the 'savage' with the 'magnificent': in the context of *hard* primitivism this identification stretches to include an avowal of a fascination for the 'abominable' and the 'hideous'. From this perspective, then, under the rags or the varnish of culture that masks what is essential, the origin would always remain present. Moreover, the memory of the vital, foundational 'savagery' is considered to be the origin of everything that is synonymous with greatness. All these historical-empirical schemes are nonetheless subverted by Philippe's analyses of African art. For Philippe, in fact, what is thrilling in the African 'incomprehensible frenzy' (96) – a frenzy which is of course far from limited to Africa – is not so much 'the thought of their humanity' (96) as is still the case for Marlow, but the opposite. African art, Philippe writes – in the context of aesthetic considerations that make his anti-racist inclinations clear – represents not so much the 'human(ity) in (of) man, but what we could risk calling the (in)human(ity) in (of) man [*l'(in) humain dans (de) l'homme*]' (197). For him, at the heart of these artistic representations of man is a secret intimacy that opens up to a pure outside, an *extime* that places humanity in an ecstatic state. Here is how he continues his discussion of primitive art in general and in Lobi art in particular. The echoes with 'The Horror of the West' are clearly audible:

> (In)humanity, here, is not inhumanity, that is, the loss of humanity or its negation. On the contrary, it is the most secret heart [*le coeur le plus secret*], the most sheltered side of humanity . . . . It is not a sort of whatever 'transcendence.' Augustine calls it God, but he says: *interior intimo meo*, what is most interior than my intimacy itself. And we can guess that this intimacy of intimacy, beyond intimacy, opens onto a prodigious exteriority, a pure outside that places humanity in an ecstatic condition [*qui extasie l'humain*] . . . a way of *figuring* . . . extricated from the eidico-spiritualist constraint that preserved philosophy.[6]

*

Philippe knew Michel Leiris well, and he strongly advised me to read *L'Afrique fantôme*.[7] As an homage to Leiris, he had entitled a conference that he had given in Benin, in 1991, 'La philosophie fantôme'.[8] And, to me, Leiris's lucidity about Africa is in fact what Philippe's irreproachable probity generally evokes. Coming from this avatar of Romanticism that is Surrealism, in Africa, Leiris did not cease to discover an intimate fissure or wound inside himself: he discovered an insuperable difference that divided him from this mythic continent, from this land of origins which, for him too, was the land of trances and possessions. 'A sinister thing it is to be a European' he notes in his journal upon returning from this failed initiatory journey that had been the Dakar–Djibouti mission (2 September 1931).[9] For Leiris, what was at stake in this physical journey was a metaphysical journey, somewhat like in *Heart of Darkness*, where the ascent of the river Congo is metaphorically associated to 'travelling back to the earliest beginnings of the world' (92). And yet, the origin proved to be both frightful and terrifying; eventually, it ended up retreating and disappearing evermore. This is exactly what happened to Africa: it remained indistinguishable from the phantoms and projections of that European in need of redemption he was. His Africa remains, in all respects, *L'Afrique fantôme*. In a slightly displaced form, we find the same disillusioned theme in Philippe's conference on Africa, a theme that will be even more sharply brought into focus in 'The Horror of the West'. As he demonstrates, the domination of the West is both definitive and complete. As such, it is identical with the becoming-world of philosophy. From the bottom of that prison which is ours we can thus only glimpse what this continent has been prior to the domination of the West: we can only 'guess at its fragile image (from the) outside'.[10]

'Lucidity is the wound which is closest to the sun', wrote René Char, at the time of *Feuillets d'Hypnos*.[11] How could one best translate what constitutes the entire difficulty, as well as the entire 'truth', of Philippe and his 'emotion of thought'? The kind of lucidity that makes us see the irremediable wound of separation, that prevents us from still being pious is, paradoxically, the tracing of the vanishing gods. And this is the only proximity that is emotionally thinkable, as well as possible, in relation to this 'sun', which, no more than death itself, cannot be faced directly.

This intense and complex relationship with Africa started very early and via the intermediary of an artistic object. Philippe, who had borrowed Michel Leiris's and Jacqueline Delange's book on African art (printed in the collection directed by André Malraux), always passionately loved what Europeans call *primitive* or *primal art*. As soon as he had a bit of money, during a visit to Paris, he purchased a Bambara *Tyi Wara* helmet crest [*cimier*]. As his brother Dominique recently told me, he was, at the time, only 13 years old. The first letter that I received from him was a passionate note in which he thanked me for the small idol made out of clay that I had left, during his absence, on his desk, in Strasbourg. In a text that still echoed the lament [*plainte*] of the exiled thinker, he said how deeply he had been moved:

I am embarrassed [*gêné*] and very happy at the same time: [I feel] a connection that I am incapable of expressing . . . . I am all the more touched as it is very beautiful and, let's say, moving. This touches, thus, very precisely, on what restrains me [*ce qui me contraint*] because the proximity risks to be excessive and unbearable [*insupportable*] in relation to the preservation of too great a distance. The presence of this object will reanimate this wound. There are few things of which this can be said.

And how many times in the years that followed did I bring back from Africa some of the last relics of primitive art, associated generally with the cult of the dead (see Fig. 6.2 below). What emotion every time I saw, in his apartment in Paris, all these statues carefully set on top of an old fireplace, and all these masks hanging on the walls!

*

To be sure, this African path had long been opened. Philippe had entered politics during the Algerian War, and it is the anti-colonial struggle that had permanently structured him. Both of us could thus maintain friendly relations with Africans, relations free from all kinds of prejudices. What we had learned from Conrad's tale was now given to us to experience: Africa was, for us, the return of the real that unmasked the Western pretention to 'civilize' indigenous people. As always, colonization and the 'civilizing mission' it entails had proved to be a total failure. This also means that there is always, at the heart of each of us, a Mr Kurtz, ready to be awakened, a Mr Kurtz intoxicated with power and possessed by a logorrhea as sinister as it is vain, by an ideology that places colonization – for all the 'missionaries' and 'pilgrims' – in the service of the Idea. Kurtz, this Belgian with a German name is indeed a 'hero' who is, quite literally, swallowed up by the colonial 'muddy hole' (150). As some scholars seem to think, Kurtz is also a shortened version of Conrad's own name (Korzeniowski). Hence he is a double: his double, but also our double – and the incarnation of the West: 'All Europe contributed to the making of Kurtz' (117). Kurtz collected ivory in the same way others would collect works of art.

I have never seen anyone respond with such a vibrating intensity as Philippe did to the spectacle that we were given to witness during our somewhat adventurous expeditions in the savannah. I recall the happiness the prodigious African gaiety roused in us, the same gaiety that had also fascinated Nietzsche. But I also recall the simple and warm hospitality whereby we had always been welcomed. I remember in particular the powerful emotional effect upon Philippe when, during his first African voyage, we visited a Dogon village at the far eastern extremity of the Bandiagara cliffs: 'One should write a book, write something', he had told me. The mythic isolation in which the Dogons live has always triggered this kind of enthusiasm: 'Exceptional religiosity; the sacred swims in every corner of life', writes the honest Leiris.[12] It has also generated an entire onto-mythology: that of the French school of anthropology, a school for which myth, and myth only, had been the royal road to study these people's identity and history. The Dogons are somewhat like the Pre-Socratics: had their discovery not been for us a bit like what the discovery of a Greece before Socrates had been for Nietzsche or Heidegger?

Upon his return to Europe, in order to describe his stay in Africa, Philippe spoke of a true *mystical experience*. In Africa, we had not felt the need to speak of this feeling of transport, this happiness, at all. And, besides, in which language could we have done so? Later, I discovered that my feeling had been confirmed, in a precise way, in an interview where Jean-Christophe Bailly asked Philippe about his furtive, but nonetheless essential, contacts with Africa.[13] In this 'kind of immense night that is Africa', he said:

> we were crushed by a feeling of . . . of sacredness [*sacré*] . . . .
> In this immense African darkness (it was cold, as always during the night over there, it was windy and there were those noises . . . .) we were haunted, haunted, which means inhabited [*habités*] too . . . and I have felt, in a very, very impressive way, this feeling of . . . this feeling of, yes, of sacredness [*sacré*]. We had the impression to be facing what, by definition, is not, what can only be thematized under the name of void. This is why it is very difficult to write about this. One cannot say this, but all of a sudden, one had the impression of being in the presence of what is other [*en presence d'autre*], an otherness which is not one thing [*une chose*]—one cannot even say 'something other' [*autre chose*]. There is a form of vacillation [*bascule*] that has taken place. . .[14]

*

Among the strongest experiences that we underwent, I recall those Dagara funerals that we chanced upon. Not unlike Conrad's Marlow, it seemed to us that this time we had ascended the river, travelled towards the origin, in order to be finally confronted with the horror – the horror of death. The great violence of this ritual had strongly impressed us: the display of the deceased, sitting for three days on a podium, the ritual laments and the heartrending cries of an entire village ready to confront the transgression of death. In reality, the Africans had turned death into a holy day; they could also dance in front of this 'dark sun', as Georges Bataille would have put it, or in front of the 'Open' [*l' Ouvert*] that is at the foundation of things, as Lacoue-Labarthe would have said. But along with its violence, what we were also given to think and feel was the great wisdom of this ceremony, a cathartic or purgative ceremony, now ingeniously erased by our Western 'techniques of death' whose function is to prevent us from facing the horror of *la disparition*.

This picture (Fig. 6.1), taken by André Vila in 1955,[15] is to my knowledge the only existing photographic testimony representing the funeral cries, or laments, as they take place in a ritualized form, in Africa, among the Lobi people of Burkina Faso. In the midst

FIGURE 6.1   André Vila, *Lamentations funéraires lobi*, 1955.

of the savannah, a crying woman wearing a *labret* on her upper lip, tragically stretches out her naked arms, in an attitude that is simultaneously one of imploration and of terror.[16] In front of her, an immobilized man seems prostrated, hypnotized, completely paralysed by a horror that is without name.

This Lobi statue (Fig. 6.2) is also intimately associated with the cult of the dead. Such statues are sculpted in order to ward off a destiny of misfortune, but also in order to signal, or take upon themselves, an unbearable and unspeakable pain. Certain statues, like the one represented here, characterized by an extreme tension and concentration, reproduce the attitude of these funerary

FIGURE 6.2 *Lobi sculpture. Lamentation funéraire,* collection J. L. Despiau, photo. F. Warin.

FIGURE 6.3   André Vila, *Funérailles lobi*, 1955.[17]

lamentations. In its making, the sculptor alone, without mediators, is exposed to occult forces and to malefic geniuses that can, at any time, strike him with madness or disease. His task is to attempt to exorcise fear and to help humans face the ever-present menace of death.

If, as Bataille puts it, 'the seriousness of death and pain is the slavery of thought',[18] then, it is likely that slavery will remain, for a long time, our common burden. Here we find ourselves, 'ceasured', in a state of mourning, exiled from cults, as well as from myths and rituals. Unlike these Africans, we shall remain fully incapable of expulsing, through ritual laments, the excessive pain that the death of our friend, Philippe, provokes in us. We will certainly have to learn to live with this void, but also with the memory of someone who chose – deliberately, there is no doubt – a brief life.

Coda: The darkness at the heart of genocide

[N]ever, never before, did this land . . . appear to me so hopeless and so dark, so impenetrable to human thought, so pitiless to human weakness

Conrad, *Heart of Darkness*

When, some time ago, I was invited to speak after the screening of a film on the Rwandan Genocide,[19] I could not help but think about 'The Horror of the West'. Like so many others, I was horrified: my spirit was broken by the unspeakable cruelty of this event, and I asked myself in which language I would have been able to speak. Then, suddenly, it appeared to me that the only mode through which one could approach it was in the mode of the *Lessons of Darkness*, a canonical text from the Catholic Liturgy which, at some level, equally informs Philippe's reading of *Heart of Darkness*.[20] The *Lessons of Darkness* are undoubtedly *lessons* in the sense that they are a form of teaching. But, above all, they are a funeral hymn, a hymn not so much turned towards *kenosis* but, rather, towards an unthinkable *black hole*.[21] From the horror of sacrificial death to the horror of the genocide, I felt like I was continuing, in the company of Philippe's thought, our African adventure into what Conrad called the 'heart of darkness'. But, this time, in Philippe's physical absence, and under omens more terrible than ever before. As it was also the case in Conrad's tale, under the 'savage clamour' (105) of nature lay hidden an artifice and an abyss of another, more intimate clamour that was going to reverberate and resonate without end. Conjuring with a stubborn degree of mimeticism what, for lack of better words, I shall call absolute evil *[l'absolu du mal]* – and this in the very year that marked the commemoration of the fiftieth anniversary of the crushing of the 'Nazi barbarity' – this genocide, in which to varying degrees 'we' were implicated belongs, in full right, to what Philippe calls 'The Horror of the West'.

As we know, *Heart of Darkness* tells an initiatory journey whereby the protagonist/narrator of the tale, Marlow, ascending the river Congo, travels in quest of the origin in order to finally find himself face to face with the horror of Kurtz's sacrificial rites. But what exactly is the vertiginous horror to which Kurtz, this *artiste maudit* avatar of Rimbaud, eventually capitulates? What is the horror that contaminates all those who approach him? As Lacoue-Labarthe puts it, it is not so much 'the *de facto* horror of savagery', (119) as the horror of the Thing or *la Chose*: the Lacanian name for the 'malignity of being' discussed by Heidegger, but also the malignity Georges Bataille – a figure obsessed by the horror of sacrifice – experienced at the time of *Acéphale*.[21] The Thing is not some-*thing*, a being among other beings but, rather, no-*thing* [*a-chose*], an unspeakable void, the yawning abyss of chaos itself, the horror that is at the 'foundation of things' as Chardonne says. Or, alternatively, the Thing is the absolute lack of foundation [*sans-fond*] that allows us to touch the Real. It is that which, by definition, cannot be expressed and, perhaps, it is also that which motivated Philippe's silences. 'The horror', he says – and we shall verify this in the precise case of Rwanda – is, indeed, '*of* the West' (italics added) which also means that the horror *is* the West itself, that is, the West that defended itself from the fascination with the Thing by constituting a *techne* that works as a dangerous supplement and the West that defended itself through a technical and colonial inspection of the totality of the planet. By instituting the modern subject that produces and realizes itself, the West has been the only 'civilization' that could give birth to a new form of evil, a devastating and characteristically modern evil. And if it is true that, in the case of Rwanda, those who looked into the darkest side of evil may have been the Africans, it is equally true that they were subjected to a properly modern form of evil, a radical evil that is inextricably tied to the name of Auschwitz. This evil, as Philippe put it, 'cesured' our own history. This evil does not come from elsewhere; it is wanted by man himself. This evil has no meaning; it is a form of evil that defies representation and that is beyond reparation.

'The horror! The Horror!' These are the only words that one of the main witnesses could find, upon his return from Kigali, as he was interrogated by the International Criminal Tribunal for Rwanda (ICTR), at the very beginning of the genocide.[23] These words obviously echo Kurtz's last, dying words, as he looked, one last time, into that abyss of darkness, which is his heart: '"The horror! The horror!"' (149). And, indeed, what closer re-enactment of Kurtz's atrocities than the Rwandan genocide? The Hutus would align children in their schools in order to cut them up with an axe or crush them under the blows of their clubs. In some instances they would give the bodies of the Hutus opponents (the first victims) for pigs to devour . . . The furore, the unchained rage, the complacency in sheer atrocity put us in the presence of an outbreak of hatred that exceeds the pure malice of human action. As Heidegger puts it, this hatred relies on 'the malignity of furor' that is at the heart of being itself.[24]

When evil transgresses a certain boundary, as Kurtz at the heart of the jungle also experiences, moral categories seem, indeed, to lose their pertinence. Evil is then liberated from human intentions; it becomes autonomous and organizes itself as a system that transcends humanity and becomes exterior to it. Its malignity without boundaries, its virulence and destructive frenzy [frénésie], as Isaiah also puts it, becomes, then, capable of 'destroy[ing] the foundations of the earth'.[25] The enigma, as we see it, is all here: like Kurtz, we are capable of producing a blind evil, an unpredictable evil that goes beyond us, and that retrospectively presents itself as a fatality. And yet, we, Westerners, are nevertheless responsible for it, if only because we could have prevented it from happening. Among those who partook in the Rwandan genocide are those who realized in what kind of infernal spiral, in what kind of exterminating vortex, they had been progressively caught up. They got carried away and none could escape this 'dynamic of the Devil'. As they testify: 'you cut up so many of them that you can't even count them; it is Satan that has pushed us to the bottom of ourselves'.[26] While saying this, they appear to be less devastated than overcome [dépassés], transported by an incomprehensible effect of excitement and amplification, an uncontrollable effect that resonated deeply with unspeakable actions, actions beyond understanding, that inspire anger as well as a certain sense of compassion. The sombre magnificence whereby Kurtz plunges into death reminds us that there is nothing prosaic about evil; evil is not of the body but of the spirit.

Genocide, this hybrid word with a double root, both Greek and Latin, is of recent formation (1944). It is now used everywhere, in those languages that founded the voracious West, a West that has now swallowed up the entire world. Despite revisionists' denials, what has taken place in Rwanda undoubtedly belongs to the category of genocide. That is, to the destruction of a *genos*, of a population deemed guilty from birth. This is not simply yet another massacre. A genocide is indeed an effect of a project concerned with the extermination of a *race*, a project instituted by the State – that is, a project in the service of what Conrad already called an 'idea': 'What redeems it is the idea' says Marlow, 'the unselfish belief in the idea – something you can set up, and bow down before, and offer a sacrifice to . . .' (51). Philippe would have said that this idea proceeds from what he calls *techne*, that is, knowledge as determined by the Greeks. This *techne* is endowed with an unequal power; it has been capable of assimilating all forms of knowledge coming from elsewhere; it is a form of knowledge that will end up by being determined as power and that will accomplish itself in the lure of the colonial and technical scramble for the entire world. And, as Philippe also reminds us, that which deploys the effects of this *techne* is what the Greeks called *logos*, that is, a discourse, an argumentation, a plan, a logistics. . . We should not forget that those who have assumed the control of this *logos* are intellectuals or, to speak plainly, 'philosophers' – figures always in quest of power. As it was already the case in Conrad's Congo, in Rwanda, those who planned the horror and who sent people to 'do the work' on the hills were professors, journalists, lawyers, politicians – figures who, as the manager in *Heart of Darkness* puts it, 'have no entrails' (74). Here, words and actions have been strung together, and it is language – the realm where Kurtz, this hollow man who is also a journalist, excelled – that has been the other side of a double-edged machete. The weapon of this recent genocide, which was initially taken to be only a rural and artisanal phenomenon, was of course the machete, but also, and perhaps even more so, the radio: the most powerful and dangerous media, the mass-medium that penetrates without restraint into the profound intimacy of people. This medium will realize the 'total mobilization' (E. Jünger)[27] of the forces of the State and feed, in a continuous stream, the genocidal frenzy.

As Conrad's descriptions of the horrors of colonialism with its continuous stream of greedy devils craving for ivory already make it clear, both time and preparation are necessary to set the genocidal machine in motion and to transform an entire country into a slaughterhouse. The 'pretty rags' of 'principles', to borrow Marlow's formula, 'fly off at the first good shake' (97).

Each country can then give way, in all impunity and serenity, to 'aggravated murder on a great scale' (50) and, while following blindly white forms of Western will to power as a model, hope for a general 'extermination'. And, indeed, the efficacy of this machine of death has been impressive. The Hutus only needed one week in order to actualize 'their' project and to engage in an 'extermination plan' that was among the fastest (from 800,000 to 1 million deaths in 3 months) and had the highest daily death rate.[28]

Notice that the critical state of a country plunged in a civil war does not explain these massacres, insofar as they were perpetuated outside of a combat situation. Women were, indeed, among the principal victims of these horrors. They were persecuted, raped, massacred, even when pregnant. Newborns were burned alive, smashed against walls or simply abandoned at places of carnage. Machetes were used to open the wombs of women, 'like bags', as it was said,[29] and the murderers could then directly destroy the foetus with the feeling that they could thus exterminate, within the egg itself, a much-detested breed. One is indeed reminded of Marlow's realization, early on in the novella, that this horror begins perhaps already with 'the first arrival of the Romans' who, fascinated by the 'abominable', are going to turn England into 'one of the darkest places of the earth' (48). Didn't Roman law inaugurate the political history of exclusion that will find a form of completion in totalitarian regimes? As it was the case for the Roman *homo sacer*,[30] the Tutsis expelled in the 'nakedness of life' see the simple fact of living within the bounds of the juridical order uniquely in the possibility of being killed.

More than 100 years after the publication of *Heart of Darkness*, the bodies of colonial ideology continue to intoxicate the world. And yet, the genocide is not at all the spontaneous product of the atavism of so-called primitive populations supposedly destined, for all eternity, to the brutal savagery of 'tribal' wars. The genocide is the poisonous fruit of a politics that has deliberately instrumentalized the ethnic factor, which the West itself constituted. For centuries, the Hutus and the Tutsis shared the same culture, the same language (*kinyarwanda*) and the same religion. Then, the Belgian colonists, stigmatized by Conrad, under the influence of a more pervasive Western *raciology* based on physical anthropology – *en vogue* in all Europe – created and developed what Lacoue-Labarthe would have probably called the *myth* of the Tutsis, and affirm, on the basis of morphological and biometric data, the genetic and aesthetic superiority of these 'feudal lords', Caucasian aristocrats with delicate features, high brows, straight nose, coming from the north. This thesis, directly inspired from Arthur de Gobineau, advocates the power of the 'unique Idea'.[31] Then, via theology and philosophy, via a theologico-political totalitarianism, via what Philippe in his career-long struggle against totalitarian horrors eventually called 'national-aestheticism', this blind belief in the idea will slowly model and fashion the mentality of a people in a plastic, typographic way and introduce, as Philippe also puts it, 'quite simply the Terror'.[32]

Such a process of 'racialization' of every sort of category would open up the racist rut in which the most extremist Hutus and Tutsis will quickly founder. There are no reasons to doubt this: it is colonialism, itself founded on racist ideology, that is at the origin of the constitution of two separate communities of fear, communities whose antagonism became explosive in 1994. The Whites have, indeed, 'spoiled the hearts of the Hutus'. And this also – along with the work of death that has been its consequence – belongs to the 'horror of the West'. The Western will to export its own practices of ethnic cleansing to those very borders of the Congo that fascinated Conrad contributed to the enactment of the most murderous conflict that the planet has known since World War II.

We can, of course, congratulate ourselves that, in matters of international justice, the West has continued, like a guiding light towards progress, to extend what is also part of its project. The designation of genocide has finally been adopted by the United Nations, and these crimes and atrocities have not remained unpunished. And yet, many of the ancient killers have already returned to their own quarters. Moreover, the Rwanda of Kagamé that is now part of the Commonwealth carried on as if nothing had happened: it was reintegrated into globalization, into planetary forms of 'development', with a growth rate, as we still say today, previously unmatched. We are left to wonder, though, if the truth that has so often been buried does not run the risk of resurfacing, one day or the other, under the form of an explosion?

Over the past years, the judiciary enclosure of Arusha, the fortress of the ICTR, has become the anonymous and distant place where what Philippe calls the loud 'echo' of the 'savagery' (116) is allowed to resonate. Protected behind armoured windows, cut off from the public, armed with recording devices of great technological sophistication, a deterritorialized and disembodied justice seemed to retreat in front of the fear to know, defending itself from the fascination of the Thing by taking refuge, as Philippe had already anticipated, in technological manipulation. We also think of the way Conrad's tragic hero accomplishes, for Philippe, the 'entire destiny of the West' (113). We think of the seductive magic of his voice, of his eloquence, of his universal genius, of his sanguinary despotism, of his voracity, of his colonial royalty. These are indeed supplements or inversed images of the 'barren darkness of his heart' (*HD* 147) whose void and hollowness generate a vertiginous 'emotion of thought'. We also think of the horror to which, at the end, in an Africa that is destroyed, Kurtz finally succumbs, both sanctified and accursed.

'You will never be able to see the source of a genocide; it is hidden too deep under malice, under the accumulation of lack of misunderstandings. . . We have been educated to absolute obedience, to hatred, they crammed our heads with formulas, we are an unfortunate generation'.[33] The lucidity of this president of the extremist militia, accused of premeditated crimes against humanity and condemned to death, is no doubt disillusioned. But if it plunges us into the heart of darkness, by the same token it also enables us to see the obscure origins of this nasty brushwood, this evil forest and, thus, to understand that all this could, indeed, have been avoided. . . This is, in any case, the least desperate of Philippe's 'lessons of darkness'. And this lesson must be affirmed even though everything leads us to think, to use Philippe's expressions one last time, that no work will ever pacify the 'lament' of the work of 'mourning'; no work will ever suspend the curse that 'the West' has *exported* to the entire world. Henceforth, these monstrous atrocities, both unspeakable and inconceivable, will stare back at us. The black heads on the stakes, in front of Kurtz's ritual abode, with their closed, hollowed out eyes, stand as peremptory signs against future horrors to come. At the same time, at the present moment, the genocidal absolute is already there for all of us to face. And what is the point of thinking – if we do not think through this Thing?

Trans. Nidesh Lawtoo[34]

Notes

For more than two months, repeatedly during the week, I had to live up to Nidesh Lawtoo's demanding expectations. And that is how, in these back and forth exchanges, the text came to be progressively rewritten *à deux mains* and the author and friend has become my translator. I would like to express my gratitude to him.

1   François Warin, 'Coeur des ténèbres', *Lignes* 22 (2007): 143–8. This piece, on which the first part of what follows is based, has been substantially revised and extended in order to fit the present volume [editor's note].

2   Despite their linguistic differences, Dagara people are close to Lobi people and live in Western Burkina Faso.

3   I lived in Africa for 11 years, where I taught philosophy at the ENSup of Bamako first, and then at the University of Ouagadougou. I have often been in the field, particularly in Dogon, Dagara and Lobi regions, whose peoples I introduced to Philippe and Claire. For my recent take on postcolonial issues related to Lacoue-Labarthe's concerns, see 'La haine de l'Occident et les paradoxes du postcolonialisme'. *EspacesTemps.net*, 22 June 2009. *http://www. espacestemps.net/document7783.html*, accessed 1 September 2011.

4   Friedrich Hölderlin, *Remarque sur Œdipe et Antigone*, trans. François Fédier (Paris: 10/18, 1965). A few years later, Lacoue-Labarthe translated Hölderlin's translation of *Antigone* and *Oedipus Rex* into French [trans. note].

5   Sally Price, *Arts primitifs; regards civilisés* (Paris: énsb-a, 1995). In William Rubin, ed., *Le primitivisme dans l'art du 20ᵉ siècle* (Paris: Flammarion, 1987), one can find references to Conrad's tale (96). See also François Warin, *La passion de l'origine: Essai sur la généalogie des arts premiers* (Paris: Ellipses, 2006) and 'Le primitivisme en question(s)', *L' homme* 201 (2012): 165–71.

6   Philippe Lacoue-Labarthe, *Ecrits sur l'art* (Genève: Les presses du réel, 2009), 197.

7   Michel Leiris, *L'Afrique fantôme*, in *Miroir de l'Afrique* (Paris: Gallimard, 1995), 91–868.

8   Philippe Lacoue-Labarthe, 'La philosophie fantôme', *Lignes* 22 (2007): 205–14.

9   Quoted in Michel Beaujour, *Terreur et Rhétorique: Breton, Bataille, Leiris, Paulhan, Barthes & Cie* (Paris: J.-M. Place, 1999), 121.

10   Lacoue-Labarthe, 'La philosophie fantôme', 214.

11 René Char, *Œuvres complètes* (Paris: Gallimard, 1983), 216, n169.

12 Leiris, *L'Afrique fantôme*, 190–1.

13 Lacoue-Labarthe, Philippe. 'L'Afrique, ". . . cette espèce d'immense nuit. . .,"', *L'Animal: Litératures, Arts & Philosophie* 19–20 (2008): 115–16.

14 *Proëme de Philippe Lacoue-Labarthe*, DVD, dirs. Christine Baudillon and François Lagarde (Montpellier: Hors Œil édition, 2006). Reprinted in *L'Animal*, 115–16, 116.

15 André Vila, an archaeologist at the CNRS and member of the *société des explorateurs français*, passed away this year. These pictures are reproduced with the kind permission of the photographer's wife.

16 Not unlike the African mistress in *Heart of Darkness*, 146 [editor's note].

17 See the catalogue dedicated to the exhibition of the Château du Grand Jardin: BrunoFrey and François Warin, *Lobi*, Exhibition Catalogue (Joinville: 2007).

18 Georges Bataille, 'Post-Scriptum au Supplice', in *L'expérience intérieure* (Paris: Gallimard, 1954), 117–81.

19 *D'Arusha à Arusha*, film, dir Christophe Gargot (Atopic production, 2008).

20 See Jean-Luc Nancy, 'Tu aimais les Leçons de Ténèbres', *Lignes* 22 (2007): 11–15.

21 Jean Hatzfeld, *Dans le nu de la vie* (Paris: Seuil, 2002); *Une saison de machettes* (Paris: Seuil, 2005); *La stratégie des antilopes* (Paris: Seuil, 2008).

22 Georges Bataille, 'La conjuration sacrée', in *Œuvres complètes*, vol. 1 (Paris: Gallimard, 1970), 442–6.

23 Testimony of Faustin Twagiramungu, a figure of the democratic Rwandan opposition, in Christophe Gargot, *D'Arusha à Arusha*. On the question of the Rwandan genocide, I have benefited from the following works: Amselle, Jean-Loup, and Elikia M'Bokolo, eds. *Au coeur de l'ethnie: Ethnies, tribalisme et État en Afrique* (Paris: La Découverte, 1985); Ba, Medhi. *Rwanda, un génocide français* (Paris: L'esprit frappeur, 1997). Chrétien, Jean Pierre, *Le défi de l'ethnisme: Rwanda et Burundi, 1990–6* (Paris: Karthala, 1997); Franche, Dominique. *Généalogie du génocide rwandais*. Bruxelles: Tribord, 2004.

24 Martin Heidegger, *Lettre sur l'humanisme*, trans. Roger Munier (Paris: Éditions Montaigne, 1957), 157.

25   Isaiah, 24:18.

26   Hatzfeld, *Une saison de machettes*, 116–17.

27   See Ernst Jünger, 'Total Mobilization', trans. Joel Golb and Richard Wolin, in *The Heidegger Controversy: A Critical Reader*, ed. Richard Wolin (London: The MIT Press, 1993).

28   Hatzfeld, *Unesaison de machettes*, 61–2. André Guichaoua, *Rwanda, de la guerre au génocide: Les politiques criminelles au Rwanda (1990–4)* (Paris: La Découverte, 2010).

29   Hatzfeld, *Dans le nu de la vie*, 51.

30   Giorgio Agamben, *Homo Sacer: Sovereign Power and Bare Life*, trans. Daniel Heller-Roazen (Stanford, CA: Stanford University Press), 1998.

31   Lacoue-Labarthe, 'La philosophie fantôme', 209. See also Hannah Arendt, *Le système totalitaire*, trans. Jean-Louis Bourget, Robert Davreu and Patrick Lévy (Paris: Seuil, 2005).

32   Lacoue-Labarthe, 'La philosophie fantôme', 209.

33   Hatzfeld, *Une saison de machettes*, 195.

34   I wish to express my gratitude to Hannes Opelz for discussing the translation and for his careful advice, as well as to Camille Marshall for final stylistic suggestions [trans. note].

PART THREE

The Affect of Ideology

7

La lettre, Lacan, Lacoue-Labarthe: *Heart of Darkness* redux[1]

STEPHEN ROSS

I follow Hillis Miller's contention in his 'Prologue' to this volume as he states:

> [T]he narrative of *Heart of Darkness* [i]s a way of indirectly speaking about, and bearing witness to, something that cannot be spoken of literally or directly but only in parable or allegory, and that can be borne witness to only in a sequence of voices, each speaking for the one before' (26).

As his reading differs from Lacoue-Labarthe's, though, so mine deviates from Miller's in its determination to use Jacques Lacan's theories to name the 'something that cannot be spoken of' as the real of desire. I suggest that the horror in *Heart of Darkness* is Kurtz's discovery that he is 'hollow at the core'; that his subjectivity is anchored by a void that threatens to absorb consciousness and yet sustains it as well. The parallel with the barbaric dark side of Western imperialism and with the brutality underwriting imperialist eloquence is neither accidental nor inconsequential. My reading demonstrates how *Heart of Darkness* functions as a critique of

Western imperialism (as Lacoue-Labarthe has it) and as an account
of a universal aspect of human subjectivity (as Miller has it). I
contend that in addition *Heart of Darkness* illuminates the extent
to which these two elements are interwoven through the fetishistic
machinations of ideology.

There is an ethical dimension to this consideration of ideology
in *Heart of Darkness* that is also at work, though quietly and
secretly, in both Lacoue-Labarthe's and Miller's essays. *Heart of
Darkness*'s concern with imperialism, race, capitalism, fidelity and
duty makes ethics its most fundamental horizon of engagement;
its concern with alterity in all these registers and its refusal to
hypostatize alterity for hegemonic recontainment makes it a crucial
pre-text to the late twentieth century ethical theories of Emmanuel
Levinas and Jacques Derrida. This connection between Conrad and
Derrida/Levinas is precisely what functions in Lacoue-Labarthe's
and Miller's texts as their crypto-ethical engagement and, perhaps,
their fundamental *raison d'être*.

Lacoue-Labarthe's essay commences with words that could
have come verbatim from the 'Exordium' of Derrida's *Specters of
Marx*: '*Je voudrais, devant vous, ce soir, essayer de me justifier*'
(111). Lacoue-Labarthe is specific: though he has begun with what
he claims was a 'rash phrase', he seeks to justify not the phrase, but
himself. Something larger is at stake here than a simple assessment
of Conrad's novel. The discourse thus invoked fades from such
prominent display but reappears in Lacoue-Labarthe's equation of
the heart of darkness with the '*interior intimo meo* of Augustine'
(117) and in the distinction he makes between 'knowledge' and
'know-how', paralleling Levinas's distinction between wisdom and
knowledge in 'Ethics as First Philosophy'. It returns most persistently,
though, in Lacoue-Labarthe's recurrence to the word 'figure'. In
English, an important nuance is lost: though *figure* means figure –
shape, image, even *eidos* – in both English and French, in French it
has an additional meaning: face. Time and again, Lacoue-Labarthe
invokes *la figure* to describe Kurtz (115, 117), *l'artiste maudit*
(115), the artist as 'the figure par excellence of the West' (115)
and mythic heroes' buffonic counterparts, such as Sancho Panza,
Rameau's nephew, Jacques le fataliste and even the Intended (117).
I do not wish to press too hard upon these delicate indications but
only to follow Jean-Luc Nancy and Lacoue-Labarthe's lead in *The
Title of the Letter*. There, in considering metonymy in Lacan's 'The

Agency of the Letter', Lacoue-Labarthe and Nancy provide an ideal means of reading the *figure*/figure double meaning I detect as a sign of ethical engagement in 'The Horror of the West': 'metonymy is related to censorship . . . a forbidden truth is able to be inscribed in the "word to word"'.[2] For Levinas, the face is an important metonym for the Other. For Lacoue-Labarthe, invoking the two-faced nature of *figure*/figure as it looks simultaneously towards French and English, rhetoric and ethics, myth and narratology, it leads us also with its knowing glance to a subterranean ethical engagement. The semantic tangle here is awesome: *la figure* as the face of the other is also a representation or a mask behind which we hide, embedding within itself also *la figue* (fig-leaf), with which we cover up our nakedness from the other's gaze.[3] Thus does Lacoue-Labarthe's hyperbolic effort to justify himself gain heft and evoke a concern with the ethics of alterity (an ethics bound to desire through the persistent alterity of *glissage* – or *difference* – as Lacoue-Labarthe and Nancy note).[4]

The ethics of Miller's essay are less concealed, opening as he does with a claim to bear witness to difference, and begging excuse for his divergence from Lacoue-Labarthe's interpretation. They are also, however, more confusing, since Miller invokes a slightly revised version of Matthew Arnold's distinction between the Hebraic and the Hellenic to delineate the differences between himself and Lacoue-Labarthe: 'The other way to specify the methodological difference between us is to say that Lacoue-Labarthe's approach is more Greek or Hellenic, whereas mine is more Biblical' (23). Miller replaces Arnold's 'Hebraic' with 'Biblical', drawing in an explicitly ethical framework for his methodological difference from Lacoue-Labarthe. Is there a sidelong reference here to the Judaic hermeneutics of Levinas and Derrida? Miller's next reference opposes his own recourse to 'the Christian Bible' to the Greek tradition and even invokes the Gospels (25). Things are no clearer when Miller reverts to simply 'biblical' to describe his orientation, though he does thereafter invoke the apocalypse, the *Book of Revelation*, and allegory as some of his key reference points (the Bible's Greekness is inescapable). All this indicates a strong ethical concern as a prominent subtext to Miller's polite difference of interpretation with Lacoue-Labarthe. There is a coherence in contradiction, then, in the two most prominent contributions to this volume, one which may well, as Derrida has taught us, express the force of a desire.[5]

The similarity between Lacoue-Labarthe's (and Miller's) crypto-ethics and Conrad's more overt but still elusive ethics is the key to understanding both the urgency with which *Heart of Darkness* can still speak to us today and the need to understand aright Lacoue-Labarthe's insights into it. I argue that the novel is concerned with incipient global capitalism rather than a specifically nineteenth-century nation-based imperialism, that it concentrates its engagement with global capitalism on its impact upon the psyches of its subjects and that this focus links the political and the ethical directly.

As Lacoue-Labarthe suggests, the elusive kernel of the tale lies in its uncanny insights into the fusion of the psychic and the social in modernity. This aspect of the novella has been surprisingly resistant to analysis despite the virtual industry devoted to interpreting it, but 'The Horror of the West' provides the ideal stimulus for reconsidering how the psychic and the social are imbricated in *Heart of Darkness*.[6] Lacoue-Labarthe's comments go straight to the heart of the fusion of the psychic and the social which characterizes Conrad's great strengths as a writer and the particular effectiveness of *Heart of Darkness* as a critique of imperialism. The fundamental nexus of the psychic and the social in Conrad's tale is where the imperatives of Western imperialism's greed infect the structures of subjectivity: desire (and its constant chaperone, ethics). Conrad shows how ideology creates a frictionless back-and-forth between the psychic and the social, how it produces subjects ideally suited to capitalist economics and how it makes capitalism seem a natural expression of desire. His depiction of the human costs of this operation is unflinching. He undertakes this exposé with the heart of an artist, penning not just a political critique of imperialism but a sophisticated tale that advances the theory and practice of narrative itself by embedding his critique in the structure and texture of his novella.

Social organization

Conrad's engagement with his contemporary culture is best deline-ated in relation to capitalism. As the primary feature of modernity, capitalism encompasses other characteristically modern phenomena like rationalization and secularization. Capitalism's remarkable malleability answers to Marshall Berman's characterization of modernity as a cultural situation of 'permanent revolution'[7] ensuring not only its survival but also its increasing domination of all aspects of life. The single most important feature of capitalist modernity informing my discussion here is its power to produce specifically modern subjectivities. In Marx's classic formulation, capitalist modernity 'not only creates an object for the subject, but also a subject for the object'.[8] This element of modernity turns on the manipulation of desire, forming the focal point of Conrad's critique.

The social organization of *Heart of Darkness* – captured in the corporate culture of the 'Company' – is a metonym for modernity. It is powerfully linked to the psychic through the symbolic order. In the novel's primal scene, young Marlow pores over maps, lingering over the 'blank spaces'. 'The biggest – the most blank, so to speak' (52) is the heart of Africa. From the Western perspective, these blank spaces are but undiscovered dominions, lacking proper social organization, civilization and especially *enlightenment*. It is somewhat perplexing, then, to find that the exploration and mapping that take place between the time of Marlow's youth and maturity appear not as illumination but darkening:

[B]y this time it was not a blank space any more. It had got filled since my boyhood with rivers and lakes and names. It had ceased to be a blank space of delightful mystery – a white patch for a boy to dream gloriously over. It had become a place of darkness. (52)[9]

The delightful mystery of the blank spaces' utopian promise is darkened with the elimination of their promise of alterity and the evacuation of any ethical possibility that might have been latent in what Marlow understood as their pure potentiality. Just as the application of the symbolic to the real produces reality as the organized world in which subjects exist, so its application to the spaces indicated by blankness on the map produces geographical reality and eliminates alternative possibilities in its claim to make knowledge and truth align perfectly – the quintessence of the unethical, according to Levinas.[10] This production of geographical reality is an ideological procedure whose opacity masquerades as transparency and universalizing a particular perspective. And yet Marlow alerts us to the artificiality of this process when he describes the changes made to the mapped area not as filling in *representations* of geographical features but as the advent of 'lakes and rivers' themselves. Their origin in symbolic fiat is reinforced by their association in a semantic group with 'names': 'rivers and lakes and names'. The gap he thus opens up preserves something of the original alterity that exploration has sought to obliterate and creates a linguistic preserve for ethical possibility to which he will return throughout the novel.

In this case, the particular symbolic order manifest in mapping is that of capitalist modernity, culminating in monopolistic trading concerns driven by the profit motive and the steam engine (52–3).[11] Conrad lays out this ideological dimension by linking the darkening strokes of mapping to the black ink used to indicate profit in accounting. A graphological counterpart to the delineation of 'lakes and rivers' in the mapping process, the ledger-work of accounting, translates geographical exploration into figures of profit. This connection is reinforced by the chief accountant, whose importance is signalled in part by his position as the gatekeeper to the river at the Outer Station, an important point at which the symbolic map is tethered to the real landscape. His ability to create order out of chaos – to account for everything – by reducing everything to figures in a ledger forges a conceptual link with mapping's power to make order out of the unruly landscape through a symbolic grid of coordinates. This set of associations takes on the dimensions of a critique of capitalist modernity in light of the privileged position Conrad gives 'the Company' over any political entity as the driving force behind the mapping process. Conrad makes a decisive point here as he pushes aside the predominant conception of imperialism as a nationally driven endeavour, instead of making a private for-profit enterprise the chief agency at work in the region: multinational capitalism as modernity's defining feature.

The reality of the social organization thus produced is grounded in one particular signifier, a commodity which is of the essence of Africa and vital to European profit margins, which usurps the place of God – or any ethical guarantee – in the novel: ivory. 'The word "ivory" rang in the air, was whispered, was sighed. You would think [the "pilgrims"] were praying to it' (76). Lacoue-Labarthe gestures towards the role played by ivory in *Heart of Darkness* as a manifestation of the Lacanian Thing, claiming that 'the horror is Western *barbarity* itself, because it is the plain underside of the fascination with the Thing' (118). Representing the Thing, ivory functions for Kurtz as the signifier of the impossible, that which eludes and robs all power of both '*potentia* and *potestas*' (117). This philosophical register is crucial because it illuminates, as simple economic theory never can, the role played by ivory as much more than a commodity. Ivory justifies the Company's presence in the Congo and organizes all commercial activity; it lures Kurtz there in the novella's prehistory, sends Marlow after Kurtz and even draws the Intended into its web of influence at the novella's close. Though actual ivory is the object of the materialist operation of the Company's interests, its real power lies in its status as a fetishized signifier, a quasi-sacred *point de caption* grounding the ideological field of 'reality' as dictated by the profit motive. Marlow points this out when he directs our attention to 'ivory' as a mantra rather than a material good; like Kurtz, it exists as a signifier long before we see it.

Consistent with its status as a *point de caption*, 'ivory' also functions as the *objet a* – the object-cause of desire – further tightening the bonds between the psychic and the social in *Heart of Darkness*. Here, fetishization becomes explicitly psychological as the twin registers of libidinal and capitalist desire converge on a single signifier. The transferal of libidinal desire onto the object of capitalist desire replicates and reinforces the process by which exchange value transforms the product into a fetishized commodity. This entire process is bound up with the colonization of libidinal desire by capitalism as modernity transforms subjectivity. Ivory's status as both corporate and individual *point de caption/objet a* thus links corporate desire to personal desire. Marlow's emphasis on its status as a fetishized signifier foregrounds desire as both a psychological and ideological element of the novella's social organization.

Backing up the *de facto* potency/*potestas* of 'ivory' to ground the ideological field in *Heart of Darkness* is the establishment of an entire legal (but in no sense ethical) system around it. In this respect, the Company's profit-driven hegemony extends to a configuration of the law that corresponds closely to Lacan's formulation in 'The Function and Field of Speech and Language'. The most salient point of this formulation is that the law is at root the law of the signifier: 'the law of man has been the law of language since the first words of recognition presided over the first gifts'.[12] The logic of substitution and supplementarity intrinsic to the operation of language permeates all aspects of social exchange for Lacan, from gift-giving through marital contracts to larger social pacts and treaties.[13] In this, the law is both universal and local, trans-historical and contingent: it governs all exchange from the most basic offering of a signifier in place of a material item to the elaborate fusions of the libidinal with the socio-commercial in marriage and the highly specialized terms of exchange involved in pacts, prohibitions and licenses.

The law in *Heart of Darkness* operates analogously, taking its universal dimension from the Company's hegemony, and its particularity from the Company's designation of ivory as the *sine qua non* of exchange in the region, and its use of ivory to redraw the boundaries of good and evil. The Company's power to dictate the law and thus to manipulate reality itself brings us back to Lacan's emphasis on the law as the law of the signifier, via Marlow's emphasis on 'ivory' (the signifier) as the fundamental element in the ideological field he enters when he signs on with the Company. Taken together, Lacan's theory and Marlow's description bring to light the constitutive interrelationship between signification and desire in the ideological field of *Heart of Darkness*, even as they point to the larger field of modernity with which both Conrad and Lacan engaged.

Marlow's insistence that the introduction of the law has actually produced criminality exemplifies how the law's arbitrary relationship between signification and reality informs the Company's social organization of the Congo:

> A slight clinking behind me made me turn my head. Six black men advanced in a file toiling up the path . . . *They were called criminals* and the outraged law like the bursting shells had come to them, an insoluble mystery from the sea. (64; my emphasis)

The men are only criminals because the law labels them so; their relative goodness or badness is openly the result of a speech act. The absurdity of this designation manifests fully when Marlow considers the Harlequin's assertion that the heads outside Kurtz's hut are those of rebels: 'Rebels! What would be the next definition I was to hear. There had been enemies, criminals, workers—and these were—rebels' (132). Marlow links the logic behind the arbitrary law of modernity to the 'unsound methods' of Kurtz's administration at the Inner Station. Prior to the advent of the law, the men Marlow sees at the Outer Station could hardly even have been *called* criminals, let alone *been* criminals; the introduction of a social order driven by profit introduces a value system whereby there can be 'something in the world allowing one man to steal a horse while another must not look at a halter' (78). At a stroke, Marlow brings the Foucauldian insight that the law produces criminality together with the Nietzschean insight that the law's denomination of 'good' and 'evil' signify according to temporal power, not transcendental authority.

The connection between the arbitrariness of the law and the economic imperatives behind the Company's hegemony in the Congo solidifies when Marlow stumbles into the grove of death: the 'criminals' are guilty only of being physically capable of furthering the Company's interests. When this capability expires, their sentence of hard labour becomes a death sentence:

> The work was going on. The work! And this was the place where some of the helpers had withdrawn to die.
> They were dying slowly – it was very clear. They were not enemies, they were not criminals, they were nothing earthly now,—nothing but black shadows of disease and starvation lying confusedly in the greenish gloom. (66)

Neither 'enemies' nor 'criminals', these men are simply 'helpers' who have outlived their usefulness. Marlow's bizarre use of the term 'helpers' points to the difficulty of reconciling what he sees with the signification options left to him by the Company's lexicon: He cannot call them law-abiding, since they have been deemed 'criminals', nor 'slaves', since this would be to accuse the Company of behaving illegally. Calling them 'workers' would complicate matters for him even more as it would place them in the same category in which his aunt places him when she calls him a 'Worker' (59). 'Helpers' thus attempts to balance these equally inadmissible options even as it exposes the dynamic of legalistic inversion and the absence of any ethical standard at work in the Company's governance of Congo.

In the traditional order of punishment by labour, a law is instituted, the violation of which condemns the criminal to hard labour as a servant (rather than an 'enemy') of the state. The work is a corollary to the law, supplementing a reparation for damage done to the social organization. In the Company's inversion of this process, the demand for work is prior. The law is put in place to generate a captive work force, not to ensure the social organization's stability. It is legislated slavery accomplished according to the arbitrary logic of signification and the potency of speech acts. Marlow's inability to assimilate the truth of the situation indicates the difficulty of Conrad's critique and emphasizes how modernity's recognition of the arbitrariness of the law can give way to its appropriation by vested interests.

The underlying principle of the law in *Heart of Darkness* is the imperative to suspend and defer gratification of individual desire in favour of the corporate will. In this regard, the Company's law is strikingly similar to the psychic law by which the infant enters the symbolic order. Both socially and psychically, compliance with the command of the father merits admission to the community. By this mechanism, the ostensibly willing containment of desire is imbued with ethical value; it is an individual sacrifice which serves the greater good. This doubling and the problems that arise when desire is freed from constraint anchor both Lacan's and Conrad's engagements with modernity and articulate the basic interdependence which structures and textures *Heart of Darkness*.

From Marlow's first contemplation of the 'blank spaces' on the map to his participation in the darkening work of imperialism, Conrad creates a microcosm of modernity in *Heart of Darkness*. Positing incipient global capitalism as the horizon of the social organization by exposing the fetishization of ivory as the ideological *point de caption* of the social organization, Conrad makes the Company, rather than any nation, the chief power in the land. He drives home the implications of this view of modernity by focusing on the Company's power as the source and force of the law. Starting with the Company's ability to create an entire class of 'criminals' by discursive fiat, Conrad draws our attention to how such constructions not only displace people and despoil landscapes but also alter identities and reconfigure subjectivities. This final step in the establishment of a social organization, the ideological field on which the narrative unfolds, sets the stage for a closer consideration of how that ideological field impinges upon those to whom its basic principles seem inevitable, if not natural and just – people like Marlow, Kurtz and the Intended.

Family romance

The critique of modernity in *Heart of Darkness* is most compellingly articulated in the narrative of libidinal desire and disrupted family romance behind Kurtz's disintegration. Behind Marlow's journey up the river to fetch Kurtz is a domestic setting that accounts for Kurtz's decision to go to Congo and for his savage behaviour there. The claim that 'All Europe contributed to the making of Kurtz' (117), incisive as it is, masks an obscure family romance in which his father is never mentioned, and his mother is mentioned only when she dies, attended, significantly, by his fiancée, the Intended. The absence of a father places the burden of Kurtz's psychic history on his mother; when she dies in the company of his Intended, the family romance is suspended. Absent siblings or parents, the Kurtz family romance threatens to terminate, and the Intended is cathected with the entire libidinal burden of familial continuity.

The chief way Conrad draws our attention to the importance of this cathexis is by calling Kurtz's fiancée simply 'his Intended'. Conrad capitalizes on this overt signification by wedding it to his commentary on signification and its role in constructing the reality we encounter. The signifier 'Intended' marks Kurtz's fiancée's place in the symbolic order surrounding Kurtz and defines her subjectivity as a signifier for other signifiers. The capitalization of 'Intended' recalls Marlow's aunt's characterization of him as 'one of the Workers, with a capital – you know' (59), and aligns her with other characters who are defined only generically: workers, helpers, criminals, Accountant, Lawyer, etc. The Intended materializes the narrative's concern with the deflections, deferrals and suspensions of desire and raises pertinent questions about the ethics of that concern. Conrad extends the Intended's cathexis by aligning her with wealth: Kurtz speaks of 'his Intended' in the same breath as he speaks of 'his ivory' (116), making her the libidinal counterpart of the ivory, but also aligning her with the kind of intractable alterity that prevents total possession. The generality accorded by her identifier subtends her specific role in relation to Kurtz and makes her an emblem of modernity's interference with its subjects' libidos. The narrative's concern with signification comes to the fore here, as 'Intended' functions on both the subjective and the cultural levels, inscribing the differential logic of desire into the warp and woof of Marlow's tale and preserving her as the *figure* of a certain 'otherwise than being'. The designation of Kurtz's fiancée as 'his Intended' also masks the economic imperative that produces her identity as a *figure* of perpetually deferred desire. Marlow tells us:

> I had heard that her engagement with Kurtz had been disapproved by her people. He wasn't rich enough or something. And indeed I don't know whether he had not been a pauper all his life. He had given me some reason to infer that it was his impatience of comparative poverty that drove him out there. (159)

This description reveals the vulgar economic reality behind Kurtz's decision to go to Congo. For all the ethical bombast of his 'burning noble words' about exerting 'a power for good practically unbounded' (118), Kurtz goes to Congo with the pragmatic aim of making his fortune. As Lacoue-Labarthe says, 'Kurtz's eloquence is systematically linked . . . to the void that is within him or, more exactly, the void that he "is"' (116). Lacoue-Labarthe does not link this existential void to Kurtz's economic woes, but Conrad does. Kurtz finds his *déhiscence* endlessly repeated in the economic realities that prohibit libidinal gratification and even love: his penury prevents him from taking the place of the father and perverts his libidinal energy into imperialism. At root, Kurtz is a victim of the impingement of economic imperatives into the libidinal life of the subject. His desire for the Intended is thwarted by considerations of wealth; in response, he undertakes a dangerous but also lucrative enterprise to earn the satisfaction of his libidinal desire – all under the sign of such empty eloquence as assuages public uneasiness about imperialism, and private qualms about the pursuit of sexual gratification, social status and respectability.

Kurtz buys into the very system that so reduces him: he ties his own worth to his wealth and pursues the Intended as a commodity. He goes off to become a self-made man, intending to use the machinery of capitalist social climbing to gratify his libido, sacrificing ethical considerations to the pleasure principle. His determination to master the machinery that produced him leads Lacoue-Labarthe to call him 'absolutely sovereign' (116) as he both flaunts and tries to eradicate his *déhiscence*. He is ex-ceptional, ex-centric, ex-treme, ex-timate; the outward embodiment of the void at subjectivity's core. He is also uncanny, not 'only a voice' (114) but also a 'spectre', an external manifestation of an internal trauma. Driven by his frustrated libidinal desire, Kurtz makes a Faustian deal with the Company, enters the capitalist realm where satisfaction exists only in the perpetuation of desire, and pursues a career that enacts the asymptotic logic of desire – a logic that ultimately leads to his horror and death. He thus exemplifies the interplay between the social and the psychic, experiencing, in his journey towards 'the horror', the specifically capitalist exploitation of the universal psychic reality of desire.

Critics are right to assume that Kurtz loses all restraint in his quest for total domination; what they have missed is that the 'colossal scale of his vile desires' (156) is continuous with his repressed desire for the Intended. The Intended, intention itself, is the in-tension of subjectivity, the alterity, the kernel of the real of desire that ought to guarantee an ethical orientation in the world. For Kurtz, though, it becomes the impetus for a collapse that does not even rise to the level of going beyond good and evil. The monstrous desires Kurtz indulges while being the warlord of the Inner Station directly result from his frustrated desire for the Intended as it is exacerbated by his 'comparative poverty' (159) and his inability to overcome the insistent alterity within. It is no accident that the two chief outlets of his desire while in charge of the Inner Station are sexual license and the procurement of 'more ivory than all the other agents together' (113).

The flipside to this tale of repression is Kurtz's relationship with his African concubine. '[W]ild and gorgeous . . . savage and superb, wild-eyed and magnificent' (135–6), the African woman is a conventionally imperialist figure of the other as passionate savage. She has 'the value of several elephant tusks upon her' (135) in addition to her other adornment, suggesting that she is Kurtz's sexual partner. The African woman's ivory adornments replay the equation of wealth and libidinal desire that characterizes Kurtz's relationship with the Intended. The connection between libidinal and material accumulation suggested with the Intended is stated baldly here and re-focused on the *figure* of the other. Whereas Kurtz had been prevented by his economic situation from giving the Intended the all-important gift of a ring, however, he is able to adorn his concubine lavishly. Kurtz has not merely sated his lust for wealth; he has also transformed that wealth into libidinal enjoyment. The binary of African woman/Intended combines with the associative logic of enjoyment/repression to suggest that the

African woman stands for *jouissance* while the Intended stands for its suspension and deferral.[14] In contrast to the restrictively civilized conduct of the Intended's family, the African woman embodies both surplus wealth and surplus enjoyment, and perhaps articulates a secret about desire itself in her concrete figuration of alterity.

The twin forces of libidinal and economic desire reveal to Kurtz the reality of desire and prompt his famous last words. In gratifying his 'various lusts', Kurtz becomes possessed by 'the heavy mute spell of the wilderness that seemed to draw him to its pitiless breast by the awakening of forgotten and brutal instincts, by the memory of gratified and monstrous passions' (144). Supported in this 'spell' by a social organization that arbitrarily redraws the limits of good and evil to maximize profits, Kurtz exceeds even the loose limits of *laissez-faire* profiteering. His 'unsound methods' are tolerated only so long as he continues to ship ivory with the correct paperwork and to buy supplies from the Company stores. His sovereignty remains within limits that serve a larger system; he is exceptional, but not yet sovereign. All this changes when Kurtz withholds ivory and repudiates the Company's monopoly on supplies (90). With this move, he goes beyond breaking the law to eschewing all law together. He declares a state of exception that reduces everyone else in Congo to the status of *homo sacer* and provokes his own parallel reduction. Nearing the end of his desire, Kurtz abandons social restraints altogether and surrenders to instinctual gratification. Regressing to primary narcissism through the gratification of desire – as encouraged and facilitated by the Company's profit ethic – Kurtz discovers the *interior intimo meo* in its full demand for pure *jouissance* – and blasts out of all recognition the question of ethics. Alterity emerges full-blown from within instead of approaching from without and demands that he *figure* it out.

Yet Kurtz is unable finally to complete this regression, just as he is ultimately unable to satiate his desire: tenuous though it may be, subjectivity dies hard. Instead, he finds that the loss which drives him in his quest for the *objet a* is irremediable, just as there can never be enough ivory to satisfy the Company. Marlow says as much of the heads outside Kurtz's hut:

> They only showed that Mr. Kurtz lacked restraint in the gratification of his various lusts, that there was something wanting in him—some small matter which when the pressing

need arose could not be found under his magnificent eloquence. Whether he knew of this deficiency himself I can't say. I think the knowledge came to him at last—only at the very last. (131)

Marlow hits on the crux of Kurtz's tragedy: the discovery that desire remains insatiable because it originates from a deep psychic wound which *nothing* can heal: what is experienced as loss is actually lack. The 'something wanting' in him is the *déhiscence* of subjectivity, the gap between signifier and signified which structures and drives subjectivity. Having exhausted the external channels for satiation of his desire, Kurtz looks inward. He plays out a crisis of subjectivity as he takes introspection to its logical conclusion, glimpsing in his final moment that *jouissance* and death are one and the same end of desire.

> It was as though a veil had been rent. I saw on that ivory face the expression of sombre pride, of ruthless power, of craven terror—of an intense and hopeless despair. Did he live his life again in every detail of desire, temptation, and surrender during that supreme moment of complete knowledge? He cried in a whisper at some image, at some vision—he cried out twice, a cry that was no more than a breath—'The horror! The horror!' (149)

Beginning with cliché of blinding insight, Marlow focuses on vision as the primary modality of Kurtz's 'supreme moment of complete knowledge'. Kurtz's vision is of the hollowness within, of the death drive behind desire: 'desire, temptation, and surrender'. It remains beyond the reach of symbolization, beyond articulation, a vision of irremediable absence/alterity at the heart of subjectivity. The unrepresentable substance of Kurtz's vision provokes the series of expressions ('pride . . . power . . . craven terror . . . hopeless despair') as he approaches his definitive moment. Eyeballs rolling up in death as they do in *jouissance*, Kurtz glimpses *déhiscence* and expresses it the only way he can: by crying out a warning that applies equally to the universal structure of subjectivity and to the particular system which exploits it.

The circuit of desire which reaches 'the farthest point of navigation and the culminating point of . . . experience' (51) in Kurtz's final words terminates when Marlow visits the Intended. The Intended is striking in her deathly stasis: 'She came forward all in black with a pale head, floating towards me in the dusk' (156–7):

> [S]he was one of those creatures that are not the playthings of Time. For her he had died only yesterday. . . I saw her and him in the same instant of time—his death and her sorrow—I saw her sorrow in the very moment of his death. (157)

Seemingly impervious to the passage of time, the Intended lives (dies?) the suspension of desire which she also represents: her position as the object of Kurtz's desire fossilizes with his death. The sepulchral setting causes Marlow to experience a collapse of time akin to the Intended's and to re-experience Kurtz's final vision. The Intended's drawing room correlates precisely enough to Kurtz's dying vision that Marlow panics. Despite his effort to withdraw from the abyss that swallowed Kurtz, he has arrived at the same place – a letter always reaches its destination. He has a vision of Kurtz 'on the stretcher opening his mouth voraciously as if to devour all the earth with all its mankind . . . a shadow insatiable' (155). This vision 'seem[s] to enter the house with' Marlow as though the entire momentum of unrestrained instinct unleashed by Kurtz were invading the sanctuary of suspended desire: 'It was a moment of triumph for the wilderness, an invading and vengeful rush which it seemed to me I would have to keep back alone for the salvation of another soul' (156). When Marlow recalls Kurtz's final words, he both anticipates his lie to the Intended and indicates that he understands their significance. All of these images come together as Marlow, having seen the end of Kurtz's pursuit of desire, arrives at its origin only to discover that the Intended, in her full allegorical significance, is in fact coterminous with the horror of Kurtz's final vision: she is the literal object-cause of his desire and *figures* the possibility of ethics he failed to recognize.

Lacoue-Labarthe articulates Marlow's role in this regard with remarkable clarity: 'Conrad's entire undertaking consists in trying to find a witness for that which he wants to bear witness to. The Ancients invoked the gods; Conrad invents Marlow' (114). Each, that is, invents an other to account for the unaccountable. The doubling is multiple: Conrad/Marlow as witnesses, the narrator/Marlow and the narrator/Conrad as storytellers, the reader/narrator as listeners and Marlow/the reader as audiences before mesmerizing speakers. The doubling of narrative perspectives, witnesses, audiences and storytellers, all overlapping and playing multiple roles, often simultaneously, enacts the movement of *différance* that is inextricable from desire/the death drive.[15] Doubling and repetition drive the narrative, forcing it to circle back and devour its own tail as it illuminates the double-bind of incipient global capitalism. In this respect, *Heart of Darkness* adheres precisely to the model of Marlow's yarns that the narrator proffers as an interpretative guide early in the tale, and to which Lacoue-Labarthe refers:

> [T]o him the meaning of an episode was not inside like a kernel but outside, enveloping the tale which brought it out only as a glow brings out a haze, in the likeness of one of these misty halos that, sometimes, are made visible by the spectral illumination of moonshine. (48)

The novel hides its truth in plain view, with its structure, its characters, the details of its plot, its social setting and its narrative technique all pointing towards the nexus of desire/ethics as the object-cause of the narrative itself. Tracing the particular confluence of forces governing subjectivity in Kurtz's losing battle with the vagaries of desire as it is exploited by capitalist modernity, Conrad provides the consummate account of the clash of the psychic and the social on the field of modern subjectivity.

Notes

1   A substantially different version of this essay originally appeared in *Conradiana* 36.1–2 (2004): 65–91.

2   Philippe Lacoue-Labarthe, Jean-Luc Nancy, *The Title of the Letter*, trans. Francois Raffoul and David Pettigrew (Albany, NY: State University of New York Press, 1992), 82.

3   I trace here a paradigmatic of the term *figure* rather than an etymology (see Jacques Lacan, 'The Instance of the Letter', in *Écrits: A Selection*, trans. Bruce Fink with Héloïse Fink and Russell Grigg (New York: W. W. Norton & Company, 2004), 138–69. In doing so, I draw out the dialectical unconscious of Lacoue-Labarthe's explicit antipathy towards the mythic dimension of the figure as an aestheticization of totalitarian politics and resistance towards

Levinasian ethics. [On the former, see Philippe Lacoue-Labarthe, Jean-Luc Nancy, 'The Nazi Myth', *Critical Inquiry*, 16.2 (1990): 291–312, 302, 306; on the latter, see Avital Ronell, 'L'indélicatesse d'un interminable fondu au noir', *Europe* 973 (2010): 17–29, 23; on the political implications of the concept of 'figure', see also Beth Ash's contribution to this volume, 184–186 editor's note].

4   Philippe Lacoue-Labarthe, Jean-Luc Nancy, *The Title of the Letter*, 68.

5   Jacques Derrida, 'Structure, Sign and Play in the Discourse of the Human Sciences' in *Writing and Difference*, trans. Alan Bass (Chicago, IL: University of Chicago Press, 1978), 278–93, 279.

6   See, Edward Garnett, 'Unsigned review [of *Heart of Darkness*]', in *Conrad: The Critical Heritage*, ed. Norman Sherry (Boston, MA: Routledge & Kegan Paul, 1973), 131–3; Andrea White, *Joseph Conrad and the Adventure Tradition: Constructing and Deconstructing the Imperial Subject* (New York: Cambridge University Press, 1993); Kimberly J. Devlin, 'The Eye and the Gaze in *Heart of Darkness*: A Symptomological Reading', in *Modern Fiction Studies* 40.4 (1994): 711–35; Tony C. Brown, 'Cultural Psychosis on the Frontier: The Work of the Darkness in Joseph Conrad's *Heart of Darkness*', in *Studies in the Novel* 32.1 (2000): 14–28; Thomas Cousineau, '*Heart of Darkness*: The Outsider Demystified', in *Conradiana* 30.2 (1998): 140–51; Tony E. Jackson, *The Subject of Modernism: Narrative Alterations in the Fiction of Eliot, Conrad, Woolf, and Joyce* (Ann Arbor, MI: University of Michigan Press, 1994); Beth Sharon Ash, *Writing in Between. Modernity and Psychosocial Dilemma in the Novels of Joseph Conrad* (New York: St. Martin's, 1999); Marianne DeKoven, *Rich and Strange. Gender, History, Modernism* (Princeton, NJ: Princeton University Press, 1991) and Michael Levenson 'The Value of Facts in the *Heart of Darkness*', in *Heart of Darkness: An Authoritative Text, Backgrounds and Sources, Criticism*, ed. Robert Kimbrough, 3rd ed (New York: Norton, 1988), 391–405.

7   Marshall Berman, *All That is Solid Melts Into Air: The Experience of Modernity* (Toronto: Penguin Books Canada, 1988), 95.

8   Karl Marx, 'Grundrisse', in *The Marx-Engels Reader*, ed. Robert C. Tucker, 2nd ed (New York: Norton, 1978), 221–93, 230. See also Berman *All That is Solid Melts Into Air*; Matei Calinescu, *Five Faces of Modernity: Modernism, Avant-Garde, Decadence, Kitsch, Postmodernism* (Durham, NC: Duke University Press, 1987); Georg Lukács, *History and Class Consciousness. Studies in Marxist Dialectics*, trans. Rodney Livingstone (Cambridge, MA: MIT Press, 1997 [1968]); Malcolm Bradbury and James McFarlane, eds.,

Modernism: A Guide to European Literature 1890–1930 (Toronto: Penguin Books Canada, 1991); T. J. Jackson Lears, *No Place of Grace: Antimodernism and the Transformation of American Culture 1880–1920* (New York: Pantheon Books, 1981).

9   Jeremy Hawthorn, *Joseph Conrad: Narrative Technique and Ideological Commitment* (New York: Edward Arnold, 1990); Ian Watt, *Conrad in the Nineteenth Century* (Berkeley, CA: University of California Press, 1979); Benita Parry and Walter Allen have remarked upon this oddity of Marlow's narrative.

10 Emanuel Levinas, 'Ethics as First Philosophy', in *The Levinas Reader*, ed. Seán Hand (Malden, MA: Blackwell Publishing, 1989), 75–87, 77–9.

11 Michael Levenson, 'The Value of Facts in the *Heart of Darkness*', 395.

12 Jacques Lacan, 'The Function and Field of Speech and Language', in *Écrits: A Selection*, trans. Bruce Fink with Héloïse Fink and Russell Grigg (New York: W. W. Norton & Company, 2004), 31–106, 61.

13 Lacan, 'Function', 61–7.

14 See, Jackson, *The Subject of Modernism*, 102.

15 On the relation between desire and the death drive, see Dollimore's contribution to this volume [editor's note].

8

The voice of
darkness

CLAUDE MAISONNAT

In many ways, this study is a commendatory response to Philippe
Lacoue-Labarthe's 'The Horror of the West', an insightful essay
which offers a theoretical approach that is both philosophical
and psychoanalytical. That the fascination of Conrad's fiction in
general and of *Heart of Darkness* in particular should extend to
philosophers and psychoanalysts is hardly surprising if we bear
in mind that his greatest novels not only severely question the
ideological assumptions on which the alleged superiority of the
Western world is predicated but also even more radically expose
the limits of representation, the traps and the pitfalls that threaten
to trick the artist dealing with words, if his aesthetic prerequisites
are not clearly thought out. In other words, it is the self-reflexive
nature of Conrad's texts that appeals to thinkers, insofar as it also
questions the role of the interpreter in the reading process, and
highlights the conditions implied by his methodological procedures,
whether they are conscious or not, acknowledged or not.

Conrad and Lacoue-Labarthe share a common concern with the
role of language, discourse and voice, insofar as each with his own
distinctive means probes into the complex issue of representation
through art. Lacoue-Labarthe comments on the particularly twisted
narrative set up of the novella and, following Plato, he points out
the complex interplay between diegetic and mimetic modes. This
leads him to conclude that, in fact, *Heart of Darkness* is not so
much a travelogue as a play of/for voices. Indeed, very little action

takes place on board the *Nellie*, apart from the turning of the tide, while everything is the subject of discourses held by the frame narrator, Marlow, Kurtz and minor characters (the Intended, the harlequin, the manager etc.), mainly expressed through reported speech. Despite the radically innovative dimension of his piece, when dealing with the specific question of voice, Lacoue-Labarthe takes for granted a number of assumptions concerning this notion and does not fully account for the far-reaching implications of the specific function of voice in *Heart of Darkness*. The goal of this chapter will be to supplement his reading by problematizing the notion of voice within a literary and psychoanalytical context, leading to the assertion that what makes a great literary text is the presence of what could be called 'textual voice'.

The textual voice as literary artefact

Richard Pedot, and before him, Vincent Pecora, are among the first critics to consider that the issue of voice is central to *Heart of Darkness*. Relying on the traditional distinction between *phoné* and *logos*, they both argue that the novella's deliberately tortuous narrative set up, with its cascading levels of embedding, displays the typically modernist collapse of literary enunciation that subsequently leads to the hypothesis of the death of the author. If such approaches do take into account the fact that voices in *Heart of Darkness* carry the inhumanity (the horror) that lies at the core of all human voices, the binary opposition between *phoné* and *logos*, narrative voice and human voice, remains unchallenged and therefore unproductive in literary and critical terms.

To avoid this aporia what is required is a third element that does not oppose but articulates the first two in a dynamic impulse that prevents closure and problematizes meaning. This third element I call the 'textual voice' because it is both inside and outside, intimate and extimate, as Lacoue-Labarthe would say. It is precisely the locus where, and the moment when, the narrative voice is metabolized into a literary version of the human voice. In other words, the textual voice is the agency that successfully achieves the transformation and dissemination of the author's voice into the fictional voices that make up the narrative, a narrative which, as Michael Greaney puts it, functions as 'an echo chamber of decentered voices'.[1] In

this light, Lacoue-Labarthe's remark that *Heart of Darkness* ought
to be considered as an '*oratorio*' is singularly perceptive, not only
because, as he maintains, it is a dramatization of 'two voices' that
of the indistinct 'clamour' of the savages (the chorus) and that,
obviously (and audibly) [*bien entendu*], of Kurtz's (114) but also
because the etymology of the word implicitly links the signifier of
speech and song (the Latin *orare*) with the horror that is the heart of
darkness.[2] And since an *oratorio* is not only a form but also an art,
the word does suggest that its function is also to contain the horror
of the inhumanity inherent in those voices.

Now, what must be added is that the textual voice is but a fictional
version of the Lacanian object voice defined as the inaudible vocal
object that is sometimes heard as hallucination in psychotic cases.[3]
It is inherently silent and corresponds to what is dropped from the
signifying chain when meaning takes over, and this loss posits it as
an object-cause of desire. In this regard, as Lacoue-Labarthe notices,
the object voice is not unlike '*la Chose* – the *Thing* or *Ding* (another
name for being, that is, for nothingness, the 'nothingness of being'
[*le riend'étant*], which Lacan borrows from Heidegger)' (117). This is
especially true if we consider the concept beyond its clinical parameters
(pre-symbolic object, the Other, the mother, the radically unknowable
part of the subject, etc.) and concentrate on its structural function in a
speaking human being: that is, what is located beyond the signified. As
an abstract space, devoid of contents, *das Ding* can be equated with a
structural 'void', which for both Lacan and Lacoue-Labarthe is also the
real that is excluded from representation. As a consequence, the object
voice shares a similar function as the Other of the authorial voice.
Having to do with a pre-symbolic object, it is a void that is the cause of
a proliferation of affects. The object voice in *Heart of Darkness* should
thus be purged of its destructive implications; or, to put it plainly, the
textual voice is what raises the object voice to the dignity of *das Ding*.
It tames, pacifies, the threatening object voice that ruins the integrity of
a literary text, jeopardized by the threat of *jouissance*.[4]

To return to more literary matters, the term 'voice' when dealing
with a piece of fiction is richly ambiguous. What is meant by voice
has usually precious little to do with the human voice as *phoné*,
which simply vanishes the moment the writer sets pen to paper, and
exists only as a memory, a vague yearning. All attempts to recuperate
this 'always already' lost voice are doomed to fail, as *Heart of
Darkness* perfectly shows. The reader confronted with a written

text can hear neither Kurtz's voice saying 'the horror' nor Marlow's voice as a spinner of oral yarns nor even the frame narrator's voice. They can only fantasize these voices and be encouraged in this hopeless task by the eventual tentative descriptions the narrative voice offers. Therefore, they are left to their own devices to build up a representation of Kurtz's oxymoronic voice: 'A voice! a voice! It was grave, profound, vibrating, while the man did not seem capable of a whisper' (135), and hear with his mind's eye his '. . . voice of longing, with a wistfulness of tone' (143), let alone the whispers, screams, yells, shouts and various tones of voice that Marlow insists on recording, but which are bound to remain eternally silent. The only voice the reader is confronted with is the authorial voice understood as the agency in charge of the whole narration, and this is also a silent voice.

The most convenient way to apprehend *Heart of Darkness*'s textual voice is to contrast it with the authorial voice, the voice of authority which guarantees narrative consistency, coherence, continuity, in short, the readability of the text. It is the abstract voice of rhetoric that controls the enunciation and the narrative set up of the text, its grammatical and linguistic choices. But what must not be lost sight of is the fact that this abstract, silent, voice is a simulacrum whose function is to give the illusion that a precise origin of the text can be identified, thus concealing the truth that this origin, like the horizon, is elusive, irremediably lost: it recedes with the progression of the viewer/reader.

The textual voice, on the other hand, presupposes no authority and largely escapes the conscious determinations of the author, as if the latter had enough confidence in his art to allow the free play of this uncontrollable parameter that emanates from the text itself. The textual voice or, properly speaking, the voice of textuality is therefore unheard, but its existence can be ascertained through the effects it produces. In other words, it is a hypothesis verified by its consequences. It is thus an abstract agency that opens up a gap between the materiality of the signifier (the Letter) and the narrativity it builds up. If, in a literary context, we can agree that the Lacanian letter is an incarnation of the voice as object, then I would like to contend that the very modality of inscription of that voice in Conrad's fiction is the textual voice. It is indeed owing to the effect of the textual voice that the reader can hear the silent voices that haunt *Heart of Darkness,* as for instance, when Marlow reports during his meeting with the Intended that in her silence he could hear: '. . . the whisper of a voice speaking from beyond the threshold of an eternal darkness' (159).

Because of its particular status as dynamic force that propels the narrative onwards with all the means of linguistic instruments like syntax, semantics or narrative construction, the textual voice challenges the authorial voice by destabilizing the construction of meaning. Its function is to get the upper hand on the authorial voice so that interpretation becomes open to discussion and questioning. Whereas the authorial voice is the voice of mastery based on the primacy of the signified over the signifier, the textual voice, based on the primacy of the signifier over the signified, is disruptive and opens up grey areas of uncertainty. As a function of the signifier located within language, it is the prime mover that haunts Conrad's fiction and gives his prose its unique flavour of spectrality. The frame narrator puts forward the same idea when he describes the specificity of Marlow's storytelling through one of the most commented passages of the novella. The direct simplicity of the 'yarns of seamen' obviously finds its source in the predominance of the authorial voice, whereas the metaphor of the halo and the spectral illumination of moonshine supply a striking visual metaphor for the textual voice:

The yarns of seamen have a direct simplicity, the whole meaning of which lies within the shell of a cracked nut. But Marlow was not typical (if his propensity to spin yarns be excepted), and to him the meaning of an episode was not inside like a kernel but outside, enveloping the tale which brought it out only as a glow brings out a haze, in the likeness of one of these misty halos that sometimes are made visible by the spectral illumination of moonshine. (48)

The halo metaphor is textually implemented in *Heart of Darkness* through the way English, the dominant language of the narrative, is more or less openly undermined by the presence of other (foreign)[5] languages that interfere with the production of meaning, mainly through the intrusion of French.[6] French turns out to be one of the most effective modes of action of the textual voice, but what makes the device more significant for us still is the fact that it is a way of dealing with the crucial issue of ideology in the novella, because Marlow's English is the language of the paradigmatic colonizer.

Pardon my French: The linguistic conundrum as textual voice

Even if Marlow is introduced as a British sailor whose language is English, it does not take long to realize that the textual space of the novel is indeed the locus of a linguistic confrontation between English, as the main instrument of narration, and French as the linguistic backdrop against which diegesis and plot develop. Apart from the opening tableau on board the Nellie, which takes place on the Thames near London, and which serves as the scene of enunciation for Marlow, the bulk of the story unfolds in French-speaking countries, mainly Belgium and its Congo colonies. The majority of the verbal exchanges take place in that context and involve mostly French-speaking characters: the doctor, the pilgrims, the manager, the Intended and presumably most of the natives, are reputed to have been held in French. This adds a new string to Marlow's bow or should we say to his harp, since he does play the part of the bard, but of the bard as translator.

Surface traces of the friction between the two languages appear when Marlow admits that he had to give evidence of his ability to speak French during his interview with the Director of the Company (56) and there is no reason to conclude that his visit to the doctor should have been the occasion to speak another language than French. Textual evidence is provided by Marlow himself, when he quotes the very words of the doctor in French: '*Bon voyage*' (56) or '*Du calme, du calme. Adieu*' (58). Marlow's awareness of the discrepancies introduced by his ambivalent linguistic status probably accounts for his felt obligation to report the comments of the doctor about being the first Englishman to come under his observation. Conversely, Marlow feels necessary to mention that his characters spoke English, or are dealing with English objects, as the harlequin does when Marlow offers him tobacco: 'English tobacco; the excellent English tobacco!' (123).

Conrad was quite attentive to the issue, as is recorded in one of his letters, originally written in French, to his friend Kaziemierz Waliszewki in December 1903: 'I took great care to give Kurtz a cosmopolitan origin'.[7] Moreover, from the fact that Kurtz's mother was half-English and his father half-French (117), it does not follow that he spoke only English with Marlow. Given the Belgian colonial context, it seems quite improbable, even if Marlow adds the following linguistic comment: 'This initiated wraith from the back of Nowhere honoured me with *its* amazing confidence, before *it* vanished altogether. This was because *it* could speak English to me' (117; my italics). A curious linguistic sleight of hand is being performed here. Marlow's remark does not positively say that it is Kurtz who speaks English, but rather, a shade, a ghost, a wraith, which is something inhuman. What is undeniable is that Marlow finds himself in a traumatic situation and that he responds to it in his own native language, whatever language Kurtz may have used to vent his despair.

The point I would like to make here is that there is no certainty that Kurtz uttered his notorious cry in English. Perhaps he uttered it in French and Marlow subsequently translated it for us to hear. But in that case what would be the French word that Marlow translated by 'the horror'? It is, of course, impossible to settle the matter. But it is precisely this undecidability that matters, because it draws the reader's attention to the potential deceptiveness of a text that systematically, though silently, questions its own modalities of representation, namely its own language, implying that somehow English could function as a screen rather than an instrument of clarification. In this perspective, the presence of French language within statements in English can be considered as the locus where the textual voice operates, as it literally splits the enunciation, and consequently the authorial voice. Thus the phrase 'the horror' is simultaneously alleged to have been uttered in English, but the original could have been in French, and to top it all it remains a silent ejaculation being a written exclamation.

The fact that the two languages compete to establish their supremacy is sometimes revealed by apparently insignificant details. For instance, when Marlow feels the need to assert his authority over the unruly hammock carriers, he recalls: 'So, one evening, I made a speech in English with gestures, not one of which was lost to the sixty pair of eyes before me, and the next morning I started the hammock off in front all right' (71–2). What is at stake here is, in fact, the relevance of the medium of the narration, because what the reader suspects is that the efficiency of an address in English to French-speaking carriers is somewhat doubtful, as the fact that he has to supplement his speech with hot-tempered gestures attests.

Gallicisms, or faulty translations that follow in English a French linguistic pattern, are the most commonly found points of friction between languages. They are transparent to a French reader, but merely sound somewhat bizarre without being totally opaque in English, so that they really are an oblique way of introducing an element of alterity in the dominant language and in the fiction. Such is one of the major functions of the textual voice. Of course, it so happens that a number of these polyglot idioms seem to be justified on account of the fact that they are spoken by characters whose native tongue is allegedly French, but it makes no difference in the way the two languages temporarily collide. Thus, the Belgian doctor exclaims: 'Famous. Interesting, too' (58) when he hears that Marlow is bound for the Congo. What he actually means is something like 'good for you' or 'well done!' – all phrases whose function is purely phatic and denote very little concern with the fate of his visitor.

Another good case in point is the attitude of the manager who mendaciously tells Marlow that he would be sorry if Kurtz died before they reached him, using the phrase: 'I would be desolated if anything should happen to Mr. Kurtz before we came up' (106). What is 'desolated' is the country they have come to exploit, not the colonizers. Shortly after that, the same manager attempts to assert his power when he wants the boat to hurry to the Central Station, in spite of the indefinite threats of the natives by asserting: 'I authorize you to take all the risks' (106). The truth of his jurisdiction is immediately revealed when Marlow flatly refuses to obey his orders, because he knows full well that the only authority on board a ship is the captain. Thus is the credit of the manager exposed for what it is: mere pretence. In such cases, Gallicisms operate as linguistic Trojan horses, the purpose of which is to disqualify those who use them through a questioning of the language they use. On one specific occasion the narrative explicitly foregrounds the activity of translation that inevitably goes on in the wings of such a narrative. It occurs when Marlow is just about to leave his office. Possibly not wanting to appear rude, the doctor wishes to address Marlow in English and translates his own parting words using, by the way, an unidiomatic phrase that sounds exactly like a Gallicism: 'Adieu. How do you English say, eh?' (58).

Such an occurrence is a convenient reminder that what the authorial voice constantly conceals from the reader is the friction that the presence of two languages within a single utterance dividing the narrative voices, inevitably creates, so that he is made to understand that the linguistic game that is going on at that precise juncture, in fact applies to the whole text. If we accept the distinction between narrative voice, in charge of each narrative level (the primary narrator, Marlow, and other transient narrative voices), and the authorial voice (in charge of the whole story), then the confusion between the two tongues, whether deliberate or not, amounts to a vast attempt at manipulation that destabilizes English as a master discourse. One elegant way of solving the issue, as Lacoue-Labarthe does, is to speak of 'narrating voice' [*voix narratrice*] (113, my trans.).[8] *Voix narratrice* is indeed a felicitous phrase: if the textual voice is located in the space between narrative voices and authorial voice, the expression 'narrating voice' insofar as it denies the agency of a subject, reduced to an 'it', suggests that it contains the object voice in both senses of the term. It simultaneously includes it as a textual component and restrains the possibility of dangerous enjoyment that it could generate. The only drawback of the formulation is that by blurring the distinction between narrative voice and authorial voice, it somehow conceals the gap that opens between the two languages involved in the act of narration.

The case of Marlow is even more telling because he is presented as a regular British sailor, so that when he produces Gallicisms, he does exactly what Conrad himself does in his non-fictional works, as well as in his novels, when writing in English. In other words, the relationship of the (real) author[9] with his work, as implemented in the textual voice, is an oblique way of re-introducing the corporeal dimension of writing and simultaneously of dealing with the affects that necessarily attend the presence of a voice beyond 'sense'. Marlow's fascination for Kurtz's voice can be understood thus, because he is obviously deeply moved by the effects of its uncanny appeal, as he honestly apprises his listeners on more than one occasion:

Oh, yes, I heard more than enough. And I was right too. A voice. He was very little more than a voice. And I heard—him—it—this voice—other voices—all of them were so little more than voices—and the memory of that time itself lingers around me, impalpable, . . . silly, atrocious, sordid, savage, or simply mean, without any kind of sense. Voices, voices – even the girl herself—now—(115).

Marlow's emotional response to voices is unambiguously attested by the staccato rhythm created by the proliferation of dashes, as well as by the multiplication of adjectives trying to account for their distinctiveness, the impersonal 'it' implying latent inhumanity, acting as an echo of the image of the wreath 'speaking' English (117).

A good illustration of the way the textual voice works in relation to Marlow can be found in Part III when he takes a stand against the stupidity of the manager by defending Kurtz, a move that excludes him from the circle of the so-called Pilgrims of Progress: 'My hour of favour was over; I found myself lumped along with Kurtz as a partisan of methods for which the time was not ripe' (138).[10] In such a context the word 'partisan' is far from being innocent. The French idiom merely implies that, like the harlequin, Marlow might be a follower, or a disciple of Kurtz. But, in fact, the word 'partisan' as a Gallicism introduces the idea of resistance, of war, exactly as if Marlow was at war against the type of society and ideology that they stand for. The textual voice, as implemented here through linguistic duality, appears to be not only a discursive device, a vector of poeticity, but most of all an ideological instrument, as will be shown presently. The inaudibility and invisibility of the textual voice is clearly exemplified by the primary narrator's description of the scene of the enunciation:

> I listened, I listened on the watch for the sentence, for the word, that would give me the clue to the faint uneasiness inspired by this narrative that seemed to shape itself without human lips in the heavy night-air of the river. (83)

In this way, Conrad provides guidelines to invite his readers to pay attention to the fact that reading *Heart of Darkness* is nothing like listening to a sailor's yarn. It calls, rather, for an opening of ears to listen to the silent textual voice, as distanced from Marlow's and the authorial voice. The faint impression of uneasiness that is recorded by the primary narrator, however, does not come from the quasi-fantasmatic scene starring Marlow as a storyteller but, rather, from the suspicion that his story and, primarily, its narrative features, could possibly challenge the basic ideological assumptions on which their world is predicated.

Ideological darkness versus textual voice

Lacoue-Labarthe convincingly argues that one of the crucial issues of Conrad's art of writing is the question of truth and ethics or, more accurately, that it interrogates the relation between fiction and truth, that is, the possibility that fiction – a variety of lies – could be a potential medium for reaching at some kind of truth, or that truth itself could be a fiction.[11] What we must add is that *Heart of Darkness* illustrates that both possibilities can be validated, depending on the author's commitment to textual voice. This is illustrated by Marlow's predicament regarding his obsession with truth. On the one hand, he claims, somewhat tautologically, that he 'can't bear a lie' (82); on the other hand, he can't help but lie on two memorable occasions: the first one as he tears off the damning postscriptum to the report for the 'International Society for the Suppression of Savage Customs', before handing it to a journalist, and the other during his interview with the Intended. What he experiences here is naturally the double-bind of all fiction, the only possible way out of it being once again through the mediation of the textual voice. As a consequence, in Conrad's fiction, the textual voice is not transcendent, it is merely translinguistic.

In *Gaze and Voice as Love Objects*, Mladen Dolar paves the way for a conception of the textual voice as a locus of ideological confrontation, not only with the object voice as such, but also with the way language produces meaning. Indeed, Conrad's art largely depends on linguistic games that he may, or may not control entirely, but which are effective in his overall strategy of indeterminacy. Therefore, Dolar's observations concerning the object voice could equally apply to the textual voice: 'It seems that the voice, as a senseless remainder of the letter, is what endows the letter with authority, making it not just a signifier but an act'.[12] The authority in question is not to be understood as that of the author or of the authorial voice. It is the authority of language itself, insofar as it becomes active and not just illustrative or descriptive. And it does so through what we can only call textual poetics: that is, the responsibility of the author residing only in his power to ensure the ethical side of the act which takes place under his gaze.

Arguably, the textual voice does play the role of a 'lever of thought',[13] in the poetic process, and the devices it resorts to are well known.[14] In addition to the function of pronouns and punctuation,[15] there are, no doubts, many other devices involved, like free indirect discourse, multi-layered narrative embedding, selected capitalization, intertextual games, ellipses, figures of rhetorical displacement, etc., but linguistic duality remains by far the overwhelming feature in *Heart of Darkness*. My contention, however, is that this 'lever of thought' is none other than the textual voice as defined above, to the extent that it appears as a way of getting around the hermeneutic circle that jeopardizes all attempts to think. Now, the reason why the hermeneutic circle, or the circular use of arguments that necessarily presuppose each other, inevitably monitors the way we think, is that no language has ever stood outside itself in order to transcend its condition. One important aspect of Marlow's role in *Heart of Darkness* is to dramatize the role of the interpreter in the process of interpretation through his never-ending epistemological questioning, insofar as meaning is necessarily an individual response to a given cultural, historical and literary context that is not always acknowledged as such. It is a tribute to Marlow's honesty that he always attempts to broaden the context of interpretation, as he does, for instance, in his historical survey of the Roman conquest.

It should be noted in passing that the very first barrier that limits the reasoning of any individual is the prior knowledge that constitutes the hermeneutic circle within which he operates. This is eventually not so far from Lacan's position, which consists in contending that there is no such thing as a metalanguage that could speak the truth about the truth. As a result, when Marlow feels it duty bound to reveal the ugly underside of colonization, he can only do so by using a language that the very same colonizers have long before learnt to control – even if he does it with the required amount of scathing irony. This is principally true of the English tongue as a vehicle of the dominant narrative worldview. The fact that Conrad once implicitly admitted that '. . . a book is a deed, that the writing of it is an enterprise as much as the conquest of a colony,'[16] should alert his readers to the relevance of the ideological context in which a work of fiction is produced.

Peter Brooks has drawn the attention of critics to the epistemology of narrative in *Heart of Darkness* and its well-known inconclusiveness,[17] so I would simply like to link his position to the manifestation of the textual voice and argue that misreading is the very condition of reading. What makes Kurtz's report unreadable is the gap between the text itself and its postscriptum. When Marlow tears off the postscriptum he, *de facto*, makes the report readable, but at the cost of truth. Yet things are a shade more complex: if the journalist is bound to misread Kurtz's report, it is not the case for the reader of *Heart of Darkness* who is in a position to detect the lie. In that sense, Marlow's lie to the journalist does tell the truth to the reader. What he stages here is nothing else but unreadability itself which, in turn, makes Marlow's own report, the fiction of *Heart of Darkness*, readable. Paradoxically, then, Marlow's narrative is a readable report because it is unreadable, that is, it delays ultimate meaning, calling for further enquiries; and, simultaneously, it is unreadable because it is readable, that is, it can be partially paraphrased. This is made possible through the mediation of the textual voice that literally undercuts both the authorial voice and the narrative voice at the same time. In fact, I maintain that the authorial and the narrative voices deal with reality, whereas the textual voice deals with the Real.[18] To that extent, the textual voice appears to be the only possible way out of the hermeneutic circle, because it functions as a substitute for the structurally missing metalanguage, and its efficiency is in proportion to its anamorphosis-like *modus operandi*.

As a matter of fact, the duty of a writer, as Jacques Derrida opportunely reminds us, is the duty of irresponsibility, since he argues that 'refusing to reply for one's thought or writing to constituted powers, is perhaps the highest form of responsibility'.[19] This, *Heart of Darkness* successfully achieves, owing to the mediation of the textual voice, whose role as an ideological fluid operator endows it with an ethical dimension. Its chief auxiliary in that respect is a strategy of semantic undecidability. The very word 'darkness', foregrounded in the title, is also a good case in point, as its very heart baffles attempts at finalizing definitions. However, I will add one more item to the open list of tentative clues, namely, the idea that the heart of darkness can also be seen as the textual voice itself. That is to say, as the agency that effectively precludes ideological and interpretational closure and alerts the reader to his responsibility in constructing his own interpretation.

Similar areas of deliberate semantic confusion are to be found in statements that make the reader wonder what Marlow is driving at when he coins phrases like 'inner truth' or 'unspeakable rites', 'the ultimate point of navigation', 'the abomination of desolation', 'the choice of nightmares' or, even more importantly, 'the idea at the back of it' that allegedly legitimizes colonization. All of them inevitably invite speculation. The only thing beyond dispute, however, is that most of these expressions deal with the question of colonization within the context of the enlightenment/savagery binary. If Derrida is right to believe that a text is always written in opposition to a pre-existing one perceived as a menace to it, then *Heart of Darkness* is to be seen as a response to the myth on which the self-image of the Western world rests. This is also Lacoue-Labarthe's point. Indeed, as a philosopher who relentlessly interrogated the mythic power of fictional texts – from the Greeks to the Moderns – he is well equipped to perceive the deeper mythical questioning that is going on within Conrad's narrative form. This is where the writer (Conrad) and the philosopher (Lacoue-Labarthe) meet on common ground, since they share, each with his own intellectual background, the conviction that the primary myth of enlightenment that serves as the backbone of imperialistic ideology is a fraud.

What Conrad admirably captures in *Heart of Darkness* is how the horror is the condition of enlightenment, just as light presupposes darkness. Ultimately, the most pregnant reason why Marlow experiences a feeling of kinship with Kurtz and undertakes to keep his memory alive out of fidelity is that they both have experienced the fact that the savagery, which they thought was inherent in the native condition, is in fact their own. Their silent partnership resides in their confrontation with the horror of the Western world. The only difference being that Kurtz's experience is direct, unmediated, whereas Marlow's is mediated through Kurtz's voice and discourse. In other words, Kurtz has actualized into unethical practises 'the horror of good intentions'[20] because he could no longer justify his subjective position, having lost his bearings in the indefinite boundary between civilization and savagery. What Marlow learns from Kurtz's fateful death, and from his journey to the Congo, is the deeper kinship that exists between human beings, irrespective of their social and historical condition. He makes no bones about it when, describing the rites and dances he witnesses along the river, he admits to his incredulous listeners: 'what thrilled you was just the thought of their humanity – like yours – the thought of your remote kinship with this wild and passionate uproar' (96).

Because of the insistence of the textual voice in his fiction, it is difficult to agree with Pecora when he holds that *Heart of Darkness* is an allegory of reading, because an allegory presupposes the existence of a definite message that must be recovered by the interpreter. Hillis Miller makes a more convincing suggestion when he claims that the novella ought to be seen as a parable, granted that the aim of the parable is to problematize the act of interpretation itself, as Lacan aptly put it when he said: 'I will speak therefore in a parable, namely to throw people off the scent'.[21] Because of its undecidability, the parable provides the locus for an encounter with alterity in the speaker's discourse, whose objective is to appeal to the desire of the listener and to expose his ideological position. Lacoue-Labarthe on the other hand, following Coleridge, argues that myths, including Conrad's, are '*tautegorical*', suggesting that 'they do not have a different meaning from the meaning they enunciate' (120). Ultimately however, if *Heart of Darkness* is also an apocalyptic text as Hillis Miller maintains, it is under the strict condition that it allows free play to the manifestations of the textual voice. In this perspective, the textual voice appears to be the result of the conjunction of the aesthetic and ethical unconscious desires of the creator whose trust in language and in his art is so complete that it allows him to come to terms with the incontrovertible fact that the unconscious is the condition of language.

'Sometimes I have luck and I write better than I can', Hemingway wrote to a friend.[22] It seems that this statement can be seen as a tribute to the dynamic role of the textual voice in creative writing and that it can be applied to Conrad too. In Conrad, it takes the form of the voice of darkness, the darkness at the bottom of the act of creation. It is therefore possible to concur with Lacoue-Labarthe's intimation that Kurtz can be viewed as a debased Rimbaud-like figure insofar as the former never managed to fully become a poet; he lost his voice in the heart of a darkness that is above all his own darkness.

Notes

1 Michael Greaney, *Conrad, Language and Narrative* (Cambridge University Press, 2002), 69.

2 Josiane Paccaud-Huguet, 'Déchets sonores: L'esthétique du fragment de voix chez Conrad', in *l'Époque Conradienne*, 35: 45–57.

3   The object voice is not the human voice, not speech even. It is an object, the vocal object in the psychoanalytical sense. See Jacques-Alain Miller, 'Jacques Lacan et la Voix' in *Quarto*, 54 (1994): 47–52.

4   *Jouissance* is not to be understood here as enjoyment, as a striving for happiness, but as what lies beyond the pleasure principle and threatens to engulf the subject.

5   German, Italian, Spanish perform a similar function in his other works, and special attention should be paid to his mother tongue, Polish, even if he systematically banned it from his fiction and did not even bother to make his children study it.

6   See my paper, 'The French Voice of Joseph Conrad', forthcoming in *l'Époque Conradienne*, 37 (2011).

7   Joseph Conrad, *The Collected Letters of Joseph Conrad*, vols. 3 and 4, eds. F. Karl and L. Davies (Cambridge: Cambridge University Press, 1903–7), 94.

8   My translation of his French formulation: '*voix narratrice*', a category that does not fit into Genette's standard narratological classification.

9   As opposed to the 'implied author', who stands for the authorial voice.

10 A single instance is being examined here but it is symptomatic of the whole narration. See 'epoch' (122), 'rude table' (138), 'suspect yourself of being deaf' (141), 'besides that' (144), etc.

11 For a particularly illuminating approach of the question, see Jeremy Hawthorn, *Joseph Conrad: Language and Fictional Self-consciousness* (London: Edward Arnold, 1979).

12 Mladen Dolar, *A Voice and Nothing More* (Cambridge, MA: The M.I.T. Press, 2006), 27.

13 The phrase is borrowed from a presentation of Dolar's book, *A Voice and Nothing More,* and is available on the MIT Press website: *http://mitpress.mit.edu/catalog/item/default.asp?ttype*, last accessed 3 April 2011.

14 See Anthony Fothergill, 'The Poetics of Particulars: Pronouns, Punctuation and Ideology in *Heart of Darkness*', in *Conrad's Literary Career*, ed. Keith Carabine et al. (East European Monographs, Boulder, CO: Maria Curie-Slodwska University, 1992), 57–73.

15 Anthony Fothergill, 'Poetics of Particulars', 57.

16 Joseph Conrad: 'A Glance at Two Books', in *Tales of Hearsay and Last Essays* (London: J. M. Dent and Sons Ltd, 1935), 132.

17 Peter Brooks, 'An Unreadable Report: Conrad's *Heart of Darkness*', in *Reading for the Plot, Design and Intention in Narrative* (London: Vintage Books, 1984), 238–63.

18 I refer here to the Real in the Lacanian sense: what is distinct from the Imaginary and escapes the Symbolic insofar as it remains unspeakable. The Real is consequently defined as the Impossible, but it is an impossible that never ceases to write itself.

19 Jacques Derrida, 'This Strange Institution Called Literature', in *Acts of Literature* (London: Routledge, 1992), 32.

20 Karola M. Kaplan, 'Colonizers, Cannibals and the Horror of Good Intentions' in *Studies in Short Fiction*, 43.3 (1997): 323–33.

21 Jacques Lacan, 'Radiophonie', in *Autres Ecrits* (Paris: Le Seuil, 2001), 414.

22 Ernest Hemingway, in 'Conversations with Ernest Hemingway', ed. Matthew Joseph Bruccoli (University Press of Mississippi, 1986), 109–29, 124.

9

The horror of trauma: Mourning or melancholia in *Heart of Darkness*?

BETH S. ASH

My reading of *Heart of Darkness* differs from Philippe Lacoue-Labarthe's reading, not just as a dispute between interpretative claims but, as Nidesh Lawtoo has made me see, as a real *differend* in Lyotard's technical sense.[1] In 'Emma: Between Philosophy and Psychoanalysis', Lyotard writes: 'In the *differend* between philosophers and analysts . . . any philosopher, as *philosopher*, will find it impossible to intervene in Freudian affairs without redressing them'.[2] More recently, Claire Nouvet explains that Lyotard's 'Emma' renounces the hegemony of philosophy in 'an attempt to think what philosophy has long resisted thinking, but with which psychoanalysis and literature constantly deal: affect'.[3] If Lacoue-Labarthe approaches *Heart of Darkness* as a philosophical or critical myth and, thus, in his words, 'as a bearer of truth' (113), in what follows, I approach Conrad's novella less in terms of truth and more in terms of the psychoanalysis of affect. This will lead me to take a psychoanalytic view of the Kurtz-Marlow relation reframed in the context of a larger crisis in colonial identity, a crisis that Marlow, perhaps more than Kurtz, undergoes. As we shall see, this psycho-political crisis signifies for him a traumatic rupture of a

communal bond and leaves him deeply ambivalent towards Kurtz –
an ambivalence characteristic of melancholic disconsolation.

I want to emphasize from the outset, however, that the *differend*
between Lacoue-Labarthe's reading and mine is only *in some ways*
insurmountable, which, of course, means that there are salient points
of interplay that make this conflict of interpretations interesting and
illuminating. And the conflict is not entirely insurmountable because
Lacoue-Labarthe is not entirely the philosopher who corrects
psychoanalytic ideas or resists thinking about affect. Lacoue-
Labarthe does use psychoanalysis, specifically the Lacanian concept
of the 'Thing' (*la Chose*), to dramatize how Kurtz existentially loses
the ground under his feet and finds himself in the psychic reality
of an unbearable void. One is still mindful that Lacan provides a
very philosophical version of psychoanalysis,[4] but Lacoue-Labarthe
does assist with the discussion of *political* affect. He has made the
significant observation that the concepts or ideas formative of
collective subjectivity hold sway over emotions. As he and Nancy
put it in 'The Nazi Myth', collective 'emotion always joins itself
to *concepts*' (their emphasis).[5] Lacoue-Labarthe's real interest is
in anatomizing the concept and dispelling the identification more
than in the psychic reality of an agonizing loss of social identity.
Thus, we might follow Lacoue-Labarthe's direction to see Kurtz
as figuring the communal idea of colonialism, but we must also
depart from him and turn to the psycho-logy of investment and
disillusionment in order to explore how Marlow suffers the loss of
political selfhood.

Lacoue-Labarthe attends in his introduction to his own affecting
experience with *Heart of Darkness*: David Warrilow's theatrical
reading of Conrad's novella prompted Lacoue-Labarthe truly to
hear 'this *tremendous* text' (111). He recounts how this performance
evoked 'an emotion of thought' in him, and in its grip he made the
'rash declaration' that the novella holds the place of 'one of
the greatest texts of Western Literature' (111). In recounting this
affect-thought Lacoue-Labarthe subtly suggests the Kantian model
of reflective judgement: that is, in the aesthetic domain, judging relies
on sensibility and does without a concept. What must be brought
to account, for Lacoue-Labarthe, is precisely his 'rash declaration'
of the novella's greatness. For him, in particular, the alert sensibility
of reflective judgement seems utterly predisposed towards ideas.
Doesn't his use of the adjective 'rash' show some discomfort with

the signal of emotion?, a need to make it signify? Lacoue-Labarthe knows that judgement, especially aesthetic judgement, has its roots in affect. And yet, almost irresistibly, he loosens the grip of emotion, makes it yield to understanding Conrad's greatness by means of illuminating, *abstract* ideas. The *differend* of *Heart of Darkness* as critical myth (Lacoue-Labarthe's approach) and *Heart of Darkness* as affective – at points, quite crucially unconscious – text provides for the variations in our respective attention towards the central characters, Kurtz and Marlow. If Lacoue-Labarthe primarily focuses on Kurtz who, in his words 'is surely the *figure* of this myth or the hero of this *fiction*' (114), I look at Kurtz through Marlow's narration – primarily how Kurtz affects Marlow.[6]

Lacoue-Labarthe's use of the Platonic categories of mimesis and diegesis, his description of the frame narrator of *Heart of Darkness* as the diegetical voice of the author (the 'autobiographical' or 'real' Conrad) and his claim that Marlow mimetically stands in for Conrad requires a word of explanation. In 'Typography', his 1975 poststructuralist essay on Plato's *Republic*, Lacoue-Labarthe shows how Plato's attempt to distinguish his own responsible mimesis from irresponsible rivals (i.e. that 'Socrates' as a speaking figure in the text must reflect the external will or intent of the philosopher) cannot withstand the equivocality of mimesis itself.[7] And yet, in 'The Horror of the West', Lacoue-Labarthe does not problematize the structure of (external) authorial intentionality as guarantee of its own stable subjectivity within the mimesis of *Heart of Darkness*. While conceding that 'a far more meticulous analysis' (113) of the formal structure of the narrative needs to be done, it seems that Lacoue-Labarthe has given himself philosophical license to bypass Marlow altogether in favour of Conrad. Locating Conrad 'in' the text, however, isn't at all easy. Even more importantly, the very elements that Lacoue-Labarthe describes – this difficulty with enunciation, this heaviness, painfulness and obscurity – first and foremost belong to *Marlow*, to *his telling*. As Hillis Miller notes in 'Revisiting "*Heart of Darkness* Revisited"', Marlow's narrative states of 'anger', 'grief' and feelings of 'uneasiness'resonate with the reader.[8] I would add that Marlow's narrative *transmits* these affective intensities and sometimes cannot articulate any meaning at all, not even 'obscure' meaning. Kurtz may very well be 'the *figure* of this myth' (114) as Lacoue-Labarthe's brilliant reading attests, but it cannot be overlooked that Kurtz, the dead man, has captured Marlow as if he were a hostage. Marlow's telling reveals this trauma.

Elaborating on the ethical dimension of the *differend*, Lyotard writes: 'A case of *differend* between two parties takes place when the "regulation" of the conflict that opposes them is done in the idiom of one of the parties, while the wrong suffered by the other is not signified in that idiom'.[9] Isn't Marlow in a sense wronged by focusing on the 'truth' of Kurtz to the exclusion of his own pain? At the very least, we lose the fullness, the density and complexity of Conrad's narration if Marlow's traumatic experience is left uninterpreted. There is a black mood in *Heart of Darkness* that asserts itself and deserves to be read. Marlow's trauma is 'not signified' in Lacoue-Labarthe's philosophical idiom, but the psychic structures and affects concentrated in Marlow's relation to Kurtz bid to resurface or return as the 'other' of Lacoue-Labarthe's philosophical reading. My aim in what follows is to show how central motifs in 'The Horror of the West' that intriguingly denote the 'other' in the philosopher's argument can be used to read the text both sympathetically with Lacoue-Labarthe and in my contrary direction. I see three central motifs that allow for this reading strategy: the full complexity of colonial identity; loss and melancholia; and the refusal of speech or, as Lacoue-Labarthe puts it, the refusal of 'truth'. But let us proceed in order.

Affective politics: Kurtz's myth and Marlow's response

It is important to begin with Lacoue-Labarthe's reading of Kurtz as a 'figure' for breaching the myth-making powers of the Colonial West and disclosing that, in Lacoue-Labarthe's words, '*beneath* this colony is the *horror*' (119). This reading is in some ways a continuation of the project that Lacoue-Labarthe and Nancy set out in *Retreating the Political* (1979), a major text reflective of their ongoing concern with the philosphico-political 'figure'. That is to say, first, their claim that an essential identity of the social or political unit is asserted by figurative means and second, their deconstruction of 'ideal' figures of the human and the state that allows for an alternative philosophical engagement with politics (the 'retreat' of the political). Their argument perhaps in somewhat simplified terms is that the modern history of the political – of the *polis* as a collective entity – has become the attempt to preserve the Western subject, and this attempt requires the identification of the subject as such. This subject is a metaphysical or an essential and absolute type – the group Subject – which, as Simon Sparks puts it in his 'Introduction' to *Retreating*, is 'an essence in-common (a community even) on the basis of a figure in-common'.[10] The political Subject is asserted in the idiom of art – for example, the Nation as self-creating, or the National Idea as a forming force for unity, or National character traits representing a being-common. Lacoue-Labarthe and Nancy uncover, in Sparks's words, 'a whole theatrics of thinking' in the political usage of *techne*, *poeisis* and *mimesis*, namely, the essential lexicon of the figure.[11] Lacoue-Labarthe's reading of *Heart of Darkness* is consistent with the critical project of *Retreating* because both texts assert that, when the capacity for art, for 'figuration'/'fictioning', enters politics, it is used to mould totalitarian truths. This is readily seen in the fascist aestheticization of the political – for example, in the following statement made by Goebbels, Reich Minister of Propaganda, that 'the true artist, the one who molds in the most elevated sense, is the [Nazi] Statesman', a statement that Lacoue-Labarthe describes as 'a drowsy repetition of Napoleon and Nietzsche'.[12]

In 'The Horror of the West', Lacoue-Labarthe tells us that there is a temptation for Western thought and politics to confuse 'ability [*capacité*] (the gift) with power' (117). That confusion was revealed 'when Nietzsche called the gift (of art) "will to power" and when, under this name, he conceived the essence of mankind as subject' (117). In the conduct of political relations, the 'will to power' operates when relations are understood as the life of the Subject alone (e.g. 'the subject of history') and conducted exclusively on the basis of realizing a being-common (e.g. manifest destiny). The 'will-to-figure' is thus the identity principle of Western politics. In their essay, 'The Nazi Myth', Lacoue-Labarthe and Nancy further clarify the idea of the figure as identity principle. They invoke Plato's conception of myth to do so: 'Myth is a fiction, in the strong, active sense of *fashioning*'.[13] Note that 'the will-to-figure' is synonymous with 'fashioning'. Myth's role, they continue, 'is to propose, if not impose, models or types . . . in imitation of which an individual, or a city, or an entire people, can grasp themselves and identify

themselves'.[14] It is through cultural myth or, actually, any unifying
being-common (i.e. 'We, the people', 'the race', 'humanity') that the
'mimetic' identity principle operates, and does so coercively, imposing
the form of political thinking and pressuring con-formity.

Kurtz's pamphlet for 'The Society for Suppression of Savage
Customs' in part shows how he, the political journalist (the failed
artist), figures the colonial myth. The pamphlet says: 'we whites'
appear to those 'savages' as 'supernatural beings—we approach
them with the might as of a deity'; and Marlow comments that 'it
gave [him] the notion of an exotic immensity ruled by an august
Benevolence' (118). In Kurtz's discourse, the European subject is
the Subject, and in Kurtz's vision of the colonial relation, the world
is no longer the world, but rather the world-process of civilizing
domination in which the European is fully realized in the rule of
a self-creating god, 'an august Benevolence'. But, of course, Kurtz
also provides the 'valuable' postscript, 'Exterminate all the brutes!'
(118). Using Lacoue-Labarthe's term 'de-figuration',[15] it might be
said that this is precisely what happens to Kurtz – that the glory of
Kurtz's representation is de-figured by his demand for genocide.

This philosophical discussion dovetails with Lacoue-Labarthe's
insightful Lacanian view of Kurtz's darkness, the gist of which is
as follows:

[T]he *horror*, the vertigo to which Kurtz falls victim, this horror
about which we know basically nothing . . . is less the 'savage'
horror itself than the horror revealed by the echo of the clamour
within him (in his 'intimate' void); it is his 'proper' horror, or
better, it is the horror of his absence of any proper-being [*être-propre*] . . . the vertigo [that] leads him even to ecstasy, this black
hole, then, this 'heart of darkness' is him—his void—as if outside
himself. . . . I would say that the horror is *la Chose*—the *Thing*
or *Ding* (another name for being, that is, for nothingness, the
'nothingness of being' [*le riend'étant*], which Lacan borrows
from Heidegger); or, if you prefer, the 'heart of darkness' is the
extime—the *interior intimo meo* of Augustine, God, but as
internal exclusion. Perhaps evil . . . (116–17)

Understanding this section depends on several Lacanian ideas that
cluster around *la Chose*. Lacoue-Labarthe seems to be saying in
part that Kurtz's boundless enjoyment – what he terms 'ecstasy' but

what Lacan refers to as '*jouissance*' (i.e. what is most exciting to the subject, which includes disgust and horror) – voids Kurtz's symbolic existence. Kurtz's 'void' is his annulment of his existence granted by the symbolic. It is well known that the Lacanian subject is split, but perhaps less well known that the split subject can be described as split between being and existence, where being is on the side of the (Lacanian) real and existence on the side of the symbolic. We therefore can imagine a real or substantive *jouissance* before/outside of the symbolic, as Žižek puts it, *das Ding*, the Thing is 'the pure substance of enjoyment that is resistant to symbolization'.[16] But desire is able only to recover a rem(a)inder of enjoyment in fantasy, through what Lacan calls the object-cause or the object (a). Enjoyment as 'pure substance' is known to the subject in the symbolic order only as the radical otherness in the Other (or the lack in the Other), in the first instance, the mOther, who makes her *jouissance* known only as something that escapes the child or as not for him/her. What is most intimately our own – the fantasy-object as the subject's partner – is the foreign cause (the *jouissance* that the other lacks) subjectively internalized.

We are able, then, to see that in Lacoue-Labarthe's reading, when Kurtz aims at the impossible *jouissance* (the Thing), his being becomes a symbolic void (he 'dies' as a member of the symbolic network) – and so cannot be symbolized or integrated into the symbolic order. As Lacoue-Labarthe puts it, this is 'a horror about which we [who are placed in the symbolic network] know basically nothing' (116); a horror that we must 'imagine'. Yet, as *extime*, the internal other qua Thing, Kurtz's being materializes the 'void' in us, in our symbolic order. Lacoue-Labarthe goes on to describe that *extime* as our 'intimate evil' as 'a tradition turned giddy, with the infinite power of destruction that is its own, its propensity for extermination' (118–19).

This Lacanian reading of Kurtz as West's own dark void (or death drive) is truly illuminating; it also resonates with a more explicit treatment of Lacan's theory that there is a lack or a void at the heart of the symbolic order – which is found in Žižek's discussion in *The Sublime Object of Ideology*:

> The symbolic order is striving for a homeostatic balance, but there is in its kernel, at its very centre, some *strange traumatic element* which cannot be symbolized, integrated in the symbolic

order—the Thing. Lacan coined a neologism for it: *L'extimité*—
external intimacy . . . The very existence of the symbolic order
implies a possibility of its *radical effacement*, of 'symbolic death'—
not the death of the so-called 'real object' in its symbol, but the
obliteration of the signifying network itself. (my emphasis)[17]

Žižek's interpretation of Lacan supplements Lacoue-Labarthe's
because Žižek does not just supply the philosophical content of
the real as a *hole* in the symbolic order; he also focuses on this
element of lack as traumatic, which might shatter the *whole* of the
symbolic network. Lacoue-Labarthe would most likely agree with
Žižek, since the reading of the 'Thing' as the evil (will to) power of
'destruction' and 'extermination' culminates for Lacoue-Labarthe in
the *'technique of death'* (119), and by this he means to suggest the
horror of the West that extends from colonialism to the horror of
the Holocaust (on which he never ceased to meditate) and beyond.[18]
But it is nonetheless a matter of making the *traumatic* real (the
horror) explicit. Kurtz is thus the name that wounds and fissures the
symbolic order of which Marlow is a member. Kurtz's perversion
of the law (in the imperative to 'exterminate!') and his obscene
enjoyment disrupt the colonial symbolic attempt to legitimate an
idealized 'We'. Kurtz is the name of a wound, a shock. Marlow
tells us when he is waiting for Kurtz to die and for a moment finds
him missing: 'What made this emotion so overpowering was—
how shall I define it?—the moral shock I received, as if something
altogether monstrous, intolerable to thought and odious to the soul,
had been thrust upon me unexpectedly' (141) – as if recovery of
Kurtz's physical body might keep the spectre of missing meaning
(the symbolic death) out of sight.

    And in this way Kurtz becomes Marlow's dangerous/traumatic
object. In Marlow's telling, the *sense* of Kurtz (i.e. his own ability
to make Kurtz meaningful) exists primarily at the level of a 'dream-
sensation' (82; my emphasis): 'Do you see him [Kurtz]? Do you see
the story? . . . It seems to me I am trying to tell you a dream . . .
convey the dream sensation' (82). And again: it is a feeling of 'being
captured by the incredible which is of the very essence of dreams'
(82), of being held by a tangle of emotions not yet translated or
processed in thought.[19] Lacoue-Labarthe refers to 'all those who are
fascinated by him [Kurtz]' (116) and, of course, Marlow admits of
being among them as he says: 'Oh, I wasn't touched. I was fascinated'

(149). In his foundational 'intimacy' with Kurtz (143), however, Marlow isn't just fascinated by him. He suffers radically conflicting emotions: he veers between attraction and revulsion, idealization and despair, anxiety and punishment. He stands mute before the enormity of Kurtz's degradation. There are no words in Marlow's belief system to make sense of Kurtz's self-worship and terror, no words for Marlow's own complicity in imperialist atrocity. The collapse of Marlow's (illusion of) moral integrity correlates with Kurtz's disintegration, threatening Marlow with self-collapse, with following Kurtz into a 'muddy hole' (150). Marlow holds himself in a suspended relation to the dangerous object until that suspension itself breaks down into melancholia. The only real alternative to disease is a correct identification of what Kurtz represents and that, for Marlow, is unbearable: the loss of subjective integrity and ethical community.

The assertion of melancholia

I have already suggested the ways in which *Heart of Darkness* is a critical myth for Lacoue-Labarthe, that this myth shows how terrible colonial domination is the expression of the West as absolute Subject, or, in his words, 'what the West *is* [is known]through what the West *does* ("to others")' (118). Lacoue-Labarthe thereby implies that, for Conrad or, at least, as the novella represents it, what the West is – namely, its political identity – is also, in Debra Berghoffen words, a 'non-ethical We'.[20] This dark vision of the *socius* is precisely what Marlow cannot accept and suffers as an extreme threat. He is in-between: he cannot accept mimetic identification with, or interpellation by, the virtuous colonial Subject (in the General Manager's words, 'the gang of virtue' [79]), but he cannot accept a place in a new, non-ethical We either.

In Lacoue-Labarthe's argument, there is 'the long work of mourning which ... governs Marlow's narrative' (114–15), presumably mourning for what Kurtz's colonial political subjectivity is, and what it does to others. Lacoue-Labarthe also focuses on how the world beyond the West, which is scattered with the West's victims, is caught up in the work of mourning too. '[S]uch is the gloom it [the West] imposes on the whole world: pain, sadness, an endless lament, a mourning that no work will ever diminish' (119). This vision is doubtlessly compelling, and yet the idea of the destructiveness of the West leading to mourning as a permanent feature of global culture moves beyond what is said in *Heart of Darkness*. For, the lamenting natives whom Marlow hears, as his steamboat moves closer to Kurtz, aren't grieving because of the destruction Kurtz has brought down on them, but because they believe that Marlow is going to take Kurtz from them. They attack Marlow's boat to prevent Kurtz from leaving. Marlow asks Kurtz's follower, the harlequin, 'Why did they attack us?' and the harlequin responds, 'They don't want him to go' (124–5). Moreover, at the time of Kurtz's death, when Marlow hears the 'droning sound of many men chanting', he tell us that Mr Kurtz's adorers were keeping their 'uneasy vigil' (140), that is to say, they mourn for Kurtz himself, not for the injuries they have suffered under his reign. When Marlow first hears the natives' mournful wail, he also thinks of himself, how he has possibly missed his chance to hear Kurtz, and he compares 'the startling extravagance of emotion' he has felt with 'the howling sorrow of these savages' (114). But that 'distant kinship' in sorrow is too distant for Marlow to recognize in the natives's howling loss, his own civilized loss: Kurtz's effective destruction of Marlow's world. Marlow's resonance with the howling savages is, at best, a missed opportunity for working through his own howling loss, and at worst, his colonial, racist projection or use of the 'simple people' (without distance from emotions) as a receptacle for evacuating 'extravagant' feelings that would otherwise threaten the self.

Lacoue-Labarthe's focus on the global effects of Western power tells us more about him than about Conrad. And Lacoue-Labarthe is able to mourn in ways that Marlow's narration shows that Marlow (and perhaps Conrad too) is not. Mourning asks us to do what we do not want to do – namely, to give up a love object or a libidinally invested position and to find a substitute for it. As Peter Homans describes it, in cultural mourning the breach is healed by means of an introspective reinterpretation of one's cultural ethos. If the substitute for lost culture is reinvented culture, there must be something in the cultural ethos that is worth reworking. But by Lacoue-Labarthe's interpretative lights, there really isn't much in the culture of domination to rework – it must be disrupted and undone. Perhaps the only valid substitute is the registration of the real. Isn't this what Lacoue-Labarthe's Conrad, the philosophic novelist, does? But in my view, uncompromised truth-telling probably isn't the most likely form of telling for an author in the throes of a crisis in imperialism and whose narrator is seized by that trauma. We do well to be mindful of what Julia Kristeva has observed: 'The periods that witness the downfall of political and religious idols, periods of crisis, are particularly favorable to black moods. While it is true that an unemployed worker is less suicidal than a deserted lover, melancholia does assert itself in times of crisis; it is spoken of, establishes its archeology, generates its representations and its knowledge'.[21] *Heart of Darkness* is one text in the long twentieth-century's archive of melancholy writing.

Marlow provides his desolate memory about almost missing the chance to experience 'the real presence' of Kurtz's voice. He says:

> I was cut to quick at the idea of having lost the inestimable privilege of listening to the gifted Kurtz. Of course I was wrong. . . . A voice. He was little more than a voice. And I heard him—it—this voice—other voices—all of them were so little more than voices—and the memory of that time itself lingers around me, impalpable, like a dying vibration of one immense jabber, silly, atrocious, sordid, savage, or simply mean, without any kind of sense. (114–15)

The phrase, 'the memory of that time lingers around me . . . mean, without any kind of sense', expresses the disillusioning loss of Kurtz's 'real presence'. One also senses anger with 'this voice—other voices—all of them were so little more than voices', a corollary of Marlow's sense of betrayal at being 'robbed of a belief' (114). Marlow wanted Kurtz to mirror back to him an idealized image – the 'real presence' of a voice filled with the power of shared beliefs – and thereby establish a mirroring rapport. But Marlow now experiences the collapse of that ideal ('I was wrong') in terms of betrayal and desolation. Kurtz has failed him. In this terrible deceleration from an illusion of rapport to a conviction of utter senselessness, Marlow substitutes anger and despair for mourning and a gradual acceptance of loss.

The 'sadder but wiser' tonalities that are part of working through disillusionment are not part of Marlow's experience (and re-experience in the narrative dream) of Kurtz. Anger and senselessness follow each other in a futile round: Marlow is enraged by the absurdity of his experience of Kurtz and of all the other imperialist voices, but rage impedes his ability to make meaning, to allow for both reality and possibility. And if his angry devaluation of the clamouring voices gets in the way of sense and the avowal of loss, then hatred becomes a position of protest. But hatred for the betrayer (a craving to destroy what destroys) arouses feelings of guilt, and guilt is only alleviated by masochistic inversion or yet another resurrection of the narcissistic ideal. This is Marlow's melancholia, his psychological movement between the redemptive Kurtz who held the promise of light in darkness and the despair-laden Kurtz who spoke no sense and razed all value. It is a Freudian or, more precisely, a Kleinian paranoid-schizoid construction of the melancholy self, the deserted self, but one not willing to relinquish the ideal promise that nourishes it.[22]

At Kurtz's death bed Marlow paradoxically transfers meaning to the very place where it is lost (i.e. in Kurtz's emptiness) and makes an exorbitant bid for the survival of idealization. Marlow's account begins with 'Oh, I wasn't touched. I was fascinated'. That is, it begins with his ambivalent attraction. Fascination, however, gives way to sanctification. Marlow asks:

Did he live his life again in every detail of desire, temptation, and surrender during that supreme moment of complete knowledge? He cried in a whisper at some image, at some vision—he cried out twice, a cry that was no more than a breath—'The horror! The horror!' (149)

'Did he . . . ?' the interrogative, is transformed into, 'I affirm that Kurtz was a remarkable man' (151), the declarative. This shift in grammar and meaning occurs because Marlow is rejecting his own experience of extremity ('And it is not my own extremity I remember best . . . No! It is his extremity that I seem to have lived through' [151]) in favour of the powerful response to death that he finds in Kurtz. The man confronts death, with a stare that 'was wide enough to embrace the whole universe, piercing enough to penetrate all the hearts that beat in the darkness. He had summed up—he had judged. "The horror!" He was a remarkable man' (151).

In Lacoue-Labarthe's discussion of this textual moment, as I have already noted, he rightly asks, 'What has [Kurtz] seen? What has he suffered? What is he talking about?' (116). And Peter Brooks describes the exclamation ('The horror! The horror!') as a simple 'cry' of indecipherable pain, a cry that answers so poorly to a death-bed scene of settling of accounts.[23] There is also a marked inconsistency between Marlow's response in this scene and his earlier, disillusioning view of Kurtz looking into his soul: 'his soul was mad. Being alone in the wilderness, it had looked within itself, and, by heavens! I tell you, it had gone mad' (145). The narrative of Kurtz's end has many gaps. And the forced and false qualities of Marlow's narration demonstrate his great need for a narcissistic antidote to depressive anxiety (feelings of guilt). In Marlow's eyes, Kurtz has 'complete knowledge' and 'all the wisdom, and all truth, and all sincerity' has gone into his summing up – 'he had judged' (151). Kurtz has become, for Marlow, almost divine. But the 'cry, that was no more than a breadth' (149) is only a painful sound of uncertain reference; an unsaid (*non dit*) that is left to stand where there should be intense recognition and even grieving words exchanged on the committed atrocities. Kurtz does not provide that in Marlow's account, but instead provides the artifice of disowned meaning, the opacity of an ideal untenanted by guilt.

What follows next in Marlow's account is Kurtz's physical death and Marlow's self-deprecating assessment of his own ordeal. The 'manager's boy' announces 'Mistah Kurtz—he dead', and Marlow follows with 'The voice was gone . . . I am of course aware that next day the pilgrims buried something in a muddy hole. And then they nearly buried me' (150). Marlow's extended rumination comes next:

> I have wrestled with death. It is the most unexciting contest you can imagine. It takes place in an impalpable greyness . . . in a sickly atmosphere of tepid skepticism, without much belief in your own right, and still less in that of your adversary . . . And it is not my own extremity I remember best—a vision of greyness without form filled with physical pain, and a careless contempt for the evanescence of all things—even of this pain itself. No! It is his extremity that I seem to have lived through. (150–1)

Why does Marlow have suicidal thoughts ('they very nearly buried me')? And why does he have a vision of his internal struggle as taking place in 'greyness' or as a 'greyness without form'? Importantly, Marlow tells us that he seems to 'live through' Kurtz – that is to say, the subject-to-subject relation has collapsed. Therefore, Marlow's struggle with death is not something apart from Kurtz's struggle. Earlier, before the deathbed scene, Marlow and Kurtz spent long hours arguing. Or, in effect, Marlow struggled with Kurtz as an adversary: 'If anybody had ever struggled with a soul, I am the man. And I wasn't arguing with a lunatic either' (144). Is Marlow not expressing a psychically internalized struggle with Kurtz? And is Marlow's wrestle 'with death' not actually a deadly struggle with this internalized adversary? Marlow literally takes Kurtz's fury into himself and punishes himself. And does he not lock up that danger in himself rather than admit to any endangering colonial wrongdoing of his own?

Marlow destroys the worth of his own experience. He knows only 'a sickly tepid scepticism', and he feels only disdain for his 'physical [and mental] pain', 'a careless contempt for the evanescence of all things—even of this pain itself' (151). The boundary between self and other collapses in deprecation as the other's anger is installed in the self. On the one hand, 'the greyness' represents the depressive denial of the painful and insufferable connection to Kurtz, an inhibition that allows Marlow to survive, yet leaves him absent from himself. On the other hand, beyond this fog of dejection is the prospect of following Kurtz into death. Suicidal thoughts derive either from Marlow's 'loyalty' to his ideal (a negative narcissistic merging) or as self-punishment for the unavowed 'sins' that belong to him as colonial citizen. This is how melancholia asserts itself, in omnipotent illusions of repair, in destruction and in self-destruction, the frightening motives that surface in times of crisis, when loss and bereavement have been repudiated.

For Marlow, these crippling affective intensities happen, but no one bears testimony to them; he most simply endures and his listeners do not want to be affected. We see this clearly when Marlow starts to tell about his disappointment at the prospect of missing out on the privilege of hearing Kurtz's voice; his audience becomes restless and sighs with impatience. Marlow infers that someone has called him 'absurd'. He retorts: 'Why do you sigh in this beastly way, somebody? Absurd? Well, absurd. Good lord! Mustn't a man ever—' (114). It is as if the men on the Nellie were saying, 'Marlow, you know that *We* don't talk about feelings'. Marlow's jungle experience overwhelms and makes him incoherent. On the one hand, he is captive to his perceptual memories; on the other hand, emotions sweep over him, but there is no subject integrating the

emotions with the perceptions, no subject to make sense in order
to mourn. Marlow cannot do this by himself, and his listeners do
not help him with representing his 'dream-sensations'. There is no
one, not Marlow, not his listeners, to address his condition of 'non-
addressedness'.[24] After leaving Africa, Marlow admits to extreme
self-dispossession, a 'passage through some inconceivable world
[with] . . . no hope in it and no desire' (152), and tragically, he suffers
perdurable isolation: 'We live, as we dream—alone . . . .' (82).

Lacoue-Labarthe tells us that Western 'barbarity' consists in not
wanting to *know* the truth, and he focuses on emotion only as an
expedient in a cover up. As he puts it, Marlow has his

> artifice of a 'white lie.' He will not dare tell Kurtz's 'Intended' his
> last words; instead, he will leave it to love to cover up and disguise
> the fury of transgression, thus completing the work of sanctification
> that averts the Western gaze from its wickedness. (119–20)

Lacoue-Labarthe foregrounds Marlow's 'will' – his egoic agency –
but the issue for the survivor of trauma is crippling pre-egoic affect,
from which, necessarily, subjective incapacity follows. For Lacoue-
Labarthe, Marlow is the artist, the artificer of the lie and the subject
in control. The disguise of the lie works hand-in-glove with the way
in which Marlow lets love do the work. From the standpoint of a
psychoanalysis of affect, Lacoue-Labarthe errs by attributing agency
where there is incapacity and confusing artifice with a prophylactic
measure against despair.

As we look at *Heart of Darkness* from the perspective of the
present, mindful of the twentieth (now inclusive of the twenty-first)
century of Western-made disasters, we discover several truisms
that are nevertheless true. The *differend* between a philosophy and
a psychoanalysis of affect brings these axioms to light. Lacoue-
Labarthe is utterly right that (*Heart of Darkness* shows us) the
Western exercise of hegemonic power has been a 'giddy' destruction
and that we do not want to know about it. But the West also
produces traumatized subjects as a consequence of that domination.
Sometimes, more often than we care to admit, we have been able
to hear the truth, and still we shun the trauma. It continues to be
an imperative to create communal space for affectively working
through such a traumatic truth for the self. At the same time, in the
mourning process, it must be acknowledged that the traumatized

within our own ranks have done our Western work of oppression. What rightfully substitutes for untenable, lost goodness are the ethical connections we make to those we have oppressed: we must share their narratives. And if the truth of our history *recurs* (the destructive horror of the West), there is the event in that history, always singular and different – no more so than for those who are subject to it and are potentially traumatized by it. *Heart of Darkness* is one of the greatest texts of Western literature because of its fundamental heterogeneity. It is a text that opens profoundly, in both the idioms of philosophy and analytic theory, and tells a meaningful truth of our history; it is also a melancholic response to crisis, an insistence on the trauma of horror for those who have the ears to hear it.

Notes

1   Vincent Descombes succinctly defines Lyotard's *differend* as 'a disagreement between claims voiced in heterogeneous idioms (idioms that are "incommensurable" in Thomas Kuhn's sense of the word), a disagreement that is in some ways insurmountable'. Vincent Descombes, *The Barometer of Modern Reason: On the Philosophies of Current Events*, trans. Adam Schwartz (London, New York: Oxford University Press, 1993), 135.

2   Jean-François Lyotard, 'Emma: Between Philosophy and Psychoanalysis', in *Lyotard, Philosophy, Politics, and the Sublime*, ed. Hugh J. Silverman (London, New York: Routledge, 2003), 24.

3   Claire Nouvet, 'The Inarticulate Affect: Lyotard and Psychoanalytic Testimony', in *Discourse* 25.1–2 (2003): 231–47, 232.

4   See André Green, 'Conceptions of Affect', in *International Journal of Psychoanalysis* 58 (1977), where he writes that Lacan has 'amputated affect from the theoretical corpus of psychoanalysis', 799. See also Jean-Luc Nancy and Philippe Lacoue-Labarthe, *The Title of the Letter* (1973), trans. François Raffoul and David Pettigrew (Albany, NY: State University of New York press, 1992), where they deconstruct Lacan's philosophical revision of the psychoanalytic subject, and thus demonstrate that Lacan's thought is a final sublation of philosophy.

5   Philippe Lacoue-Labarthe, Jean-Luc Nancy, 'The Nazi Myth', trans. Brian Holmes, in *Critical Inquiry*, 16.2 (1990): 291–312, 294.

6 Although Lacoue-Labarthe mostly discusses Marlow in formal terms, he does comment that the death of Kurtz, directs Marlow's narrative to a 'long work of mourning' (114), a point to which I shall return.

7 Philippe Lacoue-Labarthe, 'Typography' (1975) in *Typography: Mimesis, Philosophy, Politics*, ed. and trans. Christopher Fynsk (Cambridge, MA: Harvard University Press,1989), 132.

8 Hillis Miller, Prologue to this volume, 30.

9 Jean-Francois Lyotard, *The Differend: Phrases in Dispute*, trans. Georges Van Den Abbeele (Minneapolis, MN: University of Minnesota Press, 1988), 9.

10 Simon Sparks, 'Introduction: *Politica Ficta*', in Philippe Lacoue-Labarthe and Jean-LucNancy, *Retreating The Political* (1981), ed. and trans. Simon Sparks (London, New York: Routledge, 1997), xiii–xxvi, xxiv.

11 Sparks, 'Introduction', xxi.

12 Lacoue-Labarthe, Nancy, *Retreating*, 153.

13 Lacoue-Labarthe, Nancy, 'The Nazi Myth', 297.

14 Lacoue-Labarthe, Nancy, 'The Nazi Myth', 297.

15 Lacoue-Labarthe, Nancy, 'Scène', 74, quoted by Simon Sparks in 'Introduction: *Politic Ficta*', xxii.

16 Slavoj Žižek, *Enjoy Your Symptom: Jacques Lacan in Hollywood and Out* (London, New York: Routledge, 2001), 8.

17 Slavoj Žižek, *The Sublime Object of Ideology* (London, New York, Verso, 1989), 133.

18 I want to thank Nidesh Lawtoo for his observation that Lacoue-Labarthe would substantially agree with Žižek on this point.

19 My understanding of trauma is broadly psychoanalytic, that is, an overwhelming event that requires the creation of a 'trauma narrative' and only then can be grieved. See specifically, Judith Herman, *Trauma and Recovery: The Aftermath of Violence from Domestic Abuse to Political Terror* (New York: Harper Collins, 1992). For a comprehensive discussion of trauma in psychoanalytic thought informed by Lacoue-Labarthe's work, see also Ruth Leys, *Trauma: A Genealogy* (Chicago, IL: The University of Chicago Press, 2000).

20 Debra B. Berghoffen, 'Interrupting Lyotard: Whither the We?' in *Lyotard, Philosophy, Politics, and the Sublime*, ed. Hugh J. Silverman (London, New York: Routledge, 2003), 134.

21 Julia Kristeva, *Black Sun: Depression and Melancholia* (1987), trans. Leon S. Roudiez (New York, Oxford: Columbia University Press, 1989), 8.

22 See Melanie Klein, 'A Contribution to the Psychogenesis of Manic-Depressive States'(1935), in *Contributions to Psychoanalysis, 1921–45* (London: Hogarth Press), 282, 311. Thomas Ogden's revisions of Klein's paranoid-schizoid position are also relevant. See Thomas Ogden, *The Primitive Edge of Experience* (Northvale, NJ: Jason Aronson, 1989), 9–47.

23 Peter Brooks, *Reading for the Plot: Design and Intention in Narrative* (New York: Random House, 1985), 250.

24 Non-addressedness is the word Nouvet uses in her reading of Lyotard's 'Emma', see 233.

PART FOUR

The Echo of
the Horror

10

Conrad's Dionysian elegy

HENRY STATEN

With 'The Horror of the West' Lacoue-Labarthe inscribed his
name in the long list of those who have been caught up in the
spell of Conrad's *Heart of Darkness*. There is intrinsic interest in
seeing the candid reaction to Conrad's tale of a notable intellectual
figure like Lacoue-Labarthe. He does not engage the critical
discourse that for the literary scholar stands guard around the
story, attempting instead to articulate the very essence of *Heart
of Darkness* as 'an event of thought'. What this tale gives us to
think, on Lacoue-Labarthe's account, is the Heideggerian lesson
that technology is the destiny that has seized the West, and that
the West has now imposed this destiny on all of nature, including,
perforce, the colonialized peoples of the world. Moving very
quickly, Lacoue-Labarthe equates *techne* with art, art with the
technological will to power of the West, will to power with the
void or nothingness at the centre of Western subjectivity and this
Heideggerian nothingness with Lacan's *Thing*.

There is a great deal that I find dubious in this account,
beginning with the equation of technology with *techne*, of *techne*,
defined in this sense, with art, and of Kurtz with the artist. But I
will approach this entire complex of issues indirectly, through a
single claim of Lacoue-Labarthe's that condenses all the others: that
there are 'two voices that structure Marlow's narrative: the savage,
undifferentiated clamour and the voice of Kurtz' (116). These two
voices are 'purely and simply, the voice of nature (*physis*) and the
voice of art (*techne*)' (116).

There is a striking conceptual asymmetry here. The notion of the voice of *techne* is a theoretical construction produced by Lacoue-Labarthe's demystifying interpretative apparatus, whereas that of the voice of nature, to the degree that anything in the story supports such a notion, belongs to the most mystified level of Marlow's own account of his experience, his quasi-personification of nature via the association of the jungle with the Africans who inhabit it, especially Kurtz's African mistress.

To Marlow's mystification Lacoue-Labarthe regrettably added another, apparently inspired by Heidegger, against which I am obliged, parenthetically, to register a protest. Lacoue-Labarthe writes that the voice of nature, which echoes loudly within Kurtz,

> . . . is a lament [*plainte*]—and, to tell the truth, more than of the suffering of exploitation and slavery which is nevertheless very present, I am thinking of Benjamin's celebrated phrase: if nature could speak, it would be in order to lament [*se plaindre*] (colonial exploitation being, first and foremost, the exploitation of nature). (116)

We are invited here to think that the true *profundity* of thought sees beyond 'the suffering of exploitation and slavery' – because colonial exploitation is 'first and foremost' the exploitation *not* of masses of human beings but of nature.[1]

Setting aside this surprising claim about the nature of colonialism, it could still be true that, as Lacoue-Labarthe says, the 'event of thought' constituted by *Heart of Darkness* consists in a hearkening to the lament of nature. There are a number of features of the text that point in this direction. However, the voice of nature that is heard, or *as if* heard, in *Heart of Darkness* plays a very different role than the one Lacoue-Labarthe attributes to it.

To begin with, Marlow himself evinces no concern whatever for the lament of nature in Lacoue-Labarthe's sense. Marlow has none of Heidegger's, or our, concern for the 'enframing' of the ecosphere and its reduction to a 'standing reserve';[2] he has the traditional, pre-twentieth-century view of nature as a measureless, inhuman power, one that is either entirely indifferent to human existence or inimical to it. The sense of the vast *indifference* of nature to human incursion is established early in the story in Marlow's description of the French warship that is shelling the coast, shooting 'a tiny projectile' that gives a 'feeble screech' and has no effect at all on the jungle (61–2). The blasting taking place at the Central Station is similarly ineffectual, leaving 'no change on the face of the rock' (64). Later, Marlow attributes a 'vengeful aspect' to the jungle (93), and eventually he personifies it as an incubus who has drawn Kurtz to its 'pitiless breast by the awakening of forgotten and brutal passions' (144).

The only suggestion of a cry of lament from nature will be relayed through human actors, who in no way speak for trans-human nature: the Africans who attack the steamboat, Kurtz's African mistress and the Intended, who will bring together all the tonalities of lament that *for Marlow* constitute the voice of nature in her 'cry of inconceivable triumph and of unspeakable pain' (162). I will show in what follows that this culmination is very precisely motivated by the way in which the entire tale, leading up to this moment, is structured.

The device of the 'frame narrator' has the effect, in *Heart of Darkness*, as in other narratives, notably *The Turn of the Screw*, of a kind of 'phenomenological suspension' of the framed narrative, unhinging it to an indeterminable degree from the 'objective' reality that the narrative evokes and enabling it to represent all the more intensely the subjective experience of the main narrator; hence Marlow's repeated comments that the reality he conveys has a 'nightmare' character and the imaginatively overheated character of his narration. Unlike in *The Turn of the Screw*, however, Conrad's frame continues to make its effect on the framed narrator felt throughout the course of his tale. The frame narrator introduces himself as one member of an audience who does indeed, as Lacoue-Labarthe admits might be the case, interact with Marlow in crucial ways at crucial moments, and *always*, whether he is making himself heard or not, conditions the rhetoric of his tale.

Within the tale he tells, Marlow draws an impermeable boundary between himself and, on the one hand, women, of which the chief examples are his aunt and Kurtz's Intended, and, on the other hand, those men who have no beliefs, no innards and no genuine masculinity. By underlining these exclusions in the telling of his tale, Marlow rhetorically appeals to his listeners' shared sense of this boundary, affirming the solidarity of the masculine community he and they represent. Yet, even though Marlow and his listeners on the Nellie are committed to the same masculine ideals and idea of masculinity, the lines of community that hold Marlow to them are stretched very thin by the way in which, by extending a certain recognition, first, to the Africans, and then to Kurtz, he expands and eventually deforms the categories on which their agreement is based.

Thus, *the telling of the tale*, Marlow's narrated journey to the limit of his experience, is up to a point also the journey of his narration farther and farther away from the shared premises of the narrative contract with his audience. Marlow skilfully and repeatedly appeals to this contract, yet at certain crisis points the tensions between him and his audience break through and break up his narration. Nevertheless, *he always recovers from these moments and recovers the shared masculine standpoint on moral judgement.*

The rift between Marlow and his listeners first shows up when he attributes humanity to the Africans who 'howled and leaped and spun and made horrid faces' (96). When he says this, Marlow appears to anticipate dissent from his listeners, defiantly declaring that only those with sufficient masculinity will be able to share his response to the Africans, and attacking as a 'fool' anyone who is incapable of sharing it. And the dissent indeed comes, in the form of a grunt:

> [W]hat thrilled you was, just the thought of their humanity—like yours. . . Ugly. . . . but if you were man enough you would admit to yourself that there was in you just the faintest trace of a response to the terrible frankness of that noise. . . Let the fool gape and shudder—the man knows and can look on without a wink. . . . Who's that grunting? (96–7)

'The man knows, and can look on without a wink'; this is the same rhetorical-ideological machinery that will later be at work concerning Kurtz's vision and Marlow's relation to this vision. Marlow is here preparing his listeners for what is to come, pressing them in the direction of the more difficult boundary-transgression that will come later. Kurtz has experienced much more than just a 'trace of a response' to the jungle, and Marlow must convince his listeners that Kurtz's final state of being is nevertheless in some way acceptable to their moral standpoint.

In order to achieve this, Marlow defines an alternative type of masculinity to that of his sailor companions, a 'red-eyed devil' type of man whom, he suggests, his fellow sailors ought to recognize as acceptably manly, because this kind of man, like them, is essentially different from the 'flabby', 'weak-eyed' kind of man.

'I've seen the devil of violence, and the devil of greed, and the devil of hot desire; but by all the stars these were strong, lusty, red-eyed devils, that swayed and drove men—men, I tell you. But as I stood on this hillside I foresaw that in the blinding sunshine of that land I would become acquainted with a flabby, pretending, weak-eyed devil of a rapacious and pitiless folly' (65).

'Strong, lusty, red-eyed devils' – 'we are not like that ourselves', the men on the Nellie might feel; 'yet we can see, as men, that there is nothing in this that is essentially unmasculine, that it corresponds to an aspect of that which we accept as "being a man"'. But beyond this, the question Marlow appears implicitly to pose to them is whether the devil of violence, greed and hot desire is not in fact the *core* or *essence* of masculinity, an essence that it is masculine to repress but that in certain circumstances can overpower masculine restraint, and do so precisely out of an authentically masculine impulse.

The appeal of manly group identification that Marlow makes to his listeners, and which must at the crucial moment stretch to include the difficult case of Kurtz, is initially established by opposition with women. Let us read the first appearance of this element of Marlow's rhetoric in his narration, attending in particular to Marlow's tone and what this tone implies. Only twice in his narration will he address his audience directly in such a tone of flustered self-exculpation, and we will see that the two passages, occurring far apart in the narration, are closely linked.

Here is the first passage: 'Then—would you believe it—I tried the women. I, Charlie Marlow, set the women to work—to get a job! Heavens!' (53). Marlow then introduces the figure of his aunt, who gets him the job he wants, and there follows his description of his 'initiation' at the company headquarters. Then he returns once more to his aunt, and this is where the theme of 'we men' as confronters of truth is first announced. Commenting on his aunt's sentimental views of colonialism, Marlow makes his often quoted remarks about how 'out of touch with truth women are', as opposed to 'we men' who live 'contentedly' with the reality of the real (59). These remarks are clearly intended to tighten the threads of group identification between Marlow and his listeners; yet a disturbance in this identification has already appeared in the nervous vehemence of the remarks with which Marlow has first introduced his aunt ('I, Charlie Marlow . . . Heavens!' [53]).

His anxiety is even more evident in the second passage. 'Good Lord! Mustn't a man ever—' (114), Marlow will say, and be unable for some moments to continue his narrative. The significance of this second outburst, which far exceeds that of the first, can only be appreciated by a careful reconstruction of its context. Marlow's remark occurs towards the end of his narration of the attack on the steamboat by the Africans. The Europeans in the Congo are, like the men on the *Nellie*, sitting in the darkness on an anchored boat, immobilized by fog. In the African scene, however, there is complete silence as well as complete darkness: 'not the faintest sound of any kind could be heard' (101). This silence intensifies the value of sound, amplifying its impact on the sensorium: 'About three in the morning some large fish leaped, and the loud splash made me jump as though a gun had been fired' (101). Suddenly, into this floating isolation that the splash of a fish can startle like a gunshot comes a clamour so extravagant and piercing that to Marlow it sounds 'as though the mist itself had screamed' (102). Here is the entire description of this extraordinary sequence of sounds, which occurs at very nearly the precise halfway point of the story:

[A] cry, a very loud cry as of infinite desolation, soared slowly in the opaque air. It ceased. A complaining clamour, modulated in savage discords, filled our ears. The sheer unexpectedness of it made my hair stir under my cap. I don't know how it struck the others: to me it seemed as though the mist itself had screamed, so suddenly and apparently from all sides at once did this tumultuous and mournful uproar arise. It culminated in a hurried outbreak of almost intolerably excessive shrieking . . . (101–2)

Thus is announced the presence of the Africans who a few hours later will mount a desperate 'attempt at repulse' (107) against the steamship.

I count as a single structural unit the stretch of narration from the decision to drop anchor for the night up to the disposal of the body of Marlow's native helmsman. The action for which the stage is set by the anchoring of the boat is not complete until that point; there is quite a conventional coherence of narrative sequence here, from the ominous silence preceding the uproar, through attack and repulse, to the concluding disposal of the dead body. But the effect of this conventional action-adventure sequence is to a considerable degree frustrated by the character of its telling, which is even more digressive and disruptive of chronology than the narration is elsewhere. Between the opening tumult and the attack, there is the long digression on cannibals; between the death of the helmsman and his hasty burial, there is the even longer digression on Kurtz. The coherence of the entire sequence at the level of the telling is, however, secured by a leitmotif that recurs three times after its initial appearance: the motif of the mournful cry of the Africans that shatters the mist-enclosed silence. It is by means of this cry that we return to the main narration after the digression on the cannibal crew (105). Marlow then evokes the cry a second time with unwonted, almost lyrical, eloquence, in his lecture to the pilgrims regarding the 'purely defensive' nature of the attack ('The glimpse of the steamboat had for some reason filled those savages with unrestrained grief. The danger, if any, I expounded, was from our proximity to a great human passion let loose' [107]).

There follows the account of the fighting and of the helmsman's death, and we come almost to the conclusion of the affair; but just before we get there, Marlow evokes for the third time the sorrow of the natives, and it is this evocation that results directly in the major rift between Marlow and his audience that we have been approaching for some pages. The helmsman dies, but for the moment the 'dominant thought' (113) that grips Marlow is that Kurtz must be dead, too, and this thought overwhelms him with grief: 'We are too late; he has vanished . . . I will never hear that chap speak after all—and *my sorrow had a startling extravagance of emotion, even such as I had noticed in the howling sorrow of these savages in the bush. . .*' [italics added]. Here Marlow is interrupted by the response of one of his listeners, to which he responds, 'Why do you sigh in this beastly way, somebody? Absurd? Well, absurd. Good Lord! Mustn't a man ever—Here, give me some tobacco' (114).

We are still within the resonance of that moment when, with Marlow's steamboat floating blind and deaf in the middle of the river, a cry of 'infinite desolation' (102) had shattered the silence. Marlow's response to this cry has dominated his sense of everything that has happened from that point to the death of his helmsman and the disposal of his body. And finally Marlow himself has experienced a moment of what he takes to be the same kind of 'unrestrained grief' (107) as that of the natives – in fact, as he knows in the time of narration, for the same person the natives are mourning.

This is when the second, and far more marked, moment of Marlow's discomfiture before his audience occurs. It is not with respect to the question of Kurtz's unrestraint that the agreement between Marlow and his listeners is most strained; it is with respect to a certain unrestraint of *Marlow's*. 'Good Lord! Mustn't a man ever—'. Marlow is so deeply disturbed by the ridicule of his listener, to whom we apparently should ascribe the 'absurd' that Marlow picks up, that he interrupts his narrative for some moments, and even when he tries to resume it his agitation is extreme. Four more times (for a total of six) he will repeat the offending word, the word that informs him, as he believes, that what he has described – the 'startling extravagance of emotion' that he had suddenly felt, an emotion that echoed the 'howling sorrow' of the Africans in the bush – is for his audience something a man 'mustn't ever'. As before, Marlow takes the offensive, hurling at his listeners the reproach that they are not qualified to judge what (as he had earlier said) 'the man knows' and can look at 'without a wink' (84):

'Absurd!' he cried. 'This is the worst of trying to tell. . . . Here you all are each moored with two good addresses like a hulk with two anchors, a butcher round one corner, a policeman round another, excellent appetites, and temperature normal— hear you—normal from year's end to year's end. And you say, Absurd! Absurd be—exploded! Absurd!' (114).

But already Marlow has begun to hedge. It's not just that he was out there in the jungle where a man sees strange and disturbing things, but, as he has mentioned earlier, that he was not his normal self, he had often 'a little fever' (105); hence his reference to his listeners' 'temperature normal'. And now he very quickly begins to recuperate his agreement with his listeners: 'My dear boys, what can you expect from a man who out of sheer nervousness had just flung overboard a pair of new shoes?' (114). Thus Marlow revises his account, minimizing and even rendering ridiculous the 'extravagance of emotion' that had dominated his entire narration of the encounter with the natives since the moment of that initial cry when 'it seemed the mist itself had screamed'. And in fact he proceeds to transmogrify his moment of weakness into a moment of strength, of manly restraint in the most primitive sense of that restraint as it is learnt from earliest boyhood: 'Now I think of it, it is amazing I did not shed tears. I am, upon the whole, proud of my fortitude' (114).

And now that Marlow has regained his composure, denigrating his moment of emotional extravagance and re-establishing the boundaries by which 'we men' cohere together, we are just around the corner from the corresponding reassertion of the major category by opposition to which manliness is defined. After a few lines on Kurtz, Marlow is suddenly, and as if out of nowhere, reminded of a woman: 'Voices, voices—even the girl herself—now—' (115).

Here occurs the second suspension of his narrative. 'He was silent for a long time' (115).

When he speaks again, he will repeat five times the idea that women are 'out of it'. This repetition suggests that the agitation of Marlow's earlier self-defence has not entirely spent itself. He has confessed to something that, it appears, a man 'mustn't ever', and now, to re-establish his manly credentials, he remembers lying to a woman, as men must do to keep women 'out of it' where they need to be kept.

> 'I laid the ghost of his gifts at least with a lie,' he began suddenly. 'Girl! What? Did I mention a girl? Oh, she is out of it—completely. They—the women I mean—are out of it—should be out of it. We must help them to stay in that beautiful world of their own lest ours gets worse. Oh, she had to be out of it' (115).

What are we to make of that moment in which Marlow's narration sputtered to a stop, in which the categories that constitute his narrative contract with his audience were momentarily ruptured? Marlow dissimulates this moment as a mere aberration, a moment of weakness after which he pulls himself back together. But the fact that it is out of character for Marlow and that he did in fact pull himself together afterwards are merely facts about the fictional psychology of this fictional character. What we are interested in is not this 'psychology', such as it is, but the structural design of the text that generates it as one effect among others. I have just shown how massive and sustained a presence the text of *Heart of*

Darkness allots to the grief-stricken cry of the Africans as well as to Marlow's response to this cry. And as he now moves on to what is an apparently new topic, he is in fact turning his narrative in a direction that will culminate in *another cry*, another extravagantly grief-stricken cry that like the earlier one responds to the loss of Kurtz. This second cry, the cry of Kurtz's Intended, will culminate not only the new thread of his narrative that he now begins, but also *Heart of Darkness* itself.

On the surface of the text, the surface I am surveying, *Heart of Darkness* foregrounds these cries and their associated affect in a striking way, giving them a marked structural privilege. But critics have generally followed Marlow in not making too much of this extravagant, exaggerated emotion, proper to savages and women; they have focused instead on the courageous confrontation with the insight that gives rise to horror – the insight into the abyss of Western corruption, and underneath this, the deeper abyss of human depravity ('all the hearts that beat in the darkness' [151]), and beyond even this, the void of nothingness or The Thing. Such insight is appalling, horror-inducing, but the manlier we are, the more horror we can and should bear. A man who succumbs to grief and starts to shed tears would not be able to face the horror, and women, who do so succumb, must be shielded from it. Hence, Marlow almost weeps at the thought that Kurtz might be dead, but in the end he does not. Instead, he goes to the Intended and makes her cry out with grief, while he himself remains ironic, self-possessed, courageously aware of the horror.

Why does he go to visit the Intended? Marlow is obsessed with the juxtaposition of two images in his mind, that of Kurtz's depravity and that of the perfect purity he sees in the Intended. He feels something like admiration or respect for Kurtz as a 'devil of hot desire'; yet, it is this that makes Kurtz an obscene figure of rapacity from which the Intended must be protected. And in this connection, a certain reticence in regard to the characterization of Kurtz becomes noticeable. One might think that a devil of hot desire would engage, and prominently so, in sexual excesses; but excess of this kind is only delicately hinted at in *Heart of Darkness* by the presence of the dignified, even magnificent, presence of Kurtz's African mistress, and somewhat less delicately by the personification of the jungle as an incubus that had 'seemed to draw [Kurtz] to its pitiless breast by the awakening of forgotten and brutal instincts, by the memory of gratified and monstrous passions' (144). In a Victorian context, however, Kurtz would have been automatically identified as belonging to that category of debauchees and *roués* with which the moral imagination of the period was so occupied; hence, when Marlow tells us that the Intended was 'as translucently pure as a cliff of crystal' (152), the purity in question should be understood as implying more than just innocence of the realities of empire. Kurtz is, for Marlow, a figure of obscene phallic potency in all its aspects, a rapacious prick who knows no boundaries to the indulgence of what Marlow sees as a witch's brew of lust. And yet he feels compelled to come 'deposit the memory' of *this man* with what he imagines to be an utterly pure maid.

In saying this, I am trying to articulate the full force of Marlow's fantasy of Kurtz and his associated fantasy of the Intended, in order to bring to light the complex of forces that is woven into the culminating scene. The entire thing is overheated by Marlow's imagination, and it is necessary to understand what causes this overheating. Marlow is convinced that he must protect the Intended from awareness of Kurtz's defiling maleness, and yet he comes to her house precisely to talk to her about Kurtz, and with an intense consciousness that he is bringing with him, into her presence, that very 'conquering darkness' from whose 'invading and vengeful rush' he will have to protect her (156). Why, then, does he go to see her? Marlow wonders about this himself:

> I had no clear perception of what it was I really wanted. Perhaps it was an impulse of unconscious loyalty or the fulfilment of one of those ironic necessities that lurk in the facts of human existence. I don't know. (155)

But shortly before he makes this remark, it appears that he has told us precisely why he goes to her. Commenting on the portrait of his Intended that Kurtz had left behind, Marlow says:

> She seemed ready to listen without mental reservation, without suspicion, without a thought for herself. I concluded that I would go and give her back her portrait and those letters myself. (155)

This reveals with complete explicitness that what draws him to her, to deposit the monstrous memory of Kurtz with her, is, precisely, her ingenuous, unguarded, feminine susceptibility. Marlow senses this complete receptiveness in his initial response to her portrait, and his intuition is more than fulfilled (in his fantasy of her, at least) by what he finds when he comes into her presence. 'She had a mature capacity for fidelity, for belief, for suffering', (157) he admiringly says, and develops this notion as follows:

> She carried her sorrowful head . . . as though she would say, I—I alone know how to mourn for him as he deserves. . . . I perceived that she was one of those creatures that are not the playthings of Time. For her he had died only yesterday. And by Jove, the impression was so powerful that for me too he seemed to have died only yesterday—nay, this very minute. I saw her and him in the same instant of time—his death and her sorrow—I saw her sorrow in the very moment of his death. (157)

She is, thus, in his fantasy, a pure substance of feminine passivity, of ability to love and suffer and mourn without limit for a man, and to continue to do so beyond his death. What makes this a crucial moment in the narrative is not what it tells us about the Intended (i.e. that she is a strange, rather hysterical and very theatrical person) but what it tells us about Marlow. It is *his* overheated susceptibility that produces this vision, *his* emotional investments and unconscious obsessions that manifest themselves in this way. Someone else might be repelled by the complete vacuity of a self that can give over its life to this particular species of mourning memorialization (think of the grotesque overtones that such figures have in literature, from Mrs Haversham in *Great Expectations* to the title character in Faulkner's 'A Rose for Emily'), but Marlow treats her capacity for mourning as beautiful, noble womanliness, and vibrates with exquisitely tuned sympathy to her note of mourning sorrow, raising it to an even higher level of intensity by overlaying the sorrow in the presence of which he now stands with that which he had witnessed in the jungle.

> . . . the sound of her low voice seemed to have the accompaniment of all the other sounds full of mystery, desolation, and sorrow I had ever heard—the ripple of the river, the soughing of the trees swayed by the wind, the murmurs of the crowds, the faint ring of incomprehensible words cried from afar . . . (159)

> She put out her arms, as if after a retreating figure . . .
> resembling in this gesture another one, tragic also and bedecked
> with powerless charms, stretching bare brown arms over the
> glitter of the infernal stream. . . (160)

By means of that earlier, 'tragic' figure's grief, in turn, Marlow, who
in his calmer moments is struck by how 'pitiless' and 'unmoved'
(127, 129) the jungle really is, had projected his fantasy of universal
mourning onto it:

> She was savage and superb . . . And in the hush that had
> fallen suddenly upon the whole sorrowful land, the immense
> wilderness . . . seemed to look at her, pensive, as though it had
> been looking at the image of its own tenebrous and passionate
> soul. (135–6)

It is passages like these that create the sense picked up by Lacoue-
Labarthe that nature really does lament in *Heart of Darkness*, but
this happens only in Marlow's wishful thinking, which is entirely
preoccupied with a strictly human affect of mourning for a strictly
human death. The desire in question is, evidently, the same one
that is expressed in the convention of pastoral elegy, that nature
itself must mourn the lost one, and *Heart of Darkness* is perhaps
most significant, from a literary standpoint, as a revisionary form
of that genre (and thus as comparable in significance to Baudelaire's
'Une Charogne'). But, as opposed to traditional pastoral, Marlow
indulges in the hyperbole of nature's mourning only as a consciously
figurative attribution, as in the description of Kurtz's African
mistress, or when he says that the Africans' cry of grief sounds 'as
though the mist itself had screamed'.

One's death is one's own most, no one can die it for us, and
one's authenticity lies in confronting this; what goes unmentioned
in *Being and Time* is that just as necessarily as it is I who must die,
it must be *another* who grieves for me, and that, in that childish or
feminine or savage corner of a man where he keeps those tears of
automourning that a man does not shed, he harbours also the need
to have another weep them for him, and to weep them without
measure (perhaps Mrs Heidegger, on whom Mr Heidegger was all
his life so abjectly dependent). Who would be satisfied to go and
leave no tears behind, or to be grieved in moderation? I am speaking

from a strictly masculine point of view; but that is the point of view in evidence in *Heart of Darkness*.

In case there remained any doubt, in the original published version of *Heart of Darkness*, that what draws Marlow to the Intended is the desire to drink deeply of her woman's unlimited capacity to mourn, Conrad revised one phrase to make it clear. As his life wanes on the steamboat headed downriver, Kurtz suddenly asks Marlow to close the shutter through which he can see the jungle. Then: '"Oh, but I will wring your heart yet!" he cried at the invisible wilderness' (148). In the first edition, Conrad had written: 'Oh, but I will make you serve my ends'. In this story so full of wrung hearts – those of the natives in general and the savage mistress in particular, that of the Intended, and, for one moment, that of Marlow – all of them wrung with grief over the real or imagined loss of Kurtz – the replacement phrase is peculiarly fraught with meaning. 'I will wring your heart yet' can mean that Kurtz still intends to make the wilderness serve his ends, by wringing more treasure from its geographical heart; but the ordinary, one might say, 'literal', sense of heart-wringing is the infliction of grief. Marlow says that Kurtz addresses this intention to the wilderness, and the wilderness has no heart to wring, at least not in this sense – but the Intended does. And in the culminating scene of the novel, Marlow, acting as Kurtz's emissary, will indeed wring the Intended's heart with grief, thus in a strange and unexpected modality satisfying Kurtz's final expressed desire or intention.

Marlow's fantasy of course reduces the difference between wringing the heart of the jungle and that of the Intended to the maximal possible degree; we have seen how freely the mourning of the Africans and the women is substituted in Marlow's imagination for that of the jungle. Nothing is more common or banal for the period than these identifications of 'primitives', women, and nature, and to the degree that *Heart of Darkness* trades on these stereotypes and squeezes emotion from them – which is a very large degree indeed – it shows itself to us today as very much of its cultural place and time. Conrad's art is, nevertheless, such that he manages to endow all this with uncommon force, for two reasons. First, that the emotion he depicts, with its two bloodcurdling cries in the middle and at the end of the tale, is so startling that it goes beyond the boundaries of cliché, throwing Marlow's narrative into that register of dream or nightmare that has haunted the imagination of so many readers. And, second, that all this, which even in its extravagance could still be felt as lurid melodrama if presented 'straight', comes wrapped in irony that itself comes wrapped in irony.

The first kind of irony is Marlow's. He wants to believe that the Intended proffers an absolute, eternal, mourning recognition of Kurtz himself, in a pure and spiritual key. He basks in this affect of hers as though it offered some refuge from or compensation for the horror of the void that men must live with – as though she were delegated to carry through the act of mourning that in his own case had been cut short on the steamboat. At the same time, however, he remains detached, coldly and somewhat contemptuously critical of the woman's weakness, her incapacity to confront the confounded truths that men have always lived with. Marlow's narrative thus remains double-voiced: he reports *now* how he was carried away *then* by her emotion, in language that becomes rhapsodic, but he keeps touch throughout with his man's awareness of the darkness of which she remains innocent. At the level of his ironic detachment, which, the way he tells it, triumphs in the end, Marlow retains his narrative bond with his listeners on the *Nellie*, according to the protocols of masculine identification I identified earlier. Marlow thus reports telling the Intended that Kurtz's last words were her name, but on a parallel track he stresses his own uncompromising consciousness of what these words really were. 'I was on the point of crying at her, "Don't you hear them?"' (161). Thus the sublimities of the Intended, her faith and her purity and her eternal loyalty (as Marlow imagines) to the memory of Kurtz, move Marlow to his depths; he gets all the affect of mourning out of them that he can handle and yet he also maintains his masculine detachment, portraying her faith as illusory in view of the ghostly reality that he feels to be present in her drawing room, and of which she cannot be made conscious.

The second irony is more subtle, and Marlow does not control it, as, quite possibly, neither did Conrad. The force of this irony radiates out from one immensely over-determined point, that of the final cry, the cry that is both 'exulting' and 'terrible', conveying both 'inconceivable triumph' and 'unspeakable pain', which erupts when Marlow tells the Intended that Kurtz's last words were her name. The exultation and the triumph are, of course, based on a misconception, and immediately after reporting how terrible the cry is and how it made his heart stop, Marlow introduces his note of contemptuous irony once again:

> 'I knew it—I was sure!'. . . She knew. She was sure. I heard her weeping . . . It seemed to me that the house would collapse before I could escape, that the heavens would fall upon my head. But nothing happened. The heavens do not fall for such a trifle. (162)

In this way, Marlow attempts to contain even the force of this cry by the same strategy of detachment based on superior, masculine knowledge. But the strains on this strategy are now such that we might question its success. The 'trifle' to which Marlow refers is the fact that he has lied to her; but earlier he had said that lies are what he most hates, detests and cannot bear because 'there is a taint of death, a flavour of mortality, in lies' and lying makes him 'miserable and sick like biting something rotten would do' (82). Yet now that he has actually tasted this flavour of putrescence by lying to the Intended, now that he has 'breathed dead hippo' (117) – as he puts it earlier, when he sets up an excuse for the lie he knows he is going to confess – he wants to dismiss the entire affair as nothing but a trifle, another of those startling, feminine, extravagances of emotion that come over Marlow when he hears these cries of mourning, but which really do not mean anything.

Why the woman feels triumph as well as pain is clear: Kurtz is dead, but she believes (falsely, according to Marlow, but things are not so simple) that she stood in sole possession of his being at the moment of his death. But why does she express these feelings with such a bloodcurdling scream? Of the elements of *Heart of Darkness* that depart from realism, this is perhaps the most extreme; whatever they might do in reality, bourgeois women in realist novels simply do not act this way. Her cry belongs to a different register of textuality than that defined by the realist novel, a register close to that of Nietzsche's *Birth of Tragedy*. Marlow's description of the cry so closely parallels Nietzsche's description of the Dionysian cry that one finds it hard not to suspect that Conrad had encountered it somehow, perhaps from a secondary source.[3] The Dionysian experience, Nietzsche says, is the 'phenomenon that pain begets joy, that ecstasy may wring sounds of agony from us. At the very climax of joy there sounds a cry of horror or a yearning lamentation for an irretrievable loss';[4] here, 'nature itself seems to reveal a sentimental trait; it is as if she were heaving a sigh at her dismemberment into individuals'.[5] This is the same kind of metaphysical pastoral as the one I have been tracing in *Heart of Darkness*. Marlow's initial reaction to the cry, before he corrects it with his irony, treats it as though for him it had Dionysian force, a force that he barely manages to contain. The level of his narrative that moves along this emotionally and imaginatively overheated track, apparently corresponding to what he felt at the time of the experience, is overlaid with the critical coolness of his present perspective, the one that bonds him to his listeners. But within the frame of his irony, it remains starkly visible in all its original force, and if it does not overwhelm that containing irony, it rises all the way to its brim.

In Marlow's phantasmagoria of loathing and desire, the Intended, on the basis of the latter's gesture of mourning that the Intended repeats, is identified with Kurtz's African mistress, who is herself identified with the wilderness. The Intended, whom one might think to be as far from 'nature' as is culturally feasible, thus, bizarrely, belongs to a series of identifications that lead back to the African wilderness, itself personified as a woman – both mother and lover, much like Baudelaire's metamorphosing 'vampire' – when Marlow says that it had 'seemed to draw [Kurtz] to its pitiless breast' (144). Thus, Marlow can find the mourning voice of nature in a woman's cry; but, by the same token, woman evokes the 'pitiless breast' that takes the male back into its matrix of form-creation and form-dissolution, the matrix of primordial mud with its nauseating foulness of corruption that haunted Marlow throughout his time in Africa, and which, he says, he can *still smell* now, as he tells his story:

> . . . in and out of rivers, streams of death in life, whose banks were rotting into mud, whose waters, thickened into slime. (62)
>
> The smell of mud, of primeval mud by Jove, was in my nostrils. (81)
>
> . . . a provision of hippo-meat. . . went rotten and made the mystery of the wilderness stink in my nostrils. *Phoo! I can sniff it now.* (94; italics added)
>
> I felt an intolerable weight oppressing my breast, the smell of the damp earth, the unseen presence of victorious corruption. (138)

All these references converge on the taste and smell of lying – that taste that is 'like biting something rotten' (82), that smell that he can 'sniff now' as he tells his tale – and which, since women must be lied to, a man must endure in their presence. Everything in the logic of his tale implies that it must have smelled very bad indeed at the end of the scene in the drawing room of the Intended; but if Conrad had written *that*, the final decent veil of mystification would have been lifted from the tale.

Thus there is, indeed, in a sense, as Lacoue-Labarthe claims, a lament of nature in *Heart of Darkness*: in the sense that in the psychic soup of misogyny and gynophobia of Marlow's narrative, woman is nature, or nature is a woman, a Bacchic woman, the kind that is most threatening to the ethical individuality of the male ('the perfect woman tears to pieces', says Nietzsche[6]). No wonder Marlow stays away from women, as a rule. The Intended mourns Kurtz, but only because, in the dream-logic of this text, she *owns* him, lock, stock and barrel, in a way that transcends the mere illusion of ownership to which Marlow, in his direct appeal to his listeners on the *Nellie*, attempts to relegate her triumph.

The ideas behind Marlow's fantasy of the voice of nature are, it should now be clear, too traditional and conventional for *Heart of Darkness* to constitute an 'event of thought'. It is, nevertheless, a great work of art in its ironic layering of elegiac and Dionysian affects, which goes to show that literature does not need to be rich in thought to be great literature (I am reminded of Eliot's remark that Tennyson – another supreme elegist – was such a great poet because he had no ideas). In addition, it remains true that, as even Achebe came to recognize, *Heart of Darkness* has ethico-political value as an early denunciation of imperialism.

But it must also be said, in defence of Conrad, that the archetypally gynophobic themes that he strikes are so deeply rooted in the Western tradition that they have proven immensely difficult for writers to master – when they have at least attempted to struggle with them and not, like Heidegger, sublimely risen above such things. Lacan, to his credit, was far from such a pretence. Lacoue-Labarthe glossed 'the horror' in *Heart of Darkness* as the Thing in Lacan and claimed that this was 'another name for being, that is, for nothingness, the 'nothingness of being' [*le rien d'étant*], which Lacan borrows from Heidegger' (117). But, while it is true that Lacan learnt a good deal from Heidegger, his understanding of the nothingness, the Horror

that the Thing represents has little in common with Heidegger's
nothingness. This can be shown from that very Seminar 7 to which
Lacoue-Labarthe refers us. Using a troubadour poem as his text,
Lacan here defines the nothingness of the Thing in a way that takes
us far from Heidegger, but not so distant from the ending of *Heart
of Darkness*.(Let us recall that in this, as in *Heart of Darkness*, we
never leave the realm of male fantasy.)

> The idealized woman, the Lady, who is in a position of the Other
> and of the object, finds herself suddenly and brutally positing,
> in a place knowingly constructed out of the most refined of
> signifiers, the emptiness of a thing in all its crudity, a thing that
> reveals itself in its nudity to be the thing, her thing, the one that
> is to be found at her heart in its cruel emptiness.[7]
>   . . . at the extreme point of his invocation to the signifier, she
> warns the poet of the form she may take as signifier. I am, she
> tells him, nothing more than the emptiness to be found in my
> own internal cesspit, not to say anything worse. Just blow in that
> for a while and see if your sublimation holds up.[8]

Notes

Much of the first third of this essay (203–210) is a substantially
modified version of Chapter 6 of my book, *Eros in Mourning*
(Baltimore, MD: Johns Hopkins University Press, 1995). I am
grateful to Johns Hopkins Press for permission to reprint this
material.

1 I am aware that Lacoue-Labarthe was severely and protractedly
   critical of Heidegger's involvement with the Nazis, but this is
   reminiscent of Heidegger's notorious remark that the transformation
   of agriculture as a 'motorized food industry' is in essence the same
   as the killings in the extermination camps. No doubt what both
   Heidegger and Lacoue-Labarthe say is true, at a certain level of
   analysis, but it is not a level that can be approached without great
   ethical tact.

2 See Heidegger, 'The Question Concerning Technology', in *The
   Question Concerning Technology and Other Essays*, trans. William
   Lovitt (New York: Harper Colophon, 1977).

3 The English translation of *The Birth of Tragedy* was not published until 1909, the French in 1900, and Conrad did not read German well. See George Butte, 'What Silenus Knew: Conrad's Uneasy Debt to Nietzsche', *Comparative Literature* 41.2 (1989): 155–68.

4 Friedrich Nietzsche, *The Birth of Tragedy and The Case of Wagner*, trans. Walter Kaufmann (New York: Vintage Books, 1967), 40.

5 Friedrich Nietzsche, *Birth of Tragedy*, 104.

6 Friedrich Nietzsche, *Ecce Homo*, trans. Walter Kaufmann (New York: Vintage Books, 1968), 266.

7 Jacques Lacan, *The Seminar of Jacques Lacan: Book VII. The Ethics of Psychoanalysis 1959–60*, trans. Dennis Porter (New York: Norton, 1997), 163.

8 Lacan, *Ethics of Psychoanalysis*, 215.

11

Sounding the hollow heart of the West: X-rays and the *technique de la mort*[1]

MARTINE HENNARD DUTHEIL DE LA ROCHÈRE

*Je me demandais, je me demande encore en
quelle langue, sinon celle des morts,
cela l'avait-il traversé et s'était-il écrit.*

PHILIPPE LACOUE-LABARTHE, *Phrase*

Just as Philippe Lacoue-Labarthe, Jacques Derrida and Jean-Luc Nancy shared 'so many common paths'[2] in spite of the irreducible singularity or differences of their work, as Derrida immediately hastens to add in his introduction to *Typography* (1989), one cannot fail to notice the 'singular proximity' of Joseph Conrad's and Philippe Lacoue-Labarthe's writings on the darkness that – they both sensed – lies at the heart of Western 'civilization', understood as the myth through which the West has constituted itself. In 'The Horror of the West', Lacoue-Labarthe justifies his admiration for *Heart of Darkness* as one of the greatest texts of Western literature on the grounds of its *'mythical* power' and, indissociably, on 'what constitutes it as an *event of thought'* (112). He points out that it is impossible to separate them, because

> the myth of the West, which this narrative [*récit*] recapitulates (but only in order to signify that the West is a myth), *is*, literally, the thought of the West, is that which the West 'narrates' [*raconte*] about what it must necessarily think of itself, namely. . .that the West is the *horror* (112).

While keeping in mind the need to resist easy assimilations, I wish to suggest that Lacoue-Labarthe's reflections on the *technique de la mort* (119) (i.e. both the technology of death and death's mechanism, technique or *techne* – craft, art, practice) that he sees at work in *Heart of Darkness*, can be productively put in relation with Conrad's figuration of the hollow heart of Western man by means of the newly discovered X-ray technology. To be sure, Conrad's critique of the monstrous lie underlying the colonial machinery must be distinguished from Lacoue-Labarthe's take on *techne* as a response to Heidegger's legacy in the aftermath of the Holocaust.[3] And yet, despite their many differences, they share a common recognition of writing as a mode of thinking through the role of *techne* that cuts across traditional boundaries between poetic and philosophic inquiry. In Derrida's words, they both show that 'the experience of thought is also a poetic experience'.[4]

Specifically, they see the *tale* as a privileged form through which this experience can be articulated. While the anonymous narrator of Conrad's novella famously stresses the unique nature of Marlow's story as distinct from other sailors' yarns, because it alone has the ability to illuminate the darkness as an effect of refracted light, the word *tale* significantly appears untranslated in Lacoue-Labarthe's 1996 paper on *Heart of Darkness*.[5] 'The Horror of the West' opens with the philosopher's emotional and intellectual shock provoked by David Warrilow telling 'Conrad's *tale*' (111) in a theatrical representation, or rather a reading. The *tale*, which retains both senses of *histoire* and *récit*, *énoncé* and *énonciation*, *histoire vécue* and *conte* (fairy tale, fiction, lie) in English, becomes by virtue of its semantic ambiguity and suggestiveness a 'story to think with', as I have tried to show elsewhere.[6] Conrad's framing of the *tale* further contributes to keeping its enigmatic and paradoxical quality through complex structuring devices and 'a risky, problematic style',[7] to borrow Lacoue-Labarthe's and Nancy's distinction between philosophical thought and totalizing/totalitarian myth. The narrative indeed centres on, imitates/mimics but also undoes the rhetoric of myth analysed in this important essay, and confronts the horror that Kurtz both represents and utters, albeit in the form of a paradox:

> a truth too difficult to enunciate directly, too heavy or too painful—above all, too obscure. For Conrad, it is, of course, obscurity itself: the darkness, the horror. And it is this truth, the truth of the West, to which he seeks to bear witness in such a complex way (113–14).

Tellingly, the evidence of the truth value of Conrad's *tale* appears to Lacoue-Labarthe as an effect of Warrilow's voice and memorable performance, possibly because it re-inscribes human presence and physical suffering (denied, disavowed or ignored by Heidegger) at the core of the theatrical experience which, as Lacoue-Labarthe recognized, is also an experience of thought. Its interpellative force is heightened by the great actor's fragile but intense and compelling presence on the brink of death, in an uncanny re-enactment of Marlow's efforts to come to terms with Kurtz's last words. And yet the staying or haunting power of Conrad's *Heart of Darkness* as a tale that circulates in the fiction and outside it, passing between seamen, actors, philosophers and critics, fosters the *desistance* that Derrida, borrowing it from Lacoue-Labarthe, uses to characterize what brought them together and set them apart.[8] *Desistance*, as that which is both shared and unique about each of them, becomes a precondition for dialogue, because Conrad's text, and Lacoue-Labarthe's response to it, *resonates* differently in each of us, and every time we return to it (now with Lacoue-Labarthe's voice echoing in ours). In this sense, Lacoue-Labarthe's deliberately experimental reading of *Heart of Darkness* enacts a *disarticulation*, to cite Derrida again, that 'traces out merely the *silhouette* of a unity, and more of a rhythm [or a shared insight] than an organic configuration' (italics mine).[9]

Bearing this *desistance* or *disarticulation* in mind, *Heart of Darkness* explores the idea of a journey that reconfigures geography as anatomy, and whose body politics can be productively examined in light of Lacoue-Labarthe's metaphysical/political reading of Kurtz's 'absence of any proper being' (116). The imagery of physical hollowness in Conrad's text thematizes and enacts the disclosure of a fundamental absence of essence, or human substance, in Kurtz's demented, dematerialized and yet all too powerful voice. In turn (and by contrast), it is through Warrilow's memorable (re)telling of the story in a voice marked by terminal illness that Lacoue-Labarthe realizes most fully the dehumanization of Western man articulated by Conrad's text through its system of mediated narratives: 'Warrilow's exhausted voice, in its sovereign *detachment*, prompted an emotion of thought which I daresay remains, to this day, incomparable' (111). Indirection, mediation and recitation (in the interplay of speech and writing, live performance and retrospective reflection/meditation, story and commentary) thus become the very means through which the emotional truth of *fabulation* can be communicated, shared and variously engaged with.

Translation represents yet another modality of transmission, dialogue and response, and from the very beginning, in a to-and-fro movement between English and French. The occasion of Lacoue-Labarthe's piece is the (Irish-born) British actor's memorable reciting of *Heart of Darkness* in translation, which the French thinker engages with in the same language, except for the word *tale* that remains – as remainder of the translating process, and reminder of the original text – in English; in turn, the piece is translated into English by Nidesh Lawtoo and Hannes Opelz for this volume, thereby responding to the intellectual and ethical imperative of pursuing the dialogue with Conrad and Lacoue-Labarthe, the novelist and the thinker, together. Translation is not only an effective means to counter the horror/drama of disappearance by contributing to the *afterlife* of Lacoue-Labarthe's important work on the mutually illuminating interplay of literature and philosophy. It also stresses the role of cross-linguistic and intercultural exchange as fundamental to creative thought, keeping in mind that English was Conrad's third or fourth language. Translating across languages, cultures, discourses and disciplines thus becomes an appropriate way of paying tribute to Conrad and Lacoue-Labarthe as writers working across boundaries and testing limits.

In this chapter, I try to relate Lacoue-Labarthe's critique of *techne* with Conrad's representation of colonial figures as hollowed out bodies reminiscent of X-ray images. My argument is that the newly discovered technology serves to capture/symbolize the inhumanity of Western man in *Heart of Darkness* that Lacoue-Labarthe identifies as 'the horror'. Linking Lacoue-Labarthe's reflections on *techne* and the technology of X-rays that arguably informs Conrad's figuration of the state of Western man at the turn of the century, opens up the deeply Lacoue-Labartian question of the possibility (or impossibility) of revelation. Specifically, Lacoue-Labarthe seems to imply that *Heart of Darkness* reveals the 'essence' or 'truth' of the West. The *techne* of X-rays that symbolizes Western technological progress and alleged superiority ironically gives access to its internal hollowness or lack of substance (or proper being). And yet, what is revealed is simply a mimetic refraction of the 'truth' hidden inside (luckily, luckily, says Marlow).[10] Against the totalizing myth of a triumphant science, or political/religious ideology, or even ultimate meaning, the novelist and the thinker propose a mode of attention to what is intuited indirectly through an image, a turn of phrase, a tone of voice, the complaint of nature and an open form of writing that invites dialogue.

Body politics and the heart of the matter

Conrad's anatomy of empire draws on the familiar land-as-body analogy to represent the African landscape as an organic and feminized space penetrated by force and destroyed by those who pretend to cure it of its ills.[11] Several critics have observed that the trope functions in the production of Manichean allegories that legitimized Western power, control and possession of foreign lands, but it is now generally admitted that Conrad also uses it against itself. My contention is that the figuration of Africa in terms of body is part of a complex strategy through which Conrad articulates and enacts his critique of colonial binaries and hierarchies. A careful examination of the 'body politics' of *Heart of Darkness*, especially when read in the company of Lacoue-Labarthe, refutes accusations of racism and sexism put forward in some classic critical accounts of Conrad's novella.[12]

The widespread use of the land-as-body analogy represented as an opening up of the supposedly Dark Continent by European forces, notoriously led to the production of feminized and racialized images of Africa in the Victorian period to legitimize imperialist violence. Influenced by the heritage of the fear of the feminine and inflected towards imperialist concerns when projected upon the colonial context, these images combined the loathing of the female link to nature with anxieties about the degenerative influence attributed to foreign lands. However, instead of naturalizing colonial domination through the conventional practice of feminizing Africa, the descriptions of the jungle in *Heart of Darkness* expose the violence of the invasion, rule and exploitation of foreign lands by European forces. Quoting Benjamin, Lacoue-Labarthe observes: 'if nature could speak, it would be in order to lament [*se plaindre*] (colonial exploitation being, first and foremost, the exploitation of nature)' (116). He identifies the 'clamour' of the Africans expressing the profound sadness and pain of exploitation and slavery with the lamenting voice of nature, as opposed to the Western 'civilized' voice of *techne*. Although this conflation could be seen as problematic, the central image of a journey to the beating heart of Africa alters the significance of the trope since the heart, however inscrutable, is displaced onto the space of the jungle and its inhabitants, and seen as the site of a humanness (and an ability to feel) that Western man has lost in the colonial venture. Lacoue-Labarthe observes that *Heart of Darkness* is built on the striking contrast between images of an animated, suffering nature and its disembodied, objectified European invaders, Kurtz first and foremost among them: Lacoue-Labarthe's account of Kurtz as a hollow figure, a man without qualities (after Musil) who lacks proper being. Kurtz is presented 'as being *nothing himself*'; or as being '*no one* [personne]' (116). His eloquence is systematically linked to the 'barren darkness of his heart', to his being 'hollow at the core', to the void that is within him or, more exactly, the void that he 'is'. This is why he is only 'a voice' (116). In this sense, Kurtz represents *techne* as the gift of speech (or art) divorced from being and body, and bent on destruction. What he ultimately expresses is therefore the recognition of his own horror; he is a mere *figure*, which carries for Lacoue-Labarthe the implications of hollowness and brutal will to power. He is *nobody*, hardly a body any more, but the mere incarnation of a monstrous idea. By contrast, the African jungle is seen as a feminized and suffering being endowed with a will of its own. The theatrical framing through which Marlow's tale is told and the paradoxical truth that it communicates confirms the importance of the physical dramatization of its paradoxical message (a truth that can only be sensed, and uttered, indirectly), let alone the (moral, political) imperative to transmit it in the recognition that 'To say that the horror is "him"'—Kurtz—is to say that the horror is *us*' (117). Because it reveals that 'it is its own horror that the West seeks to dispel [*faire disparaître*]' (119).

As the title of Conrad's novel intimates, when read in light of Lacoue-Labarthe's essay, the actual source of horror lies within the heart of Western man symbolized by Kurtz. Although the 'mythomaniac' Marlow reproduces the fraught association of landscape and (feminized) body, he foregrounds the sinister aspects of the analogy when he describes the ravaging of Africa. The impact of colonial exploitation on the natural environment is seen as a ruthlessly draining of its life force, the Europeans bleeding the land dry. Before embarking on his inland journey, Marlow witnesses the extent of the destruction when he reaches the Company's Station. Littered with 'pieces of decaying machinery' (63–4) and 'rusty rails' (64), the Station is represented as a junkyard for the grotesque and useless symbols of Western technological advancement. In Lacoue-Labarthian terms, *techne* is here centrally associated with the horror, destruction and inhumanity of the colonial enterprise, causing the lament of the land and its inhabitants. Marlow describes the carving up of the land, ransacked merely as an assertion of Western control and masculine mastery over nature. Walking through this wasteland, Marlow avoids 'a vast artificial hole' (65) and nearly falls into 'a very narrow ravine, almost no more than a scar in the hillside' (65) in which 'a lot of imported drainage-pipes' (65) have been dumped. Read in the light of the land-as-body analogy, this description symbolically evokes the rape of the African land by the European invaders. The question of gender thus constitutes an important supplement to Lacoue-Labarthe's reading of the exploitation of nature via *techne*.

The figuration of the African land as body is not only used to stigmatize the brutality of colonial invasion, but also to question the oppositional logic informing colonial discourse. During his upriver journey, Marlow represents the surrounding landscape as a space that resists and undoes conventional boundaries. The image of a journey within an embodied landscape collapses the distinction not only between inner and outer space, but also between (masculine, European) self and (feminine, African) other. This could be put in relation with Lacoue-Labarthe's claim that two voices structure the tale, in counterpoint with each other: 'the indistinct "clamour" of the savages (the chorus) and that, obviously [*bien entendu*], of Kurtz' (114). By reconfiguring geography as anatomy, Conrad suggests that what was initially perceived as a radically alien space defies and unsettles the binary oppositions and hierarchies underlying colonial rhetoric and the long tradition of Western thought that Lacoue-Labarthe himself draws on (including the opposition of *physis* and *techne*, West and 'other', civilization and savagery, etc.). By both redeploying and subverting one of its central tropes, Conrad articulates a critique of the language of distinction and exclusion by which the European subject has sought to maintain relations of power, and more generally made sense of himself and the surrounding world. The appeal to music (voice, sound, song) in Lacoue-Labarthe's reading may be an attempt to move beyond these oppositions, since the opposition between inside and outside breaks down when he describes Kurtz's body as a hollow cavity (almost a musical instrument) through which the voice of the jungle resonates.

Marlow represents the jungle as breathing and as resonating with the heart's rhythmic pulsing of blood into the body. The narrator mentions 'the tremor of far-off drums' (70) at the beginning of the journey, and later the metaphor of the 'throb of drums' (144) suggests his greater proximity to the heart. But Marlow's anticlimactic meeting with Kurtz at the Central Station ends in the recognition of the opacity of the heart 'as the site where discourse meets its limit'.[13] Kurtz, Marlow's dark double, is accordingly described as a man whose eloquence hides 'the barren darkness of his heart' (147), although 'his was an impenetrable darkness' (149) which confounds understanding, like that of the jungle itself. The conflation of inner and outer space is again acknowledged retrospectively, when Marlow compares or confuses the rhythmic beating of the 'savage' drums with a human heartbeat, possibly his own. One of Marlow's most vivid memories, which keeps haunting him after his return to Europe, reveals the disturbing presence of the 'other' within the self: 'the beat of the drum, regular and muffled [was] like the beating of a heart – the heart of a conquering darkness' (155–6). By collapsing common distinctions between body and space, self and other, the narrator recognizes the presence of uncanny similarity at the heart of difference. Although short-lived, this confusion evidences a destabilization of the essentialist, racist and sexist base of colonial discourse deriving from logocentric philosophy.

But the true originality of the writer's figuration of the inhumanity of the colonial venture lies in images of the empty body probably inspired by the recent discovery of X-rays, whereby the agents of empire are emptied of their physical substance and reduced to insubstantial shadows. Despite Marlow's resorting to clichés in his descriptions of the jungle, he simultaneously sees it as a site of resistance against appropriation and possession as an embodied space that reasserts life over colonial and masculine mastery. In deliberate contrast to the indifferent or cynical colonizers, the personified jungle displays a whole range of attitudes, emotions and feelings, captured in the idea of the 'heart' of the land. Marlow's representation of a feminized landscape thus reworks traditional associations of the feminine with organic life and the abject, as well as with the realm of feelings and emotions. But it is interesting to note that, *pace* Achebe, Conrad's Africa does not serve as a foil to a celebration of white masculine values (intellect, reason, self-control, progress, science, civilization, etc.), except on a very superficial level. Rather, through his treatment of male bodies as lifeless or hollow set in strong contrast with the living body of Africa, Conrad expresses the dehumanization of Western man, the vacuity of colonial rhetoric and the destructive violence of the imperial age. *Heart of Darkness* notoriously revolves around the darkness and possible absence of a heart, on a literal, symbolic and even textual level, because it resonates with (and reveals?) what Lacoue-Labarthe aptly calls a 'hollow myth' (118). Marlow's journey to the heart of Africa brings no knowledge and no certainties other than the recognition of the 'heartlessness' of Western man revealed in the colonial context, as opposed to the beating and inscrutable heart of the jungle and, by extension, of the African woman.

Seeing through colonialism

In counterpoint to representations of a suffering and feminized nature, Marlow's X-ray vision of hollow colonial officials and 'shadow' men whose bone structure alone is visible, reflects the impact of breakthrough developments in science on the novel. Seizing on the imaginative possibilities opened up by the discovery of X-rays, Conrad makes it an apt metaphor for Marlow's ability to 'see through' the civilizing mission and its cynical representatives. The innovative X-ray imagery reveals the vacuity of colonial discourse and expresses a profound anxiety at the loss of the very foundation of ideas of humanity, civilization, technology and progress on which the myth of Western superiority and civilizing mission are founded. In this sense, *techne* functions as a *pharmakon*, both poison and cure, since it diagnoses the cause of the disease affecting the colonial machinery as symptomatic of Western ideology.

Conrad's sense of the hollowness of the colonial myth is best exemplified in images of insubstantial or reified bodies, whether of European officials or of the Africans subjected to their bloodthirsty rule. This new mode of visualizing the body, reduced to spectral figure or animated skeleton, reflects the impact of scientific innovation on the novella. The so-called new science, which included the groundbreaking discovery of X-rays by Wilhelm Conrad Röntgen in December 1895, resulted in new ways of perceiving and representing the human body. Marlow's descriptions of human beings as spectral presences and of the inner body as a dark, empty space in which only the bones are visible foreshadow Lacoue-Labarthe's philosophical insight into the void of the modern subject. As Lisa Cartwright has argued, X-rays contributed to 'the emergence of a distinctly modernist mode of representation in Western scientific and public culture'.[14] In this sense, the X-ray vision is not only a scientific technology but also an artistic *techne* which can be read in Lacoue-Labarthian terms as an extension of the Greek problematic of art based on a mimesis which is not simply reproductive (art as a degraded copy of the real) but as the condition of a creative form of re-*production* (what Lacoue-Labarthe also calls 'general mimesis').[15]

In making the interior of the live body visible for the first time in history, the invention of the X-ray apparatus had a tremendous impact not only on medicine but also on Western culture as a whole. Not surprisingly, artists of all kinds pondered the implications of the new technology in their work: 'From pulp fiction to the fine arts, writers, artists, and movie-makers played exuberantly with the idea of seeing through bodies with invisible rays, of looking for secrets beneath the surface'.[16] Lacoue-Labarthe's claim that the horror, and the horror of the *technique de la mort*, is something essential to the West is supported by the emergence of the new visual technology in European culture at the turn of the century, but also complicates it. Just as Lacoue-Labarthe and Nancy sought to identify the logic behind the 'Nazi myth' as a historically and ideologically grounded phenomenon as well as more abstract system that might reappear in another place, time and culture (as they state in the last paragraph), the horror underlying Western 'civilization' is both specific and representative.

The hollow body: Kurtz, Marlow and co.

Conrad's striking 'iconography of black and white'[17] in *Heart of Darkness* has already been much commented on. We can nevertheless consider it anew by combining Lacoue-Labarthe's association of *techne* with the horror of the West and the imagery of early X-rays in Marlow's description of men lacking human presence and substance, thereby putting them outside the pale of humanity.[18] Marlow's descriptions of Africans as shadowy figures, vague shapes and insubstantial forms have been read as providing ample textual evidence of the dehumanizing rhetoric of racist discourse. But Marlow makes it clear that the ghostliness of Africans results from the brutality and violence of the colonial system. When he gets closer to the victims of exploitation, as in the scene of the chain gang, their bone structure becomes apparent. The narrator thus describes six African men through the marks of exploitation on their bodies, which makes their 'ribs' and 'joints' visible as in an X-ray picture: 'I could see every rib, the joints of their limbs were like knots in a rope' (64).

In the scene that follows, Marlow again expresses his horror as he witnesses the ravages of disease and starvation which have reduced men to 'moribund shapes' (66), 'black bones' (66) and 'bundles of acute angles' (67). Marlow contrasts the dehumanization of the African work force through overwork and starvation to the obscene hunger for ivory, money and power of the White traders and administrators. But whether consumed by their insatiable greed, or emptied of their living substance and left to die through hunger and hard labour, human beings across the racial divide are reduced to their skeletal structure. In the case of colonial officials, Marlow's X-ray vision sees beyond appearances to gain access to the inner self, only to find out that the body is no more than a bag of bones surrounded with dark shadows, and disclose the horrific absence (or inscrutable darkness) of the heart. Instead of the rich, multi-layered thickness and many-coloured tissues disclosed by traditional anatomy, Marlow's exploration of the human body reveals a baffling obscurity.

Conrad's critique of the colonial system is most clearly articulated in the description of White traders and administrators who are compared to puppets, dummies and paper-cut illustrations. The most despicable colonial officials are 'flabby' (65) and boneless – that is, devoid of the 'backbone' possessed by Conrad's more recognizably human characters. At the head of this fantastic procession of grotesque colonial types is Kurtz, whose distinction is suggested in part by his boniness. When Marlow meets Kurtz, he describes him as a strangely animated skeleton:

I saw the thin arm extended commandingly, the lower jaw moving, the eyes of that apparition shining darkly far in its bony head that nodded with grotesque jerks...I could see the cage of his ribs all astir, the bones of his arm waving. It was as though an animated image of death carved out of old ivory had been shaking its hand with menaces at a motionless crowd of men made of dark and glittering bronze. (134)

As in the images of the skeletal system provided by the X-ray machine, Kurtz's body is shed of its flesh and blood materiality and reduced to a gesticulating assemblage of bones. Kurtz's body has become consubstantial with his obsession – the acquisition of ivory. Part of the disturbing effect of the scene results from Kurtz's embodiment of the idea of 'death-in-life' which was an essential aspect of the fascination over X-rays, shed of its soft tissues and organs, including the heart. Skeletons, which could only be seen after death before Röntgen's invention, traditionally symbolized death. Visualizing them in live bodies complicated the significance of this age-old symbol, although X-ray images remained a powerful *memento mori* which enables Conrad to reactivate and renew the old *danse macabre topos* in his depiction of 'the merry dance of death and trade' (62). Read from a contemporary perspective, however, it also disquietingly anticipates the *technique de la mort* employed by the Nazis during the Holocaust, which Kurtz, who would have made a good leader for an extremist party as Marlow acutely observes, symbolizes. Rendering the body visible as pure materiality (bones) seems to gesture towards the possibility of treating human bodies as materials, or undifferentiated spectral presences that foreshadow their own disappearance. This is in a way what even Heidegger intimates when he associates the Holocaust with mechanical/technical forms of exploitation.[19]

As Lacoue-Labarthe observes, Marlow represents Kurtz as a chamber of echoes, a resounding skull which reveals his 'hollow[ness] at the core' (131). After their meeting, Kurtz remains a creature of words, a disembodied voice that keeps haunting him. Marlow himself is less substantial than he (or we) may think, hinting at a contamination that implicates the reader himself (or herself). Besides Marlow's fascination for and resemblance to Kurtz, the storyteller is also a creature of words. Unravelling his enigmatic tale in the deepening obscurity, so that it 'seemed to shape itself without human lips' (83), Marlow and his companions are not unlike the sightless, whispering empty men of Eliot's poem. The parallel between Kurtz and Marlow becomes especially relevant when the latter alloys the local manager's nephew to believe that he has influence in Europe and is backed by those who promoted Kurtz. This implicit lie immediately transforms him into a flat and hollow character: 'I became in an instant as much a pretence as the rest of the bewitched pilgrims' (82). Although he has survived to tell the tale, Marlow bears the trace of his exposure to the 'pestiferous absurdity' (91) of Kurtz's speech that affects his own *fabulation*, probably to enable us to have a 'glimpse of what is at stake in the horror, that is, the savagery in us' (120), to quote the last words of Lacoue-Labarthe's essay.

Marlow describes the white traders and colonial administrators as boneless and hollow. In dramatic contrast with the 'black shapes' (66) of the dying Africans, the Company's chief accountant is identified as a white man dressed in immaculate white. In Marlow's ironic comment, 'That's backbone' (68), is a recognition that the chief accountant's fastidious taste for neat and elegant clothes does not express deeper moral or intellectual qualities: they merely help 'keep up appearances', since 'starched collars and got-up shirt-fronts' (68) provide structure, a false 'backbone' to a human body gone limp. Further on in his journey, Marlow meets the manager of the Middle Station, an unremarkable man whose status in the colonial hierarchy is said to result from his unique ability to resist the tropical climate. Marlow goes on to speculate that the only reason such a *nobody* holds a position of power in the colonial economy is that he has no human insides and is therefore not subject to illness, a speculation corroborated by the manager himself: 'Once when various tropical diseases had laid low almost every "agent" in the station, he was heard to say, "Men who come out here should have no entrails"' (74). Attempting to account for the manager's success, Marlow speculates, 'Perhaps there was nothing within him' (74). Marlow's efforts to read his enigmatic smile 'opening into a darkness' (74) end in bafflement, perhaps because there is, in fact, nothing to see. In Conrad's novel, hollowness thus turns out to be a prerequisite to operate in the colonial system. The dandy accountant (the 'hairdresser's dummy' [68]), the enduring manager (a literal *no-body*) and his scheming nephew (the 'papier-mâché Mephistopheles' possibly filled with 'loose dirt' [81]) not only lack 'guts' and other bodily organs, but also a heart and symbolically human essence.

In the preface to *The Nigger of the 'Narcissus'* (1897), Conrad famously defined the gift of the artist as his unique capacity to 'descend . . . within himself', and his role as an appeal 'to our less obvious capacities: to that part of our nature which . . . is necessarily kept out of sight'.[20] For Conrad, '[a]ll art . . . appeals primarily to the senses' and he notoriously declared: 'My task which I am trying to achieve is, by the power of the written word, to make you hear, to make you feel—it is, before all, to make you *see*'.[21] Conrad insists on the importance of recovering feeling over intellectual understanding. This, he goes on to argue, can be achieved especially through sight. He believes in the power of visible signs to gain access to a deeper understanding of reality and human nature, and of readable signs 'to reach the secret spring of responsive emotions'.[22] But a few years later, he was to reconsider the capacity of sight to provide insight into human nature, possibly as a result of his exposure to X-rays, which required a radical reconsideration of what vision itself meant, and of its limitations. Whereas a study of visible nature sought to confirm the idea of a created order designed for human understanding, Conrad's novella is about the failure to achieve knowledge although, as Lacoue-Labarthe argues, it paradoxically brings a fundamental and deeply distressing insight into recent Western history and metaphysics. The new X-ray technology proclaimed to provide a new mode of access to the human body and new ways of seeing beneath the skin, but in *Heart of Darkness* it only discloses a horrifying absence of essence, possibly because there is nothing to see. The claim that X-ray technology makes visible the invisible is thus both dramatized and questioned in *Heart of Darkness*, which bears witness to a deep and lasting crisis of visibility in turn-of-the-century culture.

In *Heart of Darkness*, Conrad captures this anxiety by focusing on the enigmatic opacity of the body and redefines the potency of X-ray vision as the capacity to penetrate beneath the surface of the lie that constitutes the colonial myth. Röntgen's invention thus provided Conrad with concrete images to express his disillusionment with the humanist notion of an essential, inner self, and capture what Coroneos has aptly called 'heartless modernism'[23] that hints at the fundamental inhumanity of Western *techne* that would reveal itself more fully in the course of the twentieth century. By questioning the claim that X-ray technology makes visible the invisible, Conrad states a position of epistemological, existential and even ontological doubt that draws attention to a deep and lasting crisis in European culture at the turn of the twentieth century – and beyond. *Heart of Darkness* can indeed be seen as recording the writer's fascination for, but also alertness to, the dehumanizing effects of the technological turn and more generally for *techne* that is intimately bound up with the colonial enterprise through the fabrication of new myths. The novel thus foreshadows the dehumanizing effects that Lacoue-Labarthe identifies as the ultimate manifestation of Nazi ideology (in the mass technology of death). Conrad, Warrilow and Lacoue-Labarthe, however, suggest that we cannot do away with the reality of material bodies through which the question of the human must be constantly reopened.

Notes

This essay is dedicated to Alexis. An earlier version of this article, titled 'Body Politics: Conrad's Anatomy of Empire in *Heart of Darkness*', was first published in *Conradiana* in 2004. The present article elaborates on several points of contact between my reading of Conrad's novella and Lacoue-Labarthe's critique of *techne*. I am much indebted to Nidesh Lawtoo for the stimulating and friendly exchanges out of which the revised piece grew.

1 Philippe Lacoue-Labarthe, *Phrase* (Paris: Christian Bourgois, 2000), 87–8.

2 Jacques Derrida, 'Introduction: Desistance', in Philippe Lacoue-Labarthe *Typography: Mimesis, Philosophy, Politics*, ed.Christopher Fynsk (Cambridge, MA: Harvard University Press, 1989), 7.

3 Lacoue-Labarthe's discussion on *techne* is tied to both the aesthetic question of mimetic art and the political question of the Holocaust. In addition to Philippe Lacoue-Labarthe and Jean-Luc Nancy, 'The Nazi Myth', trans. Brian Holmes, *Critical Inquiry* 16 (1990): 291–312, the key text on this question is probably *La ficiton du politique: Heidegger, l'art, et la politique* (Paris: Christian Bourgois, 1987). See especially 51–63 where these issues are clearly articulated.

4 Derrida, 'Desistance', 6.

5 Lacoue-Labarthe also refers to Conrad's novel as a fable and a *muthos*, but he refuses to see it as an allegory (120), probably in order to distinguish it from Nazi ideology as a total and totalizing myth based on 'the logic of an idea' and therefore functioning in the 'allegorical mode' as he argues in 'The Nazi Myth', 293; 302.

6 Martine Hennard Dutheil de la Rochère, '*Heart of Darkness* as a Modernist Anti-Fairytale',*The Conradian* 33.2 (2008): 1–17.

7 Lacoue-Labarthe and Nancy, 'The Nazi Myth', 293.

8 Derrida, 'Desistance'.

9 Derrida, 'Desistance', 6.

10 On the question of mimesis, see Nidesh Lawtoo's two contributions to this volume.

11 The first major study examining the significance of the gendered land-as-body metaphor in the colonial context was Edward W. Said, *Orientalism* (New York: Pantheon, 1978). Subsequent studies of novelistic constructions of Africa as female include David Spurr, *The Rhetoric of Empire: Colonial Discourse in Journalism, Travel*

Writing, and Imperial Administration (Durham, NC & London: Duke University Press, 1993); Florence Stratton, *Contemporary African Literature and the Politics of Gender* (London & New York: Routledge, 1994); Alison Blunt and Gillian Rose, *Writing Women and Space: Colonial and Postcolonial Geographies* (New York & London: Guilford Press, 1994.); and Anne McClintock, *Imperial Leather: Race, Gender, and Sexuality in the Colonial Contest* (London & New York: Routledge, 1995).

12   Chinua Achebe's influential essay indicting Conrad for racism, 'An Image of Africa: Racism in *Heart of Darkness*', in Joseph Conrad, *Heart of Darkness*, ed. Paul B. Armstrong (New York: Norton, 2006) 336–49, initiated a whole subgenre of Conrad criticism reappraising the political implications of *Heart of Darkness*. See Patrick Brantlinger, *Rule of Darkness: British Literature and Imperialism, 1830–1914* (Ithaca & London: Cornell University Press, 1988) and Benita Parry, *Conrad and Imperialism: Ideological Boundaries and Visionary Frontiers* (London & Basingstoke: Macmillan, 1983) for a nuanced position on this question.

13   Judith Butler, *Bodies that Matter: On the Discursive Limits of 'Sex'* (New York & London: Routledge, 1993), 53.

14   Lisa Cartwright, *Screening the Body: Tracing Medicine's Visual Culture* (Minneapolis & London: University of Minnesota Press, 1995), xi.

15   Philippe Lacoue-Labarthe, *L'imitation des modernes: Typographies 2* (Paris: Galilée, 1986).

16   Bettyann Holtzmann Kevles, *Naked to the Bone: Medical Imaging in the Twentieth Century* (New Brunswick, NJ: Rutgers University Press, 1997), 4. Among the writers who incorporated imagery derived from the new technology in their work were Virginia Woolf, D. H. Lawrence, and H. G. Wells. See Holtzmann Kelves, *Naked to the Bone* and Michael H. Whitworth, *Einstein's Wake: Relativity, Metaphor, and Modernist Literature* (Oxford: Oxford University Press, 2001).

17   Parry, Conrad and Imperialism, 5.

18   Lacoue-Labarthe's insistence on hollowness, emptiness of meaning, solitude, disaffection and anguish ('*Moi, la mort dans l'âme*' 84) as characteristic of the modern condition in his account of *Heart of Darkness* signals that he is probably reading Conrad's tale through Eliot's poem, as the echoes to 'Four Quartets' in 'Phrase XIV', a poem dedicated to 'Jean-Luc [Nancy]', suggests (*Phrase*, 84–7).

19   Lacoue-Labarthe, *La fiction du politique*, 58.

20 Joseph Conrad, *The Nigger of the 'Narcissus'* (New York: Doubleday, 1924), xii.

21 Conrad, The Nigger of the 'Narcissus', xiv.

22 Conrad, The Nigger of the 'Narcissus', xiii.

23 Con Coroneos, *Space, Conrad, and Modernity* (Oxford: Oxford University Press, 2002), 39.

12

The horror of mimesis: Echoing Lacoue-Labarthe[1]

NIDESH LAWTOO

There is a philosophical urgency that is no longer
possible to avoid: we are being compelled to think,
or to rethink, mimesis.

PHILIPPE LACOUE-LABARTHE, *L'imitation des modernes.*

During his career, Philippe Lacoue-Labarthe has thought and
rethought the question of mimesis, and this type of thinking equally
informs his affective reading of Conrad's *Heart of Darkness*.
Although Lacoue-Labarthe does not state it loudly, one of the main
ambitions of 'The Horror of the West' is to open up a mimetic line
of inquiry in Conrad studies. His reading of Kurtz as an artistic qua
'mythic' (115) figure characterized by the 'absence of any proper
being' [*absence de tout être-propre*]' (116) and by the 'will to
power' (117) to take control of the modern masses has a familiar
ring to readers acquainted with Lacoue-Labarthe's philosophical
work.[2] This reading is directly in-*formed* (i.e. given form) by the
fundamental 'mimetology' the French philosopher never tried to
trace, moving – with a tempo and rhythm characteristic of a 'long
distance run', says Jacques Derrida[3] – from the origins of Western

philosophical thought to the horrors of the Holocaust. That Conrad was in a position to foresee not only the ethical and political horrors of fascist will to power but also the affective and conceptual mimetic presuppositions responsible for 'the horror of the West', is one of the reasons Lacoue-Labarthe enthusiastically celebrates *Heart of Darkness* as 'an event of thought' (112).

In this chapter, I would like to follow-up on some of the mimetic implications of Lacoue-Labarthe's breathtaking reading in order to continue to bear witness to the untimeliness of *Heart of Darkness* for our contemporary times. Taking my clue from the French philosopher's insight into the hollow core of modern subjectivity, I trace the aesthetic, psychic and political manifestations of different types of mimetic moves, tropes and figures that animate the novella as a whole. Relying on Lacoue-Labarthe's foundational work on mimesis as well as on more recent developments in mimetic theory,[4] I argue that Conrad's fascination with the '*homo duplex*' is but one instance of his more general engagement with what I shall call *affective mimesis*. That is, a behavioural form of imitation whose primary characteristic consists in generating a psychological confusion between self and other(s) which, in turn, deprives subjects of their full rational presence to selfhood or, to use Lacoue-Labarthe's language, of their 'proper being' *tout court*. At work in Conrad's novella is, quite literally, an 'outbreak' of mimetic phenomena: somnambulism, compassion, hypnosis, depersonalization, suggestion, contagion and enthusiasm are all mimetic tendencies that haunt the Conradian conception of the subject. As we shall see, both the form and the content of Conrad's tale reflect the process of ideological formation of the subject in childhood, its persistent psychic malleability in adulthood, as well as the ethical and political horrors that continue to ensue when the modern masses capitulate to the power of mass media. Echoing Lacoue-Labarthe, I shall call this type of horror, the horror of mimesis.[5]

The mimetic frame

. . . if you allow me to use Plato's categories . . .

Philippe Lacoue-Labarthe, 'The Horror of the West'

Conrad's choice to filter Marlow's narrative by an anonymous frame narrator situates his 'tale' at a twice, or even three-times removed distance from Kurtz's 'original' insight into 'the horror'. The listeners on the *Nellie* listening to one of Marlow's 'inconclusive experiences' (51) in the dark, never see Kurtz's shady figure, nor do they hear the emotional pathos of his 'deep voice' (134). Rather, they are merely exposed to Marlow's mimetic reproduction of Kurtz's words. What they hear in Marlow's voice is thus but an echo of a voice which is, in turn, mediated by yet another frame narrator for us to read. The experience of mimesis comes, thus, quite literally first, in the sense that it is only through a series of narrative representations, mediations and echoes that Kurtz's original insight into 'the horror' can be approached.

This is, in a sense, also Lacoue-Labarthe's starting point. Thinking of David Warrilow's dramatic impersonation, Lacoue-Labarthe begins to account for the 'narrative complexity' of *Heart of Darkness* along the following lines:

> We are therefore confronted, it would seem, with what one might describe, following Plato's canonical terminology, as a 'mimetic' device [*dispositif 'mimétique'*], something almost 'theatrical'— and here I am thinking both of Jouanneau's stage production and of Warrilow's performance. The enunciator delegates his enunciation to someone else; the author does not speak in his own name but 'invents a fable' [*'fabulise'*].[6] (112)

As Plato famously explains in Book 3 of the *Republic*, in the context of a discussion that has the theatre as its paradigmatic model, in mimetic diction (or *lexis*) the speaker does not speak in his proper name (say, Homer speaking as Homer, or Conrad as Conrad) but, rather, he delegates his speech to someone else (say, Homer inventing Akhilleus, or Conrad inventing Marlow). A narrative doubling is thus created which, as Socrates puts it, allows the enunciator 'to deliver a speech *as if* he were someone else' (my emphasis)[7] (say Homer or, better, a rhapsode reciting Homer on the theatrical stage, speaking as if he were Akhilleus; Conrad, or better, Warrilow reciting Conrad on the theatrical stage, speaking as if he were Marlow).

How does this mimetic doubling take place? How can the self magically slip under the skin of the other 'likening [him]self in speech and bodily bearing' as Plato says, himself speaking *as if* he were Socrates?[8] By a simple, yet effective narrative device: in mimetic speech (tragedy, comedy, Platonic dialogues), the enunciator does not use a third person (indirect) narrative to talk *about* his characters ('he or she') but a first person (direct) speech which allows the speaker to impersonate his characters ('I'). This mimetic doubling does not only entail a narrative reproduction of reality but it also allows for an affective impersonation with a fictional character to take place: the speaker who adopts the speech of the other is placed in a position to feel, at least in part, the affect of the other, to partake in an experience that remains exterior, to be sure, but that the dramatic impersonation also renders interior. The rhapsode on the stage weeps or rails as Akhilleus does in order to communicate his pain or anger to the audience who, in turn, feels some of this pain too; Warrilow cries out at the wilderness like Kurtz in order to communicate something of 'the horror', and this emotion is felt by Lacoue-Labarthe too. Indeed, Lacoue-Labarthe, like Plato before him, is fundamentally aware that a mimetic manner of speech (or mimetic *lexis*) – and the mimetic identifications that ensue (or mimetic impersonation) – is endowed with a power of communication that affects the audience in the theatre and, by extension, spreads across the entire body politic (or mimetic contagion).

And yet, Lacoue-Labarthe is also aware that the text of *Heart of Darkness* does not confront readers with a direct, affective experience. Thus, he immediately qualifies the status of these mimetic duplications by focusing on the different manners of diction (or *lexis*) that inform the content (or *logos*) of the tale (or *muthos*).[9] Referring again to Plato's narratological categories, he continues to frame Conrad's text thus:

> And yet, it is not so simple. . . This 'novel' ['*roman*'] is not a narrative [*récit*], nor is it simply a narrative of a narrative [*le récit d'un récit*]. It is composed, if you allow me to use Plato's categories (in reality, they are the only ones we have) of a *diegesis*—a minimal diegesis, held together by the 'we' of the first three pages and by the rare instances of the 'I'. . .—taken over, in a mimetic mode, by a new *diegesis* which is itself interrupted by mimetic passages. (112–13)

Lacoue-Labarthe admits that to fully account for the formal complexity of the narrative, 'a far more meticulous analysis' should be pursued (113). In order to further this line of inquiry, let us notice that within this complex narratological/theatrical '*dispositif*', Marlow occupies a *central* affective and formal position. Affective because he is tied to both his listeners and to Kurtz: 'the bond of the sea' (45) ties him to his listeners, 'intimacy' (143) to Kurtz. Formal because Marlow functions as the locus of connection where diegetic and mimetic speech meet and intercalate: Marlow, the narrator, talks *about* the characters he encounters by using the third person narrative form (*diegesis*), but since Marlow is also the protagonist of his narrative, he talks about them in the characteristic form of the *propria persona* (*mimesis*). Mimesis is thus integral part of the *medium* of Marlow's message – perhaps because this medium *is* the message Conrad is attempting to convey.

Mimetic sexism and colonial ideology

> What is threatening in mimesis is feminization, instability—*hysteria.*

Philippe Lacoue-Labarthe, 'Typography'

Mimetic, identificatory affects are central to the telling of Conrad's tale and must be understood in relation to the gender divide Marlow initially sets up. From the beginning, Marlow puts his rhetoric to work in order to reinforce what Henry Staten in his contribution to this volume, calls the 'manly group identification. . . to his listeners' (205). These affective, identificatory bonds are generated by Marlow's *mimetic* speech, but even at the level of his *diegetic* speech, mimesis remains central. In fact, Marlow begins by representing women as emotional, mimetic creatures who are radically opposed to his male rational listeners. We are thus told, in a detached diegetic narrative, that Marlow encounters a 'compassionate secretary. . . full of desolation and sympathy' (56) 'with an air of taking an immense part in all [his] sorrows' (57). Compassion is a mimetic affect whereby one suffers *with* the other, perhaps even suffers *as* the other does which, in the context of Belgian colonialism, is a contradiction in terms. But compassion is not the only mimetic affect Marlow ironically invokes in order to distance his 'masculine' position from femininity. Invoking the language of psychopathology, he compares the other secretary's behaviour to a 'somnambulist' (55). A mimetic pathology much discussed in the last decades of the nineteenth century,[10] somnambulism suggests a passive, entranced disposition whereby the subject simply reproduces the orders of the dominant ideology. Both somnambulism and compassion, then, are mimetic affects in the sense that they create a psychic confusion between self and other which, in turn, dispossesses these female characters of their rational capacity to act as subjects.

Marlow's ironic, diegetic distance with respect to women continues if we turn to the third case of mimetic femininity that immediately follows: that is, the enthusiastic woman. Speaking of that 'dear enthusiastic soul' (53) who is his aunt, Marlow makes this sweeping comment about her colonial fervour:

> There had been a lot of such rot let loose in print and talk just about that time, and the excellent woman living right in the rush of all that humbug got carried off her feet. She talked about 'weaning those ignorant millions from their horrid ways' (59).

Notice that Marlow's critique does not simply concern the newspapers' ideological content but, rather, the affective impact of this medium on the psychic life of readers – in this case, feminine readers. Informed by a *fin-de-siècle* awareness of crowd psychology,[11] Conrad implies, via Marlow, that blind beliefs in civilizing missions expressed in print affect, like a virus, the psychic lives of the public. Hence, for Marlow, the aunt's thoughts are, quite literally, not her own; another speaks through her, namely, the idol of colonial ideology. The aunt is thus 'enthusiastic' in the Platonic sense of the term (from Greek *entousiazein*, to be possessed by a god): she is merely a passive medium for the message of the other [12]

Feminist critics have rightly denounced the sexist implications of Conrad's representations of women, but it is important to realize that sexism is not the only issue here. At stake in Marlow's attitude towards women is a tacit, yet fundamental, difficulty in taking hold of a *mimetic* conception of the subject insofar as mimesis is not only disavowed but also projected onto gendered others. Thus, if we sum up Marlow's diegetic account of women, the following crude mimetic evaluation ensues: for Marlow, women are somnambulistic-compassionate-enthusiastic creatures; as such, they are inevitably predisposed to get carried off their feet by all kinds of ideological 'rot' that appears in print, while men's feet and minds continue to diligently trade the path of 'facts' and 'truth'. Marlow's sexism, in short, should be qualified as *mimetic* sexism.

And yet, despite the initial diegetic distance Marlow posits between women and men, the narrative shows that such a distance is not as absolute as it appears to be. Marlow's colonial adventure is, in fact, rooted in a passive, mimetic disposition that far exceeds his mimetic representation of women. Here is a thorough explanation of the psychic origins of his colonial adventure expressed now in direct mimetic speech:

> Now when I was a little chap I had a passion for maps. I would look for hours at South America, or Africa, or Australia, and lose myself in all the glories of exploration. . . I would put my finger on it and say, When I grow up I will go there. . . [T]here was in it one river especially, a mighty big river, that you could see on the map, resembling an immense snake uncoiled, with its head in the sea, its body at rest curving afar over a vast country, and its tail lost in the depths of the land. And as I looked at the map of it in a shop-window, it fascinated me as a snake would a bird—a silly little bird. . . [I] could not shake off the idea. The snake had charmed me. (52–3)

Marlow's childish passion for the colonial instrument *par excellence* is predicated on an emotional fascination that totally deprives him of his critical presence to selfhood. The tropes of the 'snake' and the 'silly little bird' perfectly capture the state of entranced, psychic passivity characteristic of the mimetic subject. Marlow is quite literally hypnotized and deprived of mastery over his feet and thoughts. A capitulation to the *formative* power of mimesis – what Lacoue-Labarthe calls 'typography' – has thus taken place as Marlow was a 'young and tender' creature, a mimetic creature who, as Plato also recognized is 'best molded and takes the impression that one wishes to stamp upon it'.[13]

In time, Marlow the 'little chap' turns into a self-reliant 'seaman' and 'wanderer' (48), but both the map's hypnotic power and Marlow's mimetic suggestibility remain essentially the same. In fact, the suggestive tropes of the 'snake' and the 'charmed' 'bird' apply to Marlow the adult 'wanderer', walking along Fleet street – the former home of the British press[14] – not to the 'little chap'. It is, thus, no accident that precisely as he glances at the map, Marlow 'remember[s] there was a big concern, a Company for trade on that river' (52) and feels compelled to enact the colonial 'dream' he first experienced as a child to 'go there'.

At work in this passage is a critical genealogy that traces the colonizer's subjection to power back to mimetic childhood. The emotion of thought at work in this passage exposes the limits of humanist notions of free-will and rationality and confirms the subject's passive-malleable-hypnotic – that is, mimetic – status. The radicalism of Conrad's tacit critique of the subject of ideology stems from a dual realization. First, that a hypnotic state of mimetic dispossession characterizes the dominant subject and, thus, that mimesis cannot easily be displaced on the side of femininity alone. And second, that this psychic state is far from being something extraordinary. As the 'case of Marlow' suggests, it is instead such an ordinary everyday experience which can be triggered by any ideologically charged commodity – a map and the press in the old days, video games, the web and other mimetic devices in our postmodern times. Briefly put, Conrad begins to show us that the male subject of ideology is not the subject of *Aufklärung* (alias the rational man) but the subject of *mimesis* (alias the 'silly little bird').

By furthering the line of inquiry opened up by Lacoue-Labarthe, we are now in a position to see that Marlow's formal oscillation between mimetic and diegetic speech (*lexis*) also reveals an oscillation in the mimetic content (*logos*) of his tale. And what we see is that the affective mimesis he forecloses is inevitably constitutive of his own psychic life. What we must add now is that if Marlow's take on femininity cannot be dissociated from his take on mimesis, the same can be said with respect to his equally problematic take on race.

The racist pathos of mimetic rhetoric

Nothing, in effect, resembles more mimesis than enthusiasm.

Philippe Lacoue-Labarthe, *L'imitation des modernes*

Marlow's understanding of racial difference is predicated on a violent hierarchy that is reminiscent of his earlier considerations on gender.

The link is all the more clear since Marlow introduces a distinction between subjects who are in possession of themselves (White men) and subjects who are not ('prehistoric men'). And, once again, the notion of 'enthusiasm' pops up in a notorious passage in order to mark a difference between mimetic and non-mimetic subjects:

[A] burst of yells, a whirl of black limbs, a mass of hands clapping, of feet stamping, of bodies swaying, of eyes rolling, under the droop of heavy and motionless foliage. The steamer toiled along slowly on the edge of a black and incomprehensible frenzy. . . we glided past like phantoms, wondering and secretly appalled, as sane men would be before an *enthusiastic outbreak* in a madhouse. (96; my italics)

As it was already the case with Marlow's 'enthusiastic' aunt, the Africans' 'enthusiastic outbreak' deprives racial subjects of rational control over themselves. Yet, the mimetic degree of these subjects acquires a bodily, collective dimension that was lacking in the somnambulistic-compassionate-enthusiastic Belgian women. Moreover, Conrad's detailed physical description of this primal, mimetic scene suggests that he has in mind a ritual dance endowed with the affective power to induce a state of psychic (dis) possession.[15] Such a state of 'frenzy', as he calls it is well known, in both ancient and modern times: Plato calls it 'enthusiasm'; Nietzsche calls it 'Dionysian'; Girard calls it mimetic 'crisis'; Lacoue-Labarthe, thinking along Greek/Nietzschean lines, calls it 'chorus' (114).

At this stage, Marlow's account of race is based on the naïve, ethnocentric idea that the mimetic subject is always 'the other', and Lacoue-Labarthe, long-distance runner that he is, does not slow down to account for this ideological hurdle. At this stage, both literary and philosophical accounts of the 'myth' of the other seem to reinforce the violent hierarchy between nature and culture, 'savagery' and 'civilization' that famously infuriated Chinua Achebe.[16] I say 'seem' because while contemptuously dismissing this Dionysian chorus as a hysterical pathology, Marlow's narrative also oscillates in the opposite direction:

Well, you know, that was the worst of it—this suspicion of their not being inhuman. It would come slowly to one. They howled and leaped, and spun, and made horrid faces but what thrilled you was just the thought of their humanity—like yours—the thought of your remote kinship with this wild and passionate uproar. Ugly. Yes, it was ugly enough; but if you were man enough you would admit to yourself that there was in you just the faintest trace of a response to the terrible frankness of that noise, a dim suspicion of there being a meaning in it which you—you so remote from the night of the first ages—could comprehend. (96)

Marlow's narrative voice oscillates madly, back and forth, between racist injunctions that dehumanize racial others and repeated attempts to nuance such racist distinctions. His statements are, indeed, paradoxical: he seems intent in conveying *both* a critical distance *and* an affective proximity to racial others. 'Racism', as Achebe recognized, is clearly part of his rhetoric, but so are his persistent attempts to establish a connection between his White listeners and the Africans dancers, 'rational/sane' subjects and 'enthusiastic/mad' subjects.

Rather than quarrelling about the racist or anti-racist implications of these lines, I suggest we slow down and ask ourselves a more fundamental question: namely, what is the emotional and conceptual logic that motivates such paradoxical rhetorical oscillations towards/away from enthusiastic others?

Notice that this passage is not only about racism; it is also about mimesis. And at this stage in the narrative, Marlow not only uncritically displaces the mimetic conception of the subject on to subordinate others but also begins to acknowledge that mimetic responses are constitutive of the modern subject. For this reason, Marlow now claims that a 'kinship' exists between his listeners and the 'wild and passionate' 'uproar' the Africans give voice to. And for the same reason he insists that at work in such an 'enthusiastic outbreak' is a 'meaning' that the modern, 'civilized' subject can still 'comprehend'. But this apparently linear project to bring mimesis back home, on the side of 'modernity' and 'civilization', entangles Marlow's narrative in a paradoxical rhetorical situation. In fact, he attempts to convey the mimetic status of the subject to his 'civil', Victorian listeners, through the example of the 'prehistoric' enthusiastic Africans he seems to repudiate on racist grounds. A contradictory push-pull between racist and mimetic imperatives is thus at work in the narrative structure of this complex passage: if a racist conception of the subject introduces a rational distance, such a distance is nonetheless immediately challenged by the mimetic chorus that emotionally affects Marlow. In short, if half of the story is about racism, the other half is about mimesis, and Marlow's dialectical narrative trajectory (i.e. affirmations of racial distance followed by a dialectical 'but' which immediately negates distance and affirms a common mimesis) indicates that the emphasis is perhaps less on a disjunctive racial distance than on a conjunctive mimetic pathos. So much at the level of content (*logos*) of this mythic narrative; but what about the formal, narrative strategies (*lexis*) that inform Marlow's rhetorical moves?

Marlow's attempt to acknowledge the mimetic status of the modern subject through the example of the 'enthusiastic' Africans in a state of 'frenzy' threatens to disrupt the identificatory connection with his (racist) listeners. Within this impossible narrative situation, Marlow's offensive characterization of the Africans occupies a paradoxical (or hyperbological) rhetorical function. We have seen that racist injunctions, such as 'the worst of it', or 'ugly', are obviously instrumental in introducing a distance between the dominant and the subordinate; the subject of *Aufklärung* and the subject of *mimesis*. Less obvious, however, is that such a racist distance is precisely what his listeners expect to hear. If we reread this passage by paying careful attention to the rhetorical dimension informing the narrative as a whole, it is not even sure that these racist judgements originate directly from Marlow's voice. We should in fact not forget that Marlow's diegesis is interrupted by 'mimetic passages' whereby the listeners voice their discontent. Such mimetic interactions usually take place at moments of maximum tension between the Marlow's tale and his listeners' 'civil' expectations. And at such moments, Marlow tends to repeat, with indignation, the listeners' intrusive ejaculations, ejaculations we readers do not always get to hear directly. Here are a few examples: 'Yes; I looked at them as you would any human being, with a curiosity of their impulses, . . . when brought to the test of an inexorable physical necessity. Restraint! What possible restraint?' (105). Or, '[a man] must meet that truth with his own true stuff—with his own inborn strength. Principles? Principles won't do'.[17] And again: 'Who's that grunting? You wonder I didn't go ashore for a howl and a dance? Well, no—I didn't. Fine sentiments, you say? Fine sentiments, be hanged!' (97). Marlow's rhetorical pattern indicates that words like 'restraint', 'principles', 'fine sentiments' are, indeed, originally *not* his own; he simply restates, for rhetorical effect, what a listener has been saying. With this crucial formal point in mind the following passages resonate quite differently: '[the earth] was unearthly and the men were. . . No they were not inhuman'. Or, 'the thought of your remote kinship with this wild and passionate uproar. Ugly. Yes, it was ugly enough, but. . .'. The rhetorical movements at work in Marlow's mimetic voice suggests that racist injunctions like the unvoiced 'inhuman' and the voiced 'ugly' might have their origin in his listeners and that Marlow ventriloquizes them for rhetorical reasons – and for us to hear.

Perhaps, then, Marlow's racist narrative moves, while not excusable, have a specific rhetorical function: they serve to reassure his audience that he is still one of them after all and thus are instrumental in maintaining the mimetic ties with his listeners and readers. Marlow is now relying on this mimetic bond at the level of *lexis* (the medium), in order to paradoxically bring home the mimetic affects the Africans embody at the level of *logos* (the message). And yet, in order to do this, Marlow must, at the same time, constantly nuance his racist injunctions; if racial 'otherness' is exaggerated, mimetic 'sameness' cannot be conveyed. In other words, racism here functions both as a (mimetic) rhetorical strategy and, at the same time, as an impediment to the communication of the (mimetic) content of Marlow's tale. Structurally speaking, this passage is predicated on a double-bind that swings Marlow's narrative voice back and forth between contradictory poles. And it is precisely through this maddening oscillation that the narrator desperately attempts to make his sceptical listeners recognize and acknowledge their affective vulnerability to such enthusiastic, mimetic outbreaks. We are thus beginning to see that this narrative is predicated on a communication *of* mimesis *through* mimesis, where mimesis is both the content and the medium of the message.[18]

The heated controversy concerning racism and sexism in *Heart of Darkness* is indeed heavily inflected by the less visible but more fundamental – in the sense that it informs *both* racism *and* sexism – problematic of mimesis. For Marlow it is, in fact, crucial to acknowledge that the modern rational subject of *Aufklärung* continues to remain in a zone of dangerous proximity to contagious, mimetic affects initially projected onto subordinate 'others'. But why? Why is it so terribly important that his modern listeners acknowledge that they too are still vulnerable to states of mimetic dispossession? Paul Armstrong's Norton Critical edition of *Heart of Darkness* gives us access to a manuscript passage that Conrad did not include in the final version of the text but helps us answer what I take to be the fundamental question at the heart of this mythic text. In the context of Marlow's discussion about the effect of the enthusiastic frenzy in Africa, we read the following report about Europe:

> You know how it is when we hear the band of a regiment. A martial noise—and you pacific father, mild guardian of a domestic hearth-stone suddenly find yourself thinking of carnage. The joy of killing—hey?[19]

Now we can better hear the type of 'noise' Marlow has in mind when he encourages his listeners to acknowledge their mimetic 'response' to the 'frankness' of the 'African' drums. For him, the 'enthusiastic' effect of the chorus in the jungle is not any different from a modern response to the musical rhythm generated by a 'martial noise' at the heart of Europe. This is, indeed, a mimetic repetition with a vengeance: the ethico-political difference being that unlike the African dance, 'modern' ritual responses to contagious music have the power to generate the 'joy of killing' in otherwise 'pacific fathers'. We can now better understand why Marlow/Conrad is struggling to make his listeners/readers realize that mimetic forms of dispossession should not be hastily displaced onto subordinate others. It is because for Conrad/Marlow, disquieting forms of mimetic reactions are haunting the European body politic that it is essential for Western subjects to emotionally acknowledge and think through, their own vulnerability to the contagious power of affective mimesis.

The barbarity of mimesis

The recoil from the horror is Western *barbarity* itself.

Philippe Lacoue-Labarthe, 'The Horror of the West'

As Marlow and his men follow the meandering course of that hypnotic snake which is the river Congo, the presence of mimetic affects that haunt *Heart of Darkness* progressively intensifies. As the narrative unfolds, enthusiastic affects not only appear in relation to gendered subjects (Part I), nor do they exclusively qualify racial subjects (Part II) but also appear to characterize, with increasing insistence, that 'troupe of mimes' (126) who are the White male colonial figures (Part III). A mimetic conception of the subject and all it entails – that is, suggestibility to suggestion, hypnotic (dis) possession, psychic depersonalization, emotional contagion etc. – characterizes the mimetic figures whose 'absence of any proper-being' (116), as Lacoue-Labarthe puts it, haunt not only the heart of darkness, but the West as a whole.

Take the Harlequin, for instance, a figure Lacoue-Labarthe does not slow down to analyse but remains central to understand the type of mimetic 'void' the French philosopher denounces as constitutive of the 'myth of the West' (112). This figure embodies the most extreme version of the subject's suggestibility, enthusiasm and mimetic depersonalization Marlow has encountered so far. The narrator first introduces him as a subject totally devoid of individuality in familiar mimetic terms: he says that had 'absconded from a troupe of mimes, enthusiastic, fabulous' (126). And then he adds that he lacked 'all thought of self' and that 'even when he was talking to you, you forgot that it was he—the man before your eyes—who had gone through these things' (127). The Harlequin, in other words, is a mimetic nobody who can assume the psychic form of everybody, a 'man without proper qualities' (115–116) as Lacoue-Labarthe says of Kurtz. And indeed, the Harlequin's enthusiasm is primarily for that 'phantom' who is Mr Kurtz. We are told that '[t]he man filled his life, occupied his thoughts, swayed his emotions' (128). This mimetic man is not simply under the influence of another subject; he is, quite literally, possessed by that 'phantom' in such a fundamental way that the distinction between self and other, copy and original, no longer holds. This figure is but the shadow of another shady figure; his voice but an echo of another, haunting voice.

Who, then, is Mr Kurtz? And wherein lies his power of fascination? Lacoue-Labarthe stresses the fact that the 'essence' of Kurtz's being is not located in his actions, nor in his mind, but in his 'voice' (114). Relying on his account of 'general mimesis' developed in *L'imitation des modernes*, he defines Kurtz as a hollow man who 'having no property in himself. . . is capable of appropriating them all for himself' (115). For the French philosopher this 'absence of any proper-being', which he identifies in the figure of Kurtz *qua* artist, defines not only 'the genius' in the Modern tradition[20] but is also responsible for what he calls a manipulation of a '*technique de la mort*' responsible for devastating forms of Western 'will to power' (117). Reading Conrad in a way informed by his previous work on Plato and Aristotle, and also Diderot, Nietzsche and Heidegger, Lacoue-Labarthe proclaims, in an apocalyptic mood, that what is at stake in *Heart of Darkness* is nothing less and nothing more than 'the entire destiny of the West' (113). Now, it is true that in order to accept Lacoue-Labarthe's fundamental claim about 'the horror of the West', one needs to share a vertiginous number of philosophical assumptions (about *mimesis*, *poiesis*, *muthos*, *techne*, will to power, etc.), assumptions he develops in his protean *oeuvre*, and that resonate through his reading of Conrad. But it is equally true that if we continue patiently to follow, at a rhythm and tempo that is ours, the mimetic undercurrent that runs through the entire texture of *Heart of Darkness*, there is perhaps a sense in which we might finally catch up with Lacoue-Labarthe's reading of the horror.

For instance, we could notice that Kurtz's power over the masses does not rely exclusively on the supposed naivety and mimeticism of racial and gendered subjects: that is, the mimetic sexism and racism Lacoue-Labarthe deftly jumped over and slowed us down above. The mimetic Harlequin is, of course, part of the 'troupe of mimes' impressed by the typographic (will to) power of Kurtz's voice. But even Conrad's self-reliant hero is not immune to Kurtz's 'magnificent eloquence'. Thus, Marlow feels entitled to say that

> [O]f all his gifts the one that stood out preëminently, that carried with it a sense of real presence, was his ability to talk, his words— the gift of expression, the bewildering, the illuminating, the most exalted and the most contemptible, the pulsating stream of light or the deceitful flow from the heart of an impenetrable darkness. (113–14)

The heart of darkness and the darkness of mimesis are, once again, tightly strung together. And, once again, Marlow's evaluation oscillates between opposite poles. With one of his narrative voices, he openly condemns the mimetic suggestion at work in Kurtz's 'gift of expression' in terms of a 'deceitful flow'. But another voice enthusiastically celebrates it as 'illuminating' 'pulsating stream of light'. Similarly, speaking of Kurtz's 'report', he ironically notes that it was 'too high-strung' (118), and as he retrospectively meditates on this report, in diegetic speech, Marlow *the narrator* can indeed maintain an ironic distance from Kurtz's rhetorical pathos. Yet, as Marlow *the character* first reads the 'pamphlet', his critical distance seems to vacillate: recognizing that 'it was a beautiful piece of writing', 'eloquent, vibrating with eloquence' (117), he confesses his capitulation to Kurtz's 'magic current of phrases' (118), in mimetic speech: 'From that point he soared and took me with him. . . *It made me tingle with enthusiasm*' (118; my italics).

Now, why does Marlow enthusiastically accept an ideological position that he had earlier denounced as non-meditated 'devotion' (Harlequin), or 'sentimental pretence' (women)? The mimetic logic of the text we are trying to make audible indicates that the modern subject, whether in Africa or in Europe, is equally vulnerable by the 'unbounded power of eloquence—of words—of burning noble words' (118). In fact, Conrad insistently shows that while Marlow consciously struggles to distance himself from such a state of dispossession, he nonetheless repeatedly avows his proximity and vulnerability to enthusiastic, mimetic affects.

At stake in Marlow's narrative is thus not only a personal avowal of his own suggestibility to Kurtz's rhetorical (will to) power but also a realization of its political impact on the dominant body politic. *Heart of Darkness* makes clear that mimetic affects are indifferent to human, all too human, racial, gendered and cultural categorizations. Once back in Belgium, a journalist tells Marlow: '[H]eavens! How that man could talk. He electrified large meetings. . . He would have been a splendid leader of an extreme party' (154). The leader figure may move around the world, but his mimetic will to power as well as the predisposition of crowds to be mesmerized by it remains fundamentally the same. Whether 'the magic current of phrases' appears in 'print', 'talk', 'pamphlets', speeches in the jungle or 'at large meetings' in Europe, it has the power to 'electrify' subjects, dispossessing them of rational control over themselves. It should be clear by now that the power of darkness and the horrors that ensue cannot be dissociated from the ongoing threat of mimetic depersonalization. The phantom that haunts the heart of darkness *is* the phantom of imitation; the horror, for Conrad, *is* the horror of mimesis.

History, unfortunately, will prove Conrad's insights into the horrific results of mimetic behaviour prophetic. As Lacoue-Labarthe says allusively but unequivocally, 'we know what followed' (117): in the Europe of the 1910s, not to speak of the 1930s and 1940s, mass media, martial parades and electrifying speeches will soon stimulate the 'joy of killing' in usually 'pacific fathers'. In this sense, *Heart of Darkness* is prophetic of horrors yet to come; it diagnoses in advance the totalitarian power of tyrannical leader figures and the mimetic pathologies they promote. And yet, it also seems, that despite his apparent genial nature, the tyrannical leader figure (who, by the way, 'had been writing for the papers' [148]), like his mimetic follower, is but a hollow figure who does not possess political ideas to call his own. As Marlow asks, '[w]hat party' Kurtz could preside over, the visitor answers: 'Any party. . . . [h]e was an—an—extremist' (154).

This is the moment to interrogate what is perhaps the fundamental presupposition of Lacoue-Labarthe's argument in 'The Horror of the West'. I wonder: are leader figures who rely on the power of voice and techne to impress the mimetic crowd really in line with a productive form of 'general mimesis' characteristic of Romantic artists and universal geniuses? Or, alternatively, could it be that these 'hollow' figures or, as Marlow ironically says, these 'poor chap[s]', are passively in-*formed* by the power of mimetic media that mechanically reproduce opinions for them to repeat? What if so-called political types *à la Kurtz* (each country has their own) are typographically churned out by crude forms of 'restricted mimesis' that *lead them* to enthusiastically echo, in the most passive and uncritical way, the louder message in the dominant medium? What our race in the stimulating company of Lacoue-Labarthe – from Fleet Street to Kurtz's journalistic pamphlets – suggests is that the second option is the correct one: that is, that the horror in *Heart of Darkness* and, perhaps 'the horror of the West' too, is the horror generated by passive and rather shallow forms of mimetic capitulations to the reproductive power of mass media. We find a confirmation of this mimetic hypothesis in a little quoted, apparently superficial passage that prepares Kurtz's final, much-quoted, and supposedly deeper insight into the heart of darkness. With Marlow, we are left to wonder about the obscure origins of Kurtz's powerful voice as he hears it one last time, right before the end is approaching: 'Was he rehearsing some speech in his sleep, or was it a fragment of a phrase of newspaper article?' (148). That this question is asked at all indicates that Kurtz's voice may be less original than it initially sounded and that he is but an echo of 'other voices': 'this voices—other voices—all of them were so little more than voices' (115). This 'echo' does not re-*produce* any creative force, but mechanically *re*-produces a readymade mimetic message which, if expressed through the right mimetic medium, has the power to induce the joy of killing in pacific fathers. Perhaps, then, if *Heart of Darkness* constitutes an 'event of thought', it is also because it is a reminder of the power of mass media to shape mass opinion in our contemporary, hyper-mimetic times.

Finally, as a last tentative step 'I' could add, with Hillis Miller, that 'we' should be careful in locating the true origin of mimetic horrors exclusively 'in the West'. We should also specify, with Philippe Lacoue-Labarthe, that the phrase 'the horror of the West' should not be primarily understood in terms of a geographical ground where psychic and political horrors occur (though such horrors continue to take place). Rather, this phrase conveys the metaphysical realization that 'the West *is* the horror': that is, that no matter where the horror appears, its 'truth' or 'essence' continues to be founded on a Western *logos* that produces such *praxis* – from its Greek (Platonic) figuration to its Modern (Heideggerian) destination. Still, if Marlow fundamentally agrees that 'all Europe contributed to the making of Kurtz' (117) – indicating that the leader figure is but the by-product of the dominant ideology that informed him – his initial, past-oriented account of the Romans also indicates to future-oriented readers that the power of mimesis can be mobilized by different Empires and traditions. From the Romans to the Belgians, Germany to the United States, Israel to Afghanistan, Rwanda to Syria and North Korea and beyond, it is increasingly difficult, in the hybrid, mimetic, mediatized world that is ours, to foresee what the true essence of the West 'is', where the power of mimesis will 'appear', on the basis of which 'emotion of thought' it will attack and, above all, *how* – in what form, through what medium and to what end – it will strike.[21]

The lesson we might draw from *Heart of Darkness* is that the essence of mimesis is to lack a proper essence; its being, to lack any 'proper being'; its emotion to lack a proper thought; its subject, to lack a proper substance. And it is precisely this vertiginous lack of a single 'essence', 'being', 'thought' or 'substance' that –

as the general economy of Lacoue-Labarthe's thought has taught us – endows mimesis with the power to multiply masks, dissolve identities and infiltrate power itself. Hence, the difficulty to catch up with this mimetic phantom; hence, the challenge to keep up with the breathtaking rhythm of literary and philosophical writers like Conrad and Lacoue-Labarthe, writers of mimesis whose 'emotion of thought' is now passed on to us – to follow up.

Notes

1 This essay is dedicated to the memory of Philippe Lacoue-Labarthe (1940–2007) – for mimetic inspiration. It is substantially revised version of a paper that appeared in *Conradiana* 41.1–2 (2010): 45–74. I would like to thank J. Hillis Miller for his insightful comments on the present version.

2 Philippe Lacoue-Labarthe, *Typography: Mimesis, Philosophy, Politics*, ed. Christopher Fynsk (Cambridge: Harvard University Press, 1989); *L'imitation des modernes (Typographies 2)* (Paris: Galilée, 1986); *La ficiton du politique* (Paris: Christian Bourgois, 1987); Philippe Lacoue-Labarthe, Jean-Luc Nancy, 'The Nazi Myth', *Critical Inquiry*, 16.2 (1990): 291–312.

3 Jacques Derrida, 'Introduction: Desistance', in *Typography: Mimesis, Philosophy, Politics*, ed. Christopher Fynsk (Cambridge, MA: Harvard University Press, 1989), 1–42, 15.

4 In addition to the work of Lacoue-Labarthe, my understanding of mimesis is informed by René Girard's 'mimetic theory'. See, *Deceit, Desire and the Novel: Self and Other in Literary Structure*, trans. Yvonne Freccero (Baltimore: The Johns Hopkins University Press, 1966); *Violence and the Sacred*, trans. Patrick Gregory (Baltimore, MD: The Johns Hopkins University Press, 1977). It also owes much to the teaching and work of Mikkel Borch-Jacobsen, himself a former student and colleague of Lacoue-Labarthe. See Borch-Jacobsen, *The Emotional Tie: Psychoanalysis, Mimesis, Affect*, trans. Douglass Brick and others (Stanford, CA: Stanford University Press, 1992); *The Freudian Subject*, trans. Catherine Porter (Stanford, CA: Stanford University Press, 1988.

5 I take it to be a confirmation of Lacoue-Labarthe's claim that mimesis comes first, that the 'original' version of this paper – written and accepted for publication before the appearance of *'L'horreur occidentale'* – draws its source of inspiration from Lacoue-Labarthe's

philosophical work – on mimesis. For a study on modernism and mimesis, see Nidesh Lawtoo, *The Phantom of the Ego: Modernism and the Mimetic Unconscious*. Michigan State University Press (East Lansing: Michigan State University Press, 2013).

6   On Plato's narratological categories, see Hillis Miller's 'Prologue' as well as my 'Frame'. If Miller stresses the realistic (representational) implications of Lacoue-Labarthe's understanding of mimesis, I focus more on the theatrical (affective) implications of mimesis. Both tendencies inform Lacoue-Labarthe's reading and supplement each other.

7   Plato, *Republic*, in *The Collected Dialogues of Plato*, eds. E. Hamilton, H. Cairns, trans. Paul Shorey (New York: Pantheon Books, 1963), 575–844, 3.393c, 638.

8   Plato, *Republic*, 3.393c, 638.

9   For the distinction between *lexis* and *logos*, see Plato, *Republic*, 3.392d, 637.

10 On the link between somnambulism and imitation, see Gabriel Tarde, *Les lois de l'imitation* (Paris: Ed. Kimé, 1993), 82 n3.

11 I discuss Conrad's relation to crowd psychology in *The Phantom of the Ego*.

12 In *Ion*, Socrates relies on this concept in order to critique the rhapsodey and, via through him, the poet. See *Ion*, in *The Collected Dialogues of Plato*, trans. Lane Cooper, (New York: Pantheon Books, 1963), 216–28, 534c–d, 220. Lacoue-Labarthe, following Plato, considers enthusiasm a form of 'passive mimesis' that renders the 'subject absent to itself' (*Imitation*, 32–3).

13 Plato, *Republic*, 2.377b, 624. For Lacoue-Labarthe's illuminating discussion of 'the psychology of the *Republic*', see 'Typography', in *Typography*, 43–138.

14 I would like to thank William Johnsen for this reminder.

15 For an analysis of 'frenzy' in terms of mimesis and possession trance that serves as a sequel to this essay, see Nidesh Lawtoo 'A Picture of Europe: Possession Trance in *Heart of Darkness*'. Novel 45.3 (2012) (forthcoming).

16 Chinua Achebe, 'An Image of Africa: Racism in *Heart of Darkness*' in Joseph Conrad, *Heart of Darkness*, 4th ed., ed. Paul B. Armstrong (New York: W. W. Norton, 2006), 336–49, 339.

17 Conrad, *Heart of Darkness*, ed. Paul B. Armstrong (New York: W. W. Norton, 2006), 3–77, 36.

18 Hillis Miller usefully pointed out that this duality is close to his conception of 'irony', an irony which, as we shall see, is persistent in Marlow's double voice.

19 Conrad, *Heart of Darkness*, Armstrong, 91.

20 See Lacoue-Labarthe, 'Le paradoxe de la mimesis' in *L'imitation des modernes*, 15–35.

21 I mention in passing that the recent revolutionary movements in North Africa (or 'Arab Spring') offer us a striking example of the *liberating* forces of mimetic contagion, forces that use different forms of mass media (from the internet to mobile phones) to put an end to the horror of totalitarian regimes. An indication that mimesis 'itself' is beyond good and evil.

Postface: A talk with Avital Ronell (about Philippe Lacoue-Labarthe)[1]

NL: In your career you have done much to promote the thought of Philippe Lacoue-Labarthe: from introducing his work and disseminating his concepts during his lifetime, to honouring his memory and pursuing his legacy after his disappearance. You have known him as a colleague, privileged interlocutor and, above all, as a friend. Taking my clue from Nietzsche's claim that every great philosophy is a form of 'personal confession,' I would like to start by asking you to comment on the 'emotion of thought' that ties you to Lacoue-Labarthe, the man and the thinker.

AR: I had a very personal bond with Philippe, for all kinds of reasons and impulses. We can certainly start, as you suggest, with a personal confession. During one of our first meetings I remember sitting with him at table, for lunch with a group of professors in Irvine, California. He was entirely ignoring me until someone said something about my name and its Hebraity. It seemed as though the minute that Philippe heard I was Jewish, he suddenly cathected. I have to say that was the access-code for him. His philo-Semitism embarrassed me because I had never experienced it before (I experienced its opposite). I didn't know what to do with it, but I decided not to repel it, and opened myself to the sudden turn towards me, or my name, as a gift and as an offer. I thought, 'maybe that's the first doorkeeper, as in Kafka, the *Turhüter*, and I shouldn't let that door slam; maybe we can get past it because now at least I have his attention.' It was a start. And so, I didn't do anything to ever allow him to abandon his interest in me.

At the same time, I have to say that everything about Philippe and me was pathos-filled, deep, and quietly passionate. He made so much possible. He made it possible to read Heidegger – for a Jewish person.[2] The way Philippe took on Heidegger and had this ethical voice, timbre, and calming sureness moved my heart and made me feel a little more safe in the worlds that I was bounced out of. I go to places where I am not so welcome. I haven't necessarily always felt invited to the men's clubs of philosophical and literary inquiries. But something about Philippe's quiet outrage at certain persecutions and violences made me feel comfortable in his vicinity. I appreciate him – deeply.

NL: How do you recall the experience of working in his proximity when you were both teaching at Berkeley? Was there an intimidating side to his presence?

AR: I have a story that might help me address this question. One day, my editor said that we needed a blurb for my book on drugs and addiction.[3] We were short on time so, I thought: 'Philippe is teaching at Berkeley and I'm teaching at Berkeley, and I'm supposed to see him for dinner, so I'll pry a blurb out of him.' We had dinner, and I asked him. He answered, '*d'accord*'; but he immediately added: 'Tomorrow you'll read me the book. I want you to read it to me, before I come up with a blurb.' And I thought: 'We don't have time for this!' So we sat next to each other: he was like my piano teacher, or Latin teacher. But then something happened that I couldn't have anticipated. I was already bent over my text, humbled in prearranged humiliation. I was on the verge of tears having to read to him my book and translate it into my not greatly solidified French. But there was a moment when he just smiled at me and said: '*Tu as écrit ça? Non. . . c'est pas vrai!*' And I said: 'That's what it says here.' I was already waiting for a smack-down, or some kind of violent rejection, but he just smiled, and he gave every indication of being happy with my delivery. I still remember the word that toned down his severity, his acute *écoute*. He couldn't believe that I would dare to write something on narcosism!

There was indeed a protestant severity about Philippe. I may be wrong but I don't recall a sense of knee-slapping humour particularly. There was a kind of heaviness about his being and judgement that you couldn't wriggle your way out of, as sometimes I could with

Derrida – via a sudden outburst of parabasis, a spark of humour, or outrageous provocation. I have seen Philippe smile, and I've been able sometimes to put a smile on his face. But his expression always had the back-up crew of bewilderment and astonishment that might have been questioning. It was never a done deal with him; there was a severity that I even feared about him.

NL: Do you usually teach Lacoue-Labarthe? And what do you think distinguishes him from other French thinkers who are commonly grouped under the umbrella terms 'deconstruction' or 'poststructuralism'?

AR: When I love certain thinkers I want to teach them and quote them in order to make sure they stay close and are put in circulation. When Philippe left his body and left us I felt the real fragility of his legacy. I thought that all he represented was something that could vanish. So, I felt the responsibility to almost single-handedly assure its survival. I had the great fear of losing him as an oeuvre as well as losing him; or, maybe, that was the way I could deal with losing him. I had not one but two commemorations in New York.[4] I teach him as often as I can, and I feel like I have to almost artificially inseminate his work, in all sorts of places, some more plausible than others. Susan Sontag once said that friendship has destroyed letters, to the extent that friends just keep on promoting each other so that true judgement can't even be made. But in the case of Lacoue-Labarthe I don't waver in my evaluation of the importance of his work.

There is something very subtle in terms of the question that you asked about how to distinguish him from other so-called 'deconstructionists' or 'poststructuralists.' I would say that Philippe has what he calls 'rigorous hesitations' in the way he proceeds. There is something very surprisingly (in a Hölderlinian way) sober and sovereign, something very ethically pacifying about the way he goes step by step in the confrontations that he felt were essential to the unfolding of thought. There is a thoroughgoing modesty in the rhetoric of Lacoue-Labarthe that I appreciate. And not even a flirt with the motif of weakness, or deceleration of thought. What I mean by this is that he did not draw interest in his modesty or flip it into a usable concept. He did not turn weakness or metaphysical weariness into a brilliantly compelling paraconcept, as Levinas does. There was also something quietly warrior-like in the way he took on the big guns, or the big *topoi* of the day. Sometimes he would really stick to his guns in ways that seemed almost obstinate. He was as brave as he was fragile. I'm not surprised that he addressed himself to Hölderlin's *Dichtermut* (the poet's courage) because I think he must have had a great struggle with his own courageousness coming from such an abyss of needling fearfulness.

The other thing that may be mentioned is the way Lacoue-Labarthe lived his life philosophically – to a certain degree. That is to say, he encouraged a resurgence of a kind of *Lebensphilosophie*. When we talk about Philippe (and also, to a certain extent, Jean-Luc Nancy, but differently) there was always a community, a living-with, a *Mitsein* practice that reminded me of the German Romantics. There were great moments of restricted solitude, pressure zones that were nearly unbearable for him. To a great extent Philippe, for me, was a figure of extreme solitude, but he was also, at the same time, the most communal and communitarian of people.

NL: Lacoue-Labarthe's writing style, in 'The Horror of the West' and also elsewhere, is sometimes characterized by the spoken dimension of his voice. At times, he even seems to speak in an informal, casual way. In the past, this has cost him the charge of naivety. And yet, this 'naivety' is only apparent and his voice is informed by an uncompromising demand for theoretical rigor and clarity. Could you comment on the particularity of Lacoue-Labarthe's voice?

AR: As the great friend that I am capable of being, trained on Freudian ambivalence – meaning that I undermine the friend, I try to trap him and catch him off guard – I have an anecdote about that sort of tendency. There was something very solid and grounded about Philippe's presencing. So I don't want to make him out to be so fragile and modest because he was careful, but he was sure of his aim. Nonetheless, one of the offices of friendship in our experience together was for me to try to destabilize him, or dislocate him from that place of sovereignty he occupied. One day, I said to him: 'Oh, by the way, I'm going to teach Paul de Man today and did you know that he said that your reading of Nietzsche is like a first reading of a naïve person?'[5] I don't know what I thought I was doing. Perhaps delivering the message that in those days I tried to deliver: that I was the only friend that could be counted on? Or was it about an impish, troublemaking incursion that I was delighted maliciously in producing? Who knows what the hell I was doing? I couldn't help myself and I tried to provoke him in so many ways. Because he was so calm, I wanted to see if I could bring him over to my side of the barricade of obsessional neurotic or, more to the point, hysterical behavior. He was quiet for a moment, and I thought, 'I got him!' And then, very calmly, he said: '*Oui*, . . . *c'est pas faux*.' And that made him even stronger, firmer and more sovereign. It didn't work; from that moment he was unbeatable.

Let's get serious here. I am so astonished that you would want to retrieve people's statements about some sort of naivety. His writings demonstrate astonishing control and depth, a far-ranging grasp of the political consequences of every possible metaphysical move. There are talking texts that I remember where he is addressing someone pointedly,[6] but I wonder if these statements refer more to a tonality than to the content of his massive reach. It's as with Nietzsche: when Nietzsche does the auto-critical feint you realize that people picked it up and run with it, but one should never do that without considering the irony of a self-put-down that is several registers removed from what is said. Philippe Lacoue-Labarthe was as naïve as Tiresias.

NL: I am grateful that you emphasize Lacoue-Labarthe's extreme formal and rhetorical sophistication. Even texts originally prepared for oral presentations are never as spontaneous and direct as they might initially appear.

AR: And they are refreshing for the way they pull back on themselves, and don't boom out as just another assertion of truth, as you get in some philosophers. If, at times, Philippe seems to be speaking about 'truth,' or 'essence' one should thus be careful to always read such statements in the context of his highly stylized philosophical prose, his citational virtuosity and impeccable knowledge of Plato, Heidegger and Derrida and the other prime movers or suspects. Nor is his voice libidinally over invested as you get in other philosophers who are very high on themselves, very sure of themselves, or plainly arrogant. Somehow Philippe was able to say things like, 'this is provisional,' these are just 'brief remarks,' and stay rigorous without seeming to be playing around with us, or jerking us around theoretically.

NL: Many readers who will read 'The Horror of the West' might encounter Lacoue-Labarthe's thought for the first time. Since his reading of *Heart of Darkness* is particularly compressed at the conceptual level, do you have a piece of advice for these readers?

AR: I would tell those readers that Philippe can be trusted. I understand that especially in our fast-food, fast-thought cultures that force acceleration (we are result-oriented, business-oriented, under the gun of gains, and subject to the push towards scientific objectivization) his writings will stand out as requiring a different temporality and degree of attention: one has to slow down for the checkpoints, the allusive clusters and dense indicators of his text. But readers who are generous and capacious and smart enough to offer themselves the gift of a first encounter with Philippe (however dense, difficult or problematic and short-circuited it might seem) should probably feel that they can entrust themselves to his insights on Conrad and many other fields as well. Perhaps 'The Horror of the West' will work as a gateway drug. I hope so, in the sense that they will start smoking and injecting-introjecting the other texts, and investigating where his reading of Conrad might have come from, what kind of a splinter it is, what kind of a split-off part it is of a truly worthy *oeuvre*. I myself remain an amateur as concerns this particular contribution of Lacoue-Labarthe and tend to feel more at home in his larger works.

NL: Here is perhaps one of those splinters. In *Préface à la disparition*,[7] a youthful biographical text published only recently, the echoes with 'The Horror of the West' are particularly strong. For instance, Lacoue-Labarthe qualifies Conrad's tale as an 'event of thought', and the very same phrase also occurs in *Préface* in relation to a dream he had.[8] In this text he also describes 'the horror of death' in a context that resonates powerfully with *Heart of Darkness*.[9] This is not the moment to enter into the details of this scene, but perhaps you could comment on the role of the affective, lived experience in Lacoue-Labarthe's understanding of the horror?

AR: Philippe had to clear many abysses to get to the notational space that we can now calmly observe, examine and explore together. He certainly carried massive scripts of destruction that also lapsed into self-destruction. He carried monstrous worlds of demonic takedowns that he was fighting often, and he was in a place of great struggle. Particularly in the later texts he is meditating on this all the time. So yes, certainly, these texts are resonating with his own experience, a confrontation with various terrifying experiences.

But here is one thing that Philippe has said to help orient our thoughts and that your readers might be interested in; he said that in the twentieth century there were three major motifs for the thinkers that we cherish, continue to read and which continue to provoke our thought: one is the mission, the other the struggle, and the last is the task. The *mission* is something he associated with Heidegger; the *struggle* is a Marxist or Marxian motor; and the *task* he ascribed to Benjamin. Struggle, mission, task. Of course, if we were to dwell on these three kinds of tracks we would have to see not only how they operate but also how eventually they contaminate and leak into each other. He provisionally keeps them separate to show the invested relatedness to the work that has to be done. I think this comes from a very – if I may use this metaphor still today – deep place in him. I do think he struggled, and I do think he had a sense of task. He also has a very unique diction and rhetoric of ethicity in the way he approaches problems. Rather than seeing those cautionary remarks as naïve or self-deprecating, I would say that it's part of his ethics to stay clear of excess by limiting a statement to 'this is only this'. I think he had a great deal of lucidity about his own limits. I don't think he was fishing for compliments, and I don't think it was part of a narcissistic economy, but he held himself to a very high standard – with thousands of quotes – of 'authenticity.' He also felt that the mission that Heidegger enrolled for was calamitous. So I would think that Lacoue-Labarthe is politically urgent in the sense that he also takes measure of the catastrophe that a wrong turn in thought can induce.

NL: A catastrophe that culminates in what he calls, thinking of the Holocaust, 'the horror of the West.' What do you think is the relevance of Philippe's effort, in his larger works, to 'think and rethink mimesis,' in order to avoid future horrors?

AR: Lacoue-Labarthe opened the dossier of 'mimetology,' a large dossier involving sexual difference, metaphysical and hierarchical markings and blunders that we still are suffering from.[10] There is something that is still politically urgent about how he pushed up this thought in our faces. At the time, it was very hard perhaps to grasp mimesis as something that ought to be taken with utmost seriousness because it sounded so old-fashioned for the American receptor system. It's only coming through now, through some sort of delay call forwarding device to what extent we are still stuck on mimesis in very covert and unavowed ways. So the unavowable in mimesis, its desirability, its abjection and the kinds of constructions and institutions that depend on it, continue to hold their *omertà function* around mimesis. And I think we still require a good listen from Lacoue-Labarthe.

NL: In your moving homage to Lacoue-Labarthe you write: 'Philippe had access to the catastrophic intuition that informs, structures and dominates the grammar of our mimetic hell.'[11] This affirmation refers to Philippe's thought in general but also captures, with extreme precision, what is at stake in 'The Horror of the West.' In order to conclude would you be willing to unpack this dense passage for us?

AR: Lacoue-Labarthe certainly was able to critically approach certain things, to show how (let me talk Heideggerian here), how this is a *destiny* for us. What he does with mimesis is of destinal importance. It's not just a whim or caprice on the part of M. Lacoue-Labarthe to have gone there. Nor is it something that can be contained, restricted and controlled within the precincts of the philosophical, the political or the literary. It's not accidental or minoritizable. It's not a minoritized trace. He uncovered other birth texts in mimetic theory by critical thinkers as diverse as Luce Irigaray, René Girard and Jacques Derrida, for instance.[12] But what he did with them, how he has run with them, and how he insisted on mimesis as an historical-political off-shore hurricane, is what interests me. Do we continue to shutter our homes? Is this hurricane going to stay off-shore? Or are we going to be hit by the destructive velocities of mimetic slams? And by this figure I mean that there is something menacing today still. Maybe mimesis could dissipate in other formulations, figurations or disfigurations. But it could also hit us in the house of being, in a very core place where the issues are key survival issues. So, everything that Philippe touched, I felt, was heavy and destinal – even though all of these words would have to be further shaken up, as Derrida would say (*sollicités*).

NL: Thank you for sharing your *émotion de la pensée*. What you said will surely help future readers approach Lacoue-Labarthe's insights into what he calls 'the horror of the West' with the right frame of mind.

AR: Thank you for honouring Philippe; I think it's very important.

Notes

1   What follows is an abridged version of a conversation between Avital Ronell and Nidesh Lawtoo (in the company of Christopher Fynsk) held at the European Graduate School in Saas Fee, Switzerland, on 15 August 2011. All endnotes are the editor's.

2   On Avital Ronell's take on Lacoue-Labarthe's reading of Heidegger, *techne*, the Holocaust and the problematic of 'national aestheticism' (themes that are central to 'The Horror of the West'), see *The Telephone Book: Technology, Schizophrenia, Electric Speech* (Lincoln: University of Nebraska Press, 1989), 412–3, n. 7, n. 9.

3   Avital Ronell, *Crack Wars: Literature, Addiction, Mania* (Lincoln: University of Nebraska Press, 1992).

4   Traces of one of these commemorations, titled 'Catastrophe and Caesura: Philippe Lacoue-Labarthe Today' (NYU, 2007), can be found at the following website: http://www.lacoue-labarthe.org, accessed 20 October 2011.

5   Paul de Man, *Allegories of Reading: Figural Language in Rousseau, Nietzsche, Rilke, and Proust* (New Haven, CT: Yale University Press, 1979), 83.

6   See for instance, the opening addresses to Derrida and Lyotard in Philippe Lacoue-Labarthe, *L'imitation des modernes* (Paris: Galilée, 1986), 229, 257.

7   Philippe Lacoue-Labarthe, *Préface à la disparition* (Christian Bourgois Éditeur, 2009).

8   Lacoue-Labarthe, *Préface*, 17.

9   Lacoue-Labarthe, *Préface*, 33; see also 26–40.

10 See Philippe Lacoue-Labarthe, *Typography: Mimesis, Philosophy, Politics*, ed. Christopher Fynsk (Cambridge, MA: Harvard University Press, 1989); Lacoue-Labarthe, *L'imitation*.

11 Avital Ronell, 'L'indélicatesse d'un interminable fondu au noir', trans. Daniel Loayza, *Europe* 973 (2010): 24. Trans. modified.

12 Luce Irigaray, *This Sex Which is Not One*, trans. Catherine Porter (New York: Cornell University Press, 1985); René Girard, *Violence and the Sacred*, trans. Patrick Gregory (Baltimore, MD: The Johns Hopkins University Press, 1977); Jacques Derrida, 'The Double Session,' in *Dissemination*, trans. Barbara Johnson (Chicago, IL: The University of Chicago Press, 1981), 173–285.

BIBLIOGRAPHY

Achebe, Chinua. 'An Image of Africa: Racism in Conrad's *Heart of Darkness*.' In Joseph Conrad, *Heart of Darkness*, edited by Paul B. Armstrong. New York, NY: Norton, 2006, 336–49.

Agamben, Giorgio. *Homo Sacer: Sovereign Power and Bare Life*, translated by Daniel Heller-Roazen. Stanford, CA: Stanford University Press, 1998.

—. 'The *Muselmann*.' In *Remnants of Auschwitz: The Witness and the Archive*, translated by Daniel Heller-Roazen, 41–86. New York, NY: Zone Books, 2002.

Amselle, Jean-Loup and Elikia M'Bokolo, eds. *Au coeur de l'ethnie: Ethnies, tribalisme et État en Afrique*. Paris: La Découverte, 1985.

Arendt, Hannah. *Le système totalitaire*, translated by Jean-Louis Bourget, Robert Davreu and Patrick Lévy. Paris: Seuil, 2005.

Ash, Beth Sharon. *Writing In Between: Modernity and Psychosocial Dilemma in the Novels of Joseph Conrad*. New York, NY: St. Martin's, 1999.

Austin, John Langshaw. 'Other Minds.' In *Philosophical Papers*, edited by James O. Urmson and Geoffrey J. Warnock, 6–116. Oxford: Oxford University Press, 1979.

—. 'Pretending.' In *Philosophical Papers*, edited by James O. Urmson and Geoffrey J. Warnock, 253–71. Oxford: Oxford University Press, 1979.

Ba, Medhi. *Rwanda, un génocide français*. Paris: L'esprit frappeur, 1997.

Badiou, Alain. '"Dits" de Philippe Lacoue-Labarthe.' *Lignes* 22 (2007): 16–20.

Baldwin, Debra R. '"The Horror and the Human": The Politics of Dehumanization in *Heart of Darkness* and Primo Levi's *Se questo è un uomo*.' *Conradiana* 37.3 (2005): 185–204.

Bataille, George. 'La conjuration sacrée.' In *Œuvres complètes*, vol. 1, 442–6. Paris: Gallimard, 1970.

Baudillon, Christine and François Lagarde, dir. *Proëme de Philippe Lacoue-Labarthe*. Montpellier: Hors Œil édition, 2006. DVD.

Beaujour, Michel. *Terreur et rhétorique: Breton, Bataille, Leiris, Paulhan, Barthes & Cie*. Paris: J.-M. Place, 1999.

Beer, Gillian. '"Authentic Tidings of Invisible Things": Vision and the Invisible in the Later Nineteenth Century.' In *Vision in Context: Historical and Contemporary Perspectives on Sight*, edited by Teresa Brennan and Martin Jay, 83–98. New York & London: Routledge, 1996.

Bell, Michael. *Literature, Modernism and Myth Belief and Responsibility in the Twentieth Century*. Cambridge: Cambridge University Press, 1997.

Benjamin, Walter. *Ursprung des deutschen Trauerspiels*. Berlin: Ernst Rowohlt Verlag, 1928. Reprinted in Frankfurt: Suhrkamp, 1963.

—. *The Origin of German Tragic Drama*, translated by John Osborne. London: New Left Books, 1977.

—. 'The Task of the Translator.' In *Illuminations*, edited by Hannah Arendt, translated by Harry Zohn, 69–82. New York, NY: Schocken Books, 2007.

Berghoffen, Debra B. 'Interrupting Lyotard: Whither the We?' In *Lyotard, Philosophy, Politics, and the Sublime*, edited by Hugh J. Silverman, 127–39. New York & London: Routledge, 2003.

Berman, Marshall. *All That is Solid Melts Into Air: The Experience of Modernity*. Toronto: Penguin Books Canada, 1988.

Blanchot, Maurice. *The Writing of the Disaster*, translated by Ann Smock. Lincoln & London: University of Nebraska Press, 1995.

—. *L'Écriture du désastre*. Paris: Gallimard, 1980.

Bloom, Harold. Introduction to *Joseph Conrad's* Heart of Darkness: *Modern Critical Interpretations*, 1–4. New York, NY: Infobase, 2008.

Blunt, Alison and Gillian Rose. *Writing Women and Space: Colonial and Postcolonial Geographies*. New York & London: Guilford Press, 1994.

Booth, Wayne C. *The Rhetoric of Fiction*. Chicago, IL: University of Chicago Press, 1961.

Borch-Jacobsen, Mikkel. *The Freudian Subject*, translated by Catherine Porter. Stanford, CA: Stanford University Press, 1988.

—. *The Emotional Tie: Psychoanalysis, Mimesis, Affect*, translated by Douglass Brick et al. Stanford, CA: Stanford University Press, 1992.

Bradbury, Malcolm and James McFarlane, eds. *Modernism: A Guide to European Literature 1890–1930*. Toronto: Penguin Books Canada, 1991.

Brantlinger, Patrick. *Rule of Darkness: British Literature and Imperialism, 1830–1914*. Ithaca, NY: Cornell University Press, 1988.

Brooks, Peter. *Reading for the Plot: Design and Intention in Narrative*. New York, NY: Random House, 1985.

Brown, Tony C. 'Cultural Psychosis on the Frontier: The Work of the Darkness in Joseph Conrad's *Heart of Darkness*.' *Studies in the Novel* 32.1 (2000): 14–28.

Butler, Judith. *Bodies that Matter: On the Discursive Limits of 'Sex'*. New York & London: Routledge, 1993.

Butte, George. 'What Silenus Knew: Conrad's Uneasy Debt to Nietzsche.' *Comparative Literature* 41.2 (1989): 155–68.

Calinescu, Matei. *Five Faces of Modernity: Modernism, Avant-Garde, Decadence, Kitsch, Postmodernism*. Durham, NC & London: Duke University Press, 1987.

Cartwright, Lisa. *Screening the Body: Tracing Medicine's Visual Culture*. Minneapolis & London: University of Minnesota Press, 1995.

Celan, Paul. 'Aschenglorie.' In *Breathturn*, translated by Pierre Joris. Los Angeles, CA: Sun & Moon Press, 1995.

Char, René. *Œuvres complètes*. Paris: Gallimard, 1983.

Chrétien, Jean-Pierre. *Le défi de l'ethnisme: Rwanda et Burundi, 1990–6*. Paris: Karthala, 1997.

Conrad, Joseph. *Heart of Darkness, in Youth: A Narrative and Two Other Stories*. London: J. M. Dent & Sons Ltd., 1923.

—. *A Personal Record*. New York, NY: Doubleday, 1924.

—. *The Nigger of the 'Narcissus.'* New York, NY: Doubleday, 1924.

—. Preface to *The Nigger of the 'Narcissus,'* xi–xvi. New York, NY: Doubleday, 1924.

—. *Tales of Hearsay and Last Essays*. London: J. M. Dent & Sons Ltd., 1935.

—. *Nostromo*. Harmondsworth: Penguin, 1963.

—. *Au cœur des ténèbres; Amy Foster; Le Compagnon secret*, edited and translated by Jean-Jacques Mayoux. Paris: Aubier-Montaigne, 1980.

—. *The Collected Letters of Joseph Conrad*, vol. 2, 1898–1902, edited by Frederick R. Karl and Laurence Davies. Cambridge: Cambridge University Press, 1986.

—. *The Collected Letters of Joseph Conrad*, vol. 3, edited by Frederick R. Karl and Laurence Davies. Cambridge: Cambridge University Press, 1988.

—. *The Collected Letters of Joseph Conrad*, vol. 4, edited by Frederick R. Karl and Laurence Davies. Cambridge: Cambridge University Press, 1991.

—. *Heart of Darkness*, edited by Paul B. Armstrong, 3–77. New York, NY: W. W. Norton, 2006.

Coroneos, Con. *Space, Conrad, and Modernity*. Oxford: Oxford University Press, 2002.

Cousineau, Thomas. '*Heart of Darkness*: The Outsider Demystified.' *Conradiana* 30.2 (1998): 140–51.

Crangle, Richard. 'Saturday Night at the X-Rays: The Moving Picture and "The New Photography" in Britain, 1896.' In *Celebrating 1895: The Centenary of Cinema*, edited by John Fullerton, 138–44. Sydney: John Libbey & Co., 1998.

De Man, Paul. *Allegories of Reading: Figural Language in Rousseau, Nietzsche, Rilke, and Proust*. New Haven, CT: Yale University Press, 1979.

—. 'The Rhetoric of Temporality.' In *Blindness and Insight*, 187–228. Minneapolis & London: University of Minnesota Press, 1983.

—. 'Autobiography as De-Facement.'In *The Rhetoric of Romanticism*, 67–82. New York, NY: Columbia University Press, 1984.

DeKoven, Marianne. *Rich and Strange. Gender, History, Modernism*. Princeton, NJ: Princeton University Press, 1991.

Derrida, Jacques. *De la grammatologie*. Paris: Editions de Minuit, 1967.

—. 'Structure, Sign and Play in the Discourse of the Human Sciences.' In *Writing and Difference*, translated by Alan Bass, 278–93. Chicago, IL: University of Chicago Press, 1978.

—. 'The Double Session.' In *Dissemination*, translated by Barbara Johnson, 173–285. Chicago, IL: University of Chicago Press, 1981.

—. 'Plato's Pharmacy.' In *Dissemination*, tanslated by Barbara Johnson, 61–171. Chicago, IL: University of Chicago Press, 1981.

—. 'D'un ton apocalyptique adopté naguère en philosophie.' In *Les fins de l'homme*, edited by Philippe Lacoue-Labarthe and Jean-Luc Nancy, 445–79. Paris: Flammarion, 1981.

—. 'Introduction: Desistance' to *Typography: Mimesis, Philosophy, Politics*, by Philippe Lacoue-Labarthe, 1–42. Cambridge, MA & London: Harvard University Press, 1989.

—. 'This Strange Institution Called Literature,' translated by Geoffrey Bennington and Rachel Bowlby. In *Acts of Literature*, edited by Derek Attridge, 33–75. New York & London: Routledge, 1992.

Descombes, Vincent. *The Barometer of Modern Reason: On the Philosophies of Current Events*, translated by Adam Schwartz. Oxford: Oxford University Press, 1993.

Devlin, Kimberly J. 'The Eye and the Gaze in *Heart of Darkness*: A Symptomological Reading.' *Modern Fiction Studies* 40.4 (1994): 711–35.

Dolar, Mladen. *A Voice and Nothing More*. Cambridge, MA: The M.I.T. Press, 2006.

Dollimore, Jonathan. *Sexual Dissidence: Augustine to Wilde, Freud to Foucault*. Oxford: Clarendon Press, 1991.

—. *Death Desire and Loss in Western Culture*. New York & London: Routledge, 2001.

Donovan, Stephen. 'Sunshine and Shadows: Conrad and Early Cinema.' *Conradiana* 34.3 (2003): 237–56.

Eliot, George. *Middlemarch*. Oxford: Oxford University Press, 1999.

Fink, Bruce. *The Lacanian Subject: Between Language and Jouissance*. Princeton, NJ: Princeton University Press, 1995.

Fogel, Aaron. *Coercion to Speak: Conrad's Poetics of Dialogue.*
Cambridge, MA & London: Harvard University Press, 1985.
Fothergill, Anthony. 'The Poetics of Particulars: Pronouns, Punctuation
and Ideology in *Heart of Darkness.*' In *Conrad's Literary Career*,
edited by Keith Carabine, Owen Knowles, and Wieslaw Krajka, 57–73.
New York: East European Monographs, 1992.
Franche, Dominique. *Généalogie du génocide rwandais.* Bruxelles:
Tribord, 2004.
Freud, Sigmund. 'Mourning and Melancholia.' In *The Standard Edition*,
vol. 14, 237–60, edited and translated by James Strachey. London:
Hogarth Press, 1957.
—. *New Introductory Lectures on Psychoanalysis*, translated by James
Strachey, edited by James Strachey and Angela Richards. Vol. 2 of *The
Pelican Freud Library*, Harmondsworth: Penguin, 1973.
—. 'Beyond the Pleasure Principle.' In *On Metapsychology: The Theory
of Psychoanalysis*, translated by James Strachey, edited by Angela
Richards. Vol. 11 of *The Pelican Freud Library*. Harmondsworth:
Penguin, 1984.
—. 'Civilization and its Discontents.' In *Civilization, Society and Religion*,
translated by James Strachey, edited by Angela Richards. Vol. 12 of
The Pelican Freud Library. Harmondsworth: Penguin, 1985.
—. 'Why War?' In *Civilization, Society and Religion*, translated by James
Strachey, edited by Angela Richards. Vol. 12 of *The Pelican Freud
Library*. Harmondsworth: Penguin, 1985.
Fynsk, Christopher. Preface to *Typography: Mimesis, Philosophy, Politics*,
by Philippe Lacoue-Labarthe, vii–ix. Cambridge, MA & London:
Harvard University Press, 1989.
Gargot, Christophe, dir. *D'Arusha à Arusha.* Atopic production, 2008.
Film.
Garnett, Edward. 'Unsigned review [of *Heart of Darkness*], *Academy and
Literature*, 6 December 1902, 606.' Reprinted in *Conrad: The Critical
Heritage*, edited by Norman Sherry, 131–3. Boston, CA: Routledge &
Kegan Paul, 1973.
Genette, Gérard. 'Discours du récit.' In *Figures III*, 65–282. Paris: Seuil, 1972.
—. *Narrative Discourse: An Essay in Method*, translated by Jane E. Lewin.
Ithaca, NY: Cornell University Press, 1980.
—. *Narrative Discourse Revisited*, translated by Jane E. Lewin. Ithaca,
NY: Cornell University Press, 1988.
Girard, René. *Deceit, Desire and the Novel: Self and Other in Literary
Structure*, translated by Yvonne Freccero. Baltimore, MD: Johns
Hopkins University Press, 1965.
—. *Violence and the Sacred*, translated by Patrick Gregory. Baltimore,
MD: Johns Hopkins University Press, 1977.

Greaney, Michael. *Conrad, Language and Narrative.* Cambridge: Cambridge University Press, 2002.

Green, André. 'Conceptions of Affect.' *International Journal of Psychoanalysis* 58 (1977): 129–56.

Guichaoua, André. *Rwanda, de la guerre au génocide: Les politiques criminelles au Rwanda (1990–4).* Paris: La Découverte, 2010.

Hatzfeld, Jean. *Dans le nu de la vie.* Paris: Seuil, 2002.

—. *Une saison de machettes.* Paris: Seuil, 2005.

—. *La stratégie des antilopes.* Paris: Seuil, 2008.

Hawthorn, Jeremy. *Joseph Conrad: Narrative Technique and Ideological Commitment.* New York, NY: Edward Arnold, 1990.

Heidegger, Martin. *Lettre sur l'humanisme,* translated by Roger Munier. Paris: Éditions Montaigne, 1957.

—. 'The Question Concerning Technology.' In *The Question Concerning Technology and Other Essays,* translated by William Lovitt, 3–35. New York, NY: Harper Colophon, 1977.

Hennard Dutheil de la Rochère, Martine. 'Body Politics: Conrad's Anatomy of Empire in *Heart of Darkness.*' *Conradiana* 36.3 (2004): 185–204.

—. '*Heart of Darkness* as a Modernist Anti-Fairytale.' *Conradiana* 33.2 (2008): 1–17.

Herman, Judith. *Trauma and Recovery: The Aftermath of Violence from Domestic Abuse to Political Terror.* New York, NY: Harper Collins, 1992.

Hirt, André. *Un homme littéral: Philippe Lacoue-Labarthe.* Paris: Kimé, 2009.

Holtzmann Kevles, Bettyann. *Naked to the Bone: Medical Imaging in the Twentieth Century.* New Brunswick, NJ: Rutgers University Press, 1997.

Homans, Peter. *The Ability to Mourn: Disillusionment and the Social Origins of Psychoanalysis.* Chicago, IL: University of Chicago Press, 1989.

Husserl, Edmund. 'Fifth Meditation: Uncovering the Sphere of Transcendental Being as Monadological Intersubjectivity.' In *Cartesian Meditations: An Introduction to Phenomenology,* translated by Dorion Cairns, 89–151. The Hague: Martinus Nijhoff, 1960.

Irigaray, Luce. *This Sex Which is Not One,* translated by Catherine Porter. Ithaca, NY: Cornell University Press, 1985.

Jackson, Tony E. *The Subject of Modernism: Narrative Alterations in the Fiction of Eliot, Conrad, Woolf, and Joyce.* Ann Arbor, MI: University of Michigan Press, 1994.

Jünger, Ernst. 'Total Mobilization,' translated by Joel Golb and Richard Wolin. In *The Heidegger Controversy: A Critical Reader,* edited by Richard Wolin, 119–39. Cambridge, MA & London: MIT Press, 1993.

Kacem, Mehdi Belhaj. *Inesthétique et mimésis: Badiou, Lacoue-Labarthe et la question de l'art.* Paris: Lignes, 2010.

Kaufmann, Walter, ed. *The Portable Nietzsche.* Harmondsworth: Penguin, 1976.

Kimbrough, Robert, ed. *The Nigger of the 'Narcissus': An Authoritative Text, Background and Sources, Reviews and Criticism.* New York, NY: Norton, 1979.

Klein, Melanie. 'A Contribution to the Psychogenesis of Manic-Depressive States.' In *Contributions to Psychoanalysis, 1921–45,* 282–311. London: Hogarth Press, 1968.

Kristeva, Julia. *Black Sun: Depression and Melancholia,* translated by Leon S. Roudiez. New York, NY: Columbia University Press, 1989.

Lacan, Jacques. *Le séminare, livre VII: L'éthique de la psychanalyse (1959–60).* Paris: Seuil, 1986.

—. *The Seminar of Jacques Lacan, Book VII: The Ethics of Psychoanalysis (1959–60),* translated by Dennis Porter, edited by Jacques-Alain Miller. New York, NY: Norton, 1997.

—. 'The Instance of the Letter in the Unconscious, or Reason Since Freud.' In *Écrits: A Selection,* translated by Bruce Fink, Héloïse Fink and Russell Grigg, 138–68. New York, NY: Norton, 2004.

—. 'The Function and Field of Speech and Language.' In *Écrits: A Selection,* translated by Bruce Fink, Héloïse Fink and Russell Grigg, 31–106. New York, NY: Norton, 2004.

—. *Autres Ecrits.* Paris: Seuil, 2006.

Lacoue-Labarthe, Philippe. 'La césure du spéculatif.' In *L'Antigone de Sophocle,* translated by Friedrich Hölderlin and Philippe Lacoue-Labarthe, 183–223. Paris: Christian Bourgois, 1978.

—. *Le sujet de la philosophie: Typographies 1.* Paris: Flammarion, 1979.

—. *L'imitation des modernes: Typographies 2.* Paris: Galilée, 1986.

—. *La ficiton du politique: Heidegger, l'art, et la politique.* Paris: Christian Bourgois, 1987.

—. 'Neither an Accident nor a Mistake,' translated by Paula Wissing. *Critical Inquiry* 15.2 (1989): 481–4.

—. *Typography: Mimesis, Philosophy, Politics,* edited by Christopher Fynsk and Linda M. Brooks. Cambridge, MA & London: Harvard University Press, 1989.

—. 'De l'éthique: À propos d'Antigone.' In *Lacan avec les philosphes,* 21–36. Paris: Albin Michel, 1991.

—. *Musica Ficta: Figures de Wagner.* Paris: Christian Bourgois, 1991.

—. *The Title of the Letter,* translated by François Raffoul and David Pettigrew. Albany, NY: State University of New York Press, 1992.

—. *Retreating The Political,* edited and translated by Simon Sparks. New York & London: Routledge, 1997.

—. *Phrase*. Paris: Christian Bourgois, 2000.

—. *Heidegger: La politique du poème*. Paris: Galilée, 2002.

—. 'L'horreur occidentale.' *Lignes* 22 (2007): 224–34.

—. 'La philosophie fantôme.' *Lignes* 22 (2007): 205–14.

—. 'L'Afrique, ". . . cette espèce d'immense nuit. . ."' (Interview with Jean-Christophe Bailly). *L'Animal: Littératures, Arts & Philosophies* 19–20 (2008): 115–16.

—. 'Bye bye Farewell.' *L'Animal: Littératures, Arts & Philosophies* 19–20 (2008): 191–8.

—. *Ecrits sur l'art*. Genève: Les presses du réel, 2009.

—. *Préface à la disparition*. Paris: Christian Bourgois, 2009.

—. 'Tradition et vérité à partir de la philosophie.' *Europe* 973 (2010): 61–7.

Lawrence, David H. *Women in Love*, edited by David Farmer, Lindeth Vasey and John Worthen. Cambridge: Cambridge University Press, 1987.

—. *The Rainbow*, edited by Mark Kinkead-Weekes. Cambridge: Cambridge University Press, 1989.

Lawtoo, Nidesh. 'The Horror of Mimesis: "Enthusiastic Outbreak[s]" in *Heart of Darkness*.' *Conradiana* 42.1–2 (2010): 45–74.

—. *The Phantom of the Ego: Modernism and the Mimetic Unconscious*. Michigan State University Press. (East Lansing: Michigan State University Press, 2013) (forthcoming).

—. 'A Picture of Europe: Possession Trance in *Heart of Darkness*.' *Novel* 45.3 2012 (forthcoming).

Lears, T. J. Jackson. *No Place of Grace: Antimodernism and the Transformation of American Culture 1880–1920*. New York, NY: Pantheon Books, 1981.

Leavis, Frank R. *The Great Tradition*. London: Chatto and Windus, 1948.

Leiris, Michel. *L'Afrique fantôme*. In *Miroir de l'Afrique*, 91–868. Paris: Gallimard, 1995.

Levenson, Michael. 'The Value of Facts in the *Heart of Darkness*.' *Nineteenth-Century Fiction* 40 (1985): 261–80. Reprinted in *Heart of Darkness: An Authoritative Text, Backgrounds and Sources, Criticism*, edited by Robert Kimbroug, 391–405. New York, NY: Norton, 1988.

Levi, Primo. *The Drowned and the Saved*, translated by Raymond Rosenthal. New York, NY: Vintage, 1989.

Lévi-Strauss, Claude. *Tristes tropiques*. Paris: Terre humaine, 1955.

Levinas, Emmanuel. 'Ethics as First Philosophy.' In *The Levinas Reader*, edited by Seán Hand, 75–87. Malden, MA: Blackwell, 1989.

Leys, Ruth. *Trauma: A Genealogy*. Chicago, IL: University of Chicago Press, 2000.

Lukács, Georg. *History and Class Consciousness. Studies in Marxist Dialectics*, translated by Rodney Livingstone. Cambridge, MA & London: MIT Press, 1997.

Lyotard, Jean-Francois. *The Differend: Phrases in Dispute*, translated by Georges Van Den Abbeele. Minneapolis & London: University of Minnesota Press, 1988.

—. 'Emma: Between Philosophy and Psychoanalysis.' In *Lyotard, Philosophy, Politics, and the Sublime*, edited by Hugh J. Silverman, 23–45. New York & London: Routledge, 2003.

Maisonnat, Claude.'"Truth Stripped of its Cloak of Time" ou l'énigme de la littérarité dans *Heart of Darkness*.' In *Joseph Conrad 2: Une leçon des ténèbres*, edited by Josiane Paccaud-Huguet, 79–103. Paris: Les lettres modernes Minard, 2002.

—. 'The French Voice of Joseph Conrad.' *L'époque Conradienne* 37 (2011) (forthcoming).

Martis, John. *Philippe Lacoue-Labarthe: Representation and the Loss of the Subject*. New York, NY: Fordham University Press, 2005.

Marx, Karl. 'The Grundrisse.' In *The Marx-Engels Reader*, edited by Robert C. Tucker, 221–93. New York, NY: Norton, 1978.

—. 'Manifesto of the Communist Party.' In *The Marx-Engels Reader*, edited by Robert C. Tucker, 473–91. New York, NY: Norton, 1978.

McClintock, Anne. *Imperial Leather: Race, Gender, and Sexuality in the Colonial Contest*. New York & London: Routledge, 1995.

Miller, J. Hillis. '*Heart of Darkness* Revisited.' In *Conrad Revisited: Essays for the Eighties*, edited by Ross C. Murfin, 31–50. Alabama: University of Alabama Press, 1985.

Miller, Jacques-Alain. 'Jacques Lacan et la voix.' *Quarto* 54 (1994): 47–52.

Murfin, Ross C., ed. *Joseph Conrad, Heart of Darkness: Complete, Authoritative Text with Biography and Historical Contexts*. Boston & New York: Bedford Books of St. Martin's Press, 1996.

—. Introduction to *Joseph Conrad, Heart of Darkness: Complete, Authoritative Text with Biography and Historical Contexts*, edited by Ross C. Murfin, 3–16. Boston & New York: Bedford Books of St. Martin's Press, 1996.

Nancy, Jean-Luc. 'Tu aimais les Leçons de Ténèbres.' *Lignes* 22 (2007): 11–15.

—. *Corpus*, translated by Richard A. Rand. New York, NY: Fordham University Press, 2008.

—. 'D'une "mimesis sans modèle"' (interview with Philippe Choulet). *L'Animal: Littératures, Arts & Philosophies* 19–20 (2008): 107–14.

—. 'Philippe.' In *Philippe Lacoue-Labarthe: La césure et l'impossible*, edited by Jacob Rogozinski, 409–33. Paris: Éditions Lignes, 2010.

—. 'Philippe Lacoue-Labarthe à Strasbourg.' *Europe* 973 (2010): 11–16.

Nietzsche, Friedrich. *The Birth of Tragedy and The Case of Wagner*, translated by Walter Kaufmann. New York, NY: Vintage, 1967.

—. *Ecce Homo*, translated by Walter Kaufmann. New York, NY: Vintage, 1968.

—. *The Gay Science*, translated by Walter Kaufmann. New York, NY: Random House, 1974.

—. *Twilight of the Idols*. In *The Portable Nietzsche*, edited and translated by Walter Kaufmann, 464–564. New York, NY: Penguin Books, 1982.

—. 'On the Genealogy of Morals.' In *Basic Writings of Nietzsche*, translated and edited by Walter Kaufmann, 437–599. New York, NY: Modern Library, 1992.

Nordau, Max. *Degeneration*. New York, NY: Appleton and Co., 1895.

Nouvet, Claire. 'The Inarticulate Affect: Lyotard and Psychoanalytic Testimony.' *Discourse* 25.1–2 (2003): 231–47.

Ogden, Thomas. *The Primitive Edge of Experience*. Northvale, NJ & London: Jason Aronson, 1989.

Paccaud-Huguet, Josiane. 'Déchets sonores: L'esthétique du fragment de voix chez Conrad.' *L'Époque Conradienne* 35 (2010): 45–57.

Panagopoulos, Nic. *Heart of Darkness and The Birth of Tragedy: A Comparative Study*. Athens: Kardamitsa, 2002.

Parry, Benita. *Conrad and Imperialism: Ideological Boundaries and Visionary Frontiers*. London & Basingstoke: Macmillan, 1983.

Pasveer, Bernike. *Shadows of Knowledge: Making a Representing Practice in Medicine: X-Ray Pictures and Pulmonary Tuberculosis, 1895–1930*. Amsterdam: CIP-Gegevens Koninklijke Bibliotheek, 1992.

Pecora, Vincent P. *Self and Form in Modern Narrative*. Baltimore, MD: Johns Hopkins University Press, 1989.

Pedot, Richard. *Heart of Darkness de Joseph Conrad: Le sceau de l'inhumain*. Nantes: Éditions du Temps, 2003.

Phelan, James. *Living to Tell about It: A Rhetoric and Ethics of Character Narration*. Ithaca, NY: Cornell University Press, 2005.

Plato. *Republic*, translated by Paul Shorey. In *The Collected Dialogues of Plato*, edited by Edith Hamilton and Huntington Cairns, 575–844. New York, NY: Bollingen Series, 1963.

—. *Ion*, translated by Lane Cooper. In *The Collected Dialogues of Plato*, edited by Edith Hamilton and Huntington Cairns, 215–28. New York, NY: Bollingen Series, 1963.

Price, Sally. *Arts primitifs; regards civilisés*. Paris: énsb-a, 1995.

Raine, Craig. 'Conrad and Prejudice.' Review of *Hopes and Impediments: Selected Essays 1967–87*, by Chinua Achebe. *The London Review of Books* 11.12 (1989): 16–18.

Ronell, Avital. *The Telephone Book: Technology, Schizophrenia, Electric Speech*. Lincoln: University of Nebraska Press, 1989.

—. *Crack Wars: Literature, Addiction, Mania*. Lincoln: University of Nebraska Press, 1992.

—. 'L'indélicatesse d'un interminable fondu au noir,' translated by Daniel Loayza. *Europe* 973 (2010): 17–29.

Rubin, William, ed. *Le primitivisme dans l'art du 20ᵉ siècle*. Paris: Flammarion, 1987.

Said, Edward W. *Orientalism*. New York, NY: Pantheon, 1978.

—. *Culture and Imperialism*. New York, NY: Knopf, 1994.

Salecl, Renata and Zizek Slavoj, eds. *Gaze and Voice as Love Objects*. Durham, NC & London: Duke University Press, 1996.

Schelling, F. W. J. *Historical-Critical Introduction to the Philosophy of Mythology*, translated by Mason Richey and Markus Zisselsberger. Albany, NY: SUNY Press, 2007.

Schopenhauer, Arthur. *The World as Will and Idea*, 2 vols., translated by E.F.J. Payne. New York, NY: Dover, 1966.

Slavoj, Zizek. *The Sublime Object of Ideology*. London & New York: Verso, 1989.

—. *Enjoy Your Symptom!: Jacques Lacan in Hollywood and Out*. New York & London: Routledge, 2001.

—. *Bienvenue dans le désert du réel*. Paris: Flammarion, 2002.

Smith, Johanna M. '"Too Beautiful Altogether": Ideologies of Gender and Empire in *Heart of Darkness*.' In *Joseph Conrad, Heart of Darkness: Complete, Authoritative Text with Biography and Historical Contexts*, edited by Ross C. Murfin, 169–84. Boston & New York: Bedford Books of St. Martin's Press, 1996.

Spurr, David. *The Rhetoric of Empire: Colonial Discourse in Journalism, Travel Writing, and Imperial Administration*. Durham, NC & London: Duke University Press, 1993.

Staten, Henry. *Eros in Mourning*. Baltimore, MD: Johns Hopkins University Press, 1995.

Stratton, Florence. *Contemporary African Literature and the Politics of Gender*. New York & London: Routledge, 1994.

Tarde, Gabriel. *Les lois de l'imitation*. Paris: Kimé, 1993.

Tessitore, John. 'Freud, Conrad, and *Heart of Darkness*.' In *Modern Critical Interpretations. Joseph Conrad's Heart of Darkness*, edited by Harold Bloom, 91–103. New York, NY: Chelsea House Publishers, 1987.

Tucker, Robert C., ed. *The Marx-Engels Reader*. New York, NY: Norton, 1978.

Walter, Allen. *The English Novel: From* The Pilgrim's Progress *to* Sons and Lovers. *A Short Critical History*. Toronto: Penguin Books Canada, 1991.

Walter, Benjamin. 'On Language as Such and on the Language of Man' (1916). In *Selected Writings*, edited by Michael Jennings and Marcus Bullock, vol. 1, 62–74. Cambridge, MA & London: Harvard University Press, 1996.

Warin, François. *Nietzsche et Bataille: La parodie à l'infini*. Paris: PUF, 1994.

—. *La passion de l'origine: Essai sur la généalogie des arts premiers.* Paris: Ellipses, 2006.

—. 'La haine de l'Occident et les paradoxes du postcolonialisme.' *EspacesTemps.net*, June 22, 2009. Accessed September 1, 2011. http:// www.espacestemps.net/document7783.html.

—. 'Le primitivisme en question(s).' (L'homme 201 (2012): 165–71.).

Watt, Ian. 'Impressionism and Symbolism in *Heart of Darkness.*' In *Joseph Conrad: A Commemoration*, edited by Norman Sherry, 37–53. London & Basingstoke: Macmillan, 1976.

—. *Conrad in the Nineteenth Century.* Berkeley, CA: University of California Press, 1979.

White, Andrea. *Joseph Conrad and the Adventure Tradition. Constructing and Deconstructing the Imperial Subject.* Cambridge: Cambridge University Press, 1993.

Whitworth, Michael H. *Einstein's Wake: Relativity, Metaphor, and Modernist Literature.* Oxford: Oxford University Press, 2001.

Wittgenstein, Ludwig. *Remarks on Frazer's 'Golden Bough,'* edited by Rush Rees, translated by Allan C. Miles. Hereford: Brynmill Press, 1979.

INDEX